Passionate Journeys

Passionate Journeys

WHY
SUCCESSFUL
WOMEN JOINED
A CULT

Marion S. Goldman

Ann Arbor

THE UNIVERSITY OF MICHIGAN PRESS

2002   2001   2000   1999   4   3   2   1

*A CIP catalog record for this book is available
from the British Library.*

Library of Congress Cataloging-in-Publication Data

Goldman, Marion S.
    Passionate journeys : why successful women joined a cult /
Marion S. Goldman.
        p.   cm.
    Includes bibliographical references and index.
    ISBN 0-472-11101-9 (alk. paper)
    1. Rajneeshees—Oregon—Rajneeshpuram—Psychology Case studies.
2. Women—Religious life—Oregon—Rajneeshpuram Case studies.   I.
Title.
BP605.R342   G65   1999
299'.93—dc21   99-6632
                                                      CIP

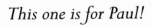

This one is for Paul!

Acknowledgments

Over the decade I have worked on this project, so many friends, colleagues, and students have helped me that I cannot possibly list them all. I hope those whom I don't name know that they are part of this book.

Ben Johnson and Norm Sundberg provided intellectual background and consistent assistance. Dave Frohnmayer and Roshani Shay shared their knowledge and contrasting perspectives, allowing me to consider many aspects of Rajneeshpuram.

Linda Long and Bernie McTigue supplied unique access to the Rajneesh Collection in the University of Oregon's Knight Library. Research grants from the University of Oregon's Office of Research and Faculty Development and the Center for the Study of Women in Society made it possible for me to begin this research.

In the UO Department of Sociology Lynne Isaacson, Shelly Kowalski, Barbara Luton, Bob O'Brien, and Arlene Stein offered creative suggestions and intellectual sustenance. Linda Kintz, Susan Moseley, and Daniel Wocjik also made unique contributions to this work.

I am deeply grateful to Eileen Barker, Lew Carter, Larry Iannaccone, Janet Liebman Jacobs, and Michael Rockland for both their scholarship and also their friendship. Rodney Stark supplied me with singular intellectual challenges and sustained encouragement. And Mary Jo Neitz is an incomparable personal and professional resource.

Dan Attias, Elaine Attias, Nancy Milton, and Pam Stacey were wise advisors and gentle critics, as were Mary Ann Linden and Robin Rokey, who prepared the manuscript, and Vik Gumbhir, who took care of the map and index. LeAnn Fields, my editor at the University of Michigan Press, has been amazingly helpful, flexible, and entertaining.

I owe a great deal to the many sannyasins who shared their lives, their joys, and their struggles with me. But, most of all, I am indebted to my two wonderful sons, Michael and Henry, and to their father, my darling Paul.

Contents

Illustrations following page 168

Introduction

PASSIONATE JOURNEYS

I would like to take readers back to the early 1980s, when Bhagwan Shree Rajneesh and his devotees, whom he called sannyasins, materialized in central Oregon to create the short-lived communal city of Rajneeshpuram. Now there are only empty buildings and tattered signs to remind passersby of the luxurious community that had briefly sprung to life in the dry canyons. Winds howl through halls where devotees once chanted homage to their spiritual master. Battered pickups travel along the road where Bhagwan once drove his Rolls-Royces through crowds of adoring followers.

My son, who was barely two when I began my research, recently asked: "Why would anyone care? It's history." But that history had a lasting impact on the Northwest. And this book is also about more than the sannyasins themselves. The Rajneeshpuram experience illuminates fundamental questions concerning achievement and ambivalence, desire and devotion.

The communal city attracted outsiders' attention for many reasons. The sannyasins' verbal and physical attacks on their opponents made national news, as did their frequent disregard of land-use, election, and immigration laws. And there were symbolic issues as well that intrigued and piqued observers, who could seldom completely articulate what bothered them so much.

One of the most important symbolic issues was the presence of hundreds of high-achieving baby boomers who had forsaken their careers to seek their true identities. The average sannyasin was about thirty-five years old, almost 70 percent of them had degrees from four-year colleges, and slightly more than half of the college graduates also held advanced professional or graduate degrees (Latkin, Hagan, Littman, and Sundberg 1987). These spiritual seekers hoped to blend materialism and spirituality in a utopian community, where everyone enjoyed basic physical comforts, meaningful labor, and possibilities for self-actualization through spiritual surrender to Bhagwan Shree Rajneesh.

The sannyasins seemed like a lost tribe, wandering from India to Oregon to recapture the hopes of the 1960s. Most of their contemporaries had already abandoned commitments to personal and social change by that time, so that the devotees' unlikely continuation of the baby boomers' great expectations provoked outsiders' wonder and anger.

Many Americans could not understand why women and men who had achieved recognition and economic security would willingly give up those hard-won rewards to recreate themselves and fill some invisible spiritual void. The residents of Rajneeshpuram, however, actually lived out long-standing American values of endless possibilities and rebirth through spiritual commitment (Fitz Gerald 1986).

Critics of Rajneeshpuram generally considered any resemblance between themselves and the sannyasins to be completely untenable. They believed that Bhagwan's devotees were deviants who had totally jettisoned the American dream. Yet second chances and new lives are embedded in our culture. Cherished popular icons have often redefined themselves and discovered new identities several times over, just as the sannyasins did. The list is almost endless. Even the American icon Dale Evans was a seventeen-year-old divorced mother, Frances Butts, from Uvalde, Texas, before she died her hair blond to sing in Chicago nightclubs and then traveled to Hollywood, where she discovered Roy Rogers and her true, brunette self (Gilbert 1996).

I mention Dale Evans because she appears so wholesome, so all-American, and yet, surprisingly, she embodied the sannyasins' dream of capturing their true identities, after a number of misadventures along the way. The discovery of one's essence, stripped of layers of social conditioning, was a central theme in Bhagwan's philosophy and in the human potential movement in general. Women and men sannyasins both sought their core identities, but they embarked on their quests in different ways.

The women of Rajneeshpuram were more interesting to me than the men, in part because they constituted the majority (54 percent) of sannyasins at Rancho Rajneesh. They were usually more attractive and, on the whole, more accomplished than their male counterparts. They had developed careers when the upper reaches of the occupational structure were just opening to women, and then they gratefully turned away from their accomplishments. Something in Bhagwan's message drew extraordinarily talented women to his remote communal city.

The unlikely redirection of feminine achievement that led accomplished women to Rajneeshpuram made me curious, but I held back and weighed other research options, until I spent an afternoon with an old friend who believed that Rajneesh therapy had changed her life. Nevertheless, when Jessica faced the choice between becoming a sannyasin and developing her career, she chose her career. Following Bhagwan to the Northwest was never a realistic possibility for her.

She talked with me about how Rajneesh's message first seduced and then repelled her. I was hooked. I wanted to discover the key. Why did some women become sannyasins while others, like Jessica, who seemed so similar, did not? This was the question that first led me up the winding road to Rajneeshpuram.

Jessica was born in 1950. She was the same age as many women sannyasins, and a major research university had granted her early tenure just a few weeks before we talked. Five years earlier Jessica was in so much emotional pain that she could barely function. While she completed her graduate work in the San Francisco Bay area, her long-term romantic relationship collapsed. Jessica was devastated. "I was so freaked out," she said, "I couldn't figure out how I got to work in the morning. It was like being completely deconstructed. You lose bits of your behavior, and you just don't know how you ended up where you ended up."

Although she was a skeptical scientist at work, in private moments Jessica found some solace in the frenetic spiritual marketplace of meditations, palmistry, and other esoteric disciplines. A friend recommended a respected psychic healer who had trained at the Shree Rajneesh Ashram. Jessica followed this advice, and the Rajneesh therapist helped her through one of the most difficult periods in her life. She recalled: "The healing objectively makes you feel better. It is kind of a grounding thing."

The therapist didn't recruit or proselytize, but he repeatedly voiced gratitude to Bhagwan for inspiring his powerful techniques. After a number of individual sessions, he suggested that Jessica could benefit from group work based on Rajneesh meditations. For four months she attended four-hour evening sessions twice each week, performing active, dynamic meditations to confront her anger and aggression. Jessica explored her feelings with other group members and learned chakra readings and aura interpretations. She also attended all-day Saturday sessions every three weeks. Rajneesh therapy became the center of her life for four months.

Jessica was thankful for the new understandings and empowerment she derived from therapy. It was very rewarding, until, during one of her last sessions, she discovered that she could not move her body. Jessica briefly feared that she was paralyzed.

In the wake of that incident, she began to withdraw her energy from the group, and she focused on her doctoral dissertation. When Jessica skipped a session because of an important job interview on the East Coast, her therapist chastised her and insisted that she absolutely must not miss any more. Jessica never went back. Yet she continued to think about and apply what she had learned about herself and other people during Rajneesh therapy.

Years afterward she continued to acknowledge her debt to the therapist, the group, and, indirectly, to Rajneesh. Jessica was certain that successful women like herself were drawn to Bhagwan Shree Rajneesh because his approach took account of the fury that sometimes fueled their achievement. She believed that Rajneesh therapy also allowed them to understand the sadness they experienced when they were subtly penalized for being too successful in their careers. Jessica said, "There are certain terrible, awful conflicts that successful women have and a particular kind of pain that this therapy addresses better than most."

After spending time at Rajneeshpuram and getting to know a number of sannyasins, I found that Jessica was right about the ways in which Bhagwan's philosophy, meditations, and therapy groups met successful women's needs. But that was only one part of the puzzle. If escape from sexism were the attraction, almost every talented woman in America might have gone to Rajneeshpuram. They did not, however, because they usually held more pragmatic expectations about success and about life in general.

Jessica's story clearly indicated that the high-achieving sannyasins were not brainwashed or fundamentally different from other women like them, but her narrative also indicated that they might have experienced somewhat more extreme hopes and more intense feelings of pain and anger than she did. The stories that the sannyasins told me make it possible to better understand Jessica's and other women's many difficulties reconciling achievement and femininity. Their life histories also illuminate the ways in which some women, like those at Rajneeshpuram, experience those contradictions more intensely and seek exceptional personal solutions.

It is important to consider the many rewards successful women found in connection with their spiritual teacher and in living at Rajneeshpuram. It is equally important to think about their uncommon need for those rewards and to consider the kinds of family configurations that fostered those needs.

As I talked with women sannyasins, I often thought of Jessica. She resembled them, yet she terminated Rajneesh therapy and never seriously contemplated becoming a devotee. Like the sannyasin baby boomers, Jessica also had to make choices about careers and relationships without preparation or clear, guiding values. Difficult as those uncharted choices were, she was not as emotionally vulnerable as the sannyasins, so she never experienced the same kinds of intense frustration and anger when her achievements failed to provide her with complete happiness. Jessica was also significantly different from the sannyasins because she had no religious reference points. Her family was unfailingly antireligious, and she had never learned to experience the rewards of spirituality. Jessica was tone-deaf to the siren songs of the sacred.

There may have been other differences and similarities, but Jessica and I never discussed them. Although she wanted to talk about her Rajneesh therapy, we were too close for me to request full, dispassionate disclosure about her personal journeys. The women of Rajneeshpuram were equally generous with their time and honest in our discussions, and, because we had no history of friendship and no continuing relationship, we could somehow talk with far more depth and ease. This book is about their life histories and the paths they took to become sannyasins.

The first chapter describes Rajneeshpuram, Bhagwan, and his philosophy. Chapter 2 recounts my own adventures in central Oregon and the strategies I used to construct composite characters. Each of the next three chapters deals with a different composite sannyasin: Shanto, Dara, and Tanmaya, respectively. This is an unusual approach designed to allow the women's voices to be heard fully while still protecting their anonymity.

The first composite woman, Shanto, grew up in the 1940s and 1950s. She dropped out of college to marry a successful contractor and have three children. Although the prevailing feminine mystique suggested that she should be happy, she thirsted for education and self-discovery. After many years of marriage, Shanto divorced her loyal husband and embarked on her own quests.

Dara, the second woman, was an early baby boomer from Tacoma, Washington, who went to graduate school in Berkeley and was active in movements against the war in Vietnam and in support of women's liberation. She married, had a child, and then divorced after she discovered a meaningful career. Like many other women of her generation, she tried to fuse the personal and the political in a number of different ways. Eventually, her yearning for both self-actualization and social justice led Dara to central Oregon.

The third woman, Tanmaya, came of age during the 1960s. Although she always expected to have some kind of a career, her success as a fashion model in London took Tanmaya by surprise. No matter how much she earned, Tanmaya's work was always secondary to relationships with men. For many years she felt strong only when she was involved with a man who she believed possessed the powers to help and protect her in some way. Tanmaya had used relationships with men to feel safe, but she did not find contentment until she found Bhagwan Shree Rajneesh.

All three sannyasins' life stories illustrate the myriad ways that women attempt to find themselves through achievement, intimate relationships, or charismatic connections. Many of us who did not take such dramatic steps will recognize our own experiences and longings through the sannyasins' accounts. Eight shared experiences marked the women's paths to spiritual commitment, and those are examined in the final chapter.

Although Rajneeshpuram had collapsed by 1986, the women have all continued to pursue alternative spiritual paths. The epilogue describes their current activities and how their years at Rajneeshpuram changed their lives.

If Jessica or I or most women readers had passed through all eight shared experiences to the same extent as the sannyasins, we might well have become devotees. Most of us did not. Nevertheless, I expect that readers will see parts of themselves, their mothers, their sisters, and their friends in these seekers, that many aspects of the three women's lives will resonate with them in surprising ways.

Chapter 1

BHAGWAN SHREE RAJNEESH
AND THE WORLD
HIS SANNYASINS MADE

Driving down the dust-choked highway between Antelope and Fossil, in central Oregon, at the end of the 1990s, most people find it difficult to remember back a dozen years ago, when the row of untended frame buildings near the county road mesmerized national and international media. Not so long ago, there were fashionable boutiques, a bookstore, excellent restaurants, coffee and wine bars, a cavernous lecture hall, and a university of meditation and personal growth on what is now, once again, the Big Muddy Ranch. The communal city was designed for visitors and residents to absorb the presence of Bhagwan Shree Rajneesh,[1] the Indian master who advocated blending materialism and spirituality in the service of personal growth and self-transcendence.

Worried Oregonians speculated that Bhagwan Shree Rajneesh's sannyasins would overrun their state. Conscientious advocates helplessly criticized the exploitation of homeless women and men bussed into the community to vote for its candidates for Wasco County commissioner during the elections of 1984. Most Americans, watching from afar, simply gasped at the incredible combinations of self-discipline and self-indulgence that allowed several thousand devotees to create a pulsing utopian community around their spiritual master.

Rajneeshpuram began on July 10, 1981, and the experiment was over by late fall of 1985. Bhagwan Shree Rajneesh, who claimed the name of Osho in his final years, died in January 1990. A small but thriving international movement continues, however. Sannyasins keep Osho's spirit alive in the old Shree Rajneesh Ashram near Pune, formerly known as Poona. The Osho Commune International remains the movement's spiritual center, and it attracts sannyasins and seekers from all over the world.

There are also intentional communities of twenty to one hundred sann-yasins in many countries, including the United States.

Although much has disintegrated, the skeleton of Rancho Rajneesh remains a significant symbol to old hands and new recruits alike. It is also an important memory to disillusioned former members and to embattled outsiders, many of whom consider the movement's Rajneeshpuram days to have been the worst of times.

In February 1998 the Montana millionaire who had purchased the Big Muddy Ranch during foreclosure a decade earlier donated its airstrip, deserted shopping mall, human-made Krishnamurti Lake, and everything else to the evangelical Christian ministry Young Life. Bhagwan's com-pound was destroyed in the summer forest fires of 1996, although the rest of the community was merely charred.

Officials in Young Life hope that they can erase memories of the short-lived communal city. The Big Muddy is closed to the steady stream of pil-grims, current and former sannyasins who regularly came through the town of Antelope, up the winding road past the old commune. Worried neighbors remember the Rajneeshpuram days and even remain suspi-cious of Young Life's wholesome representatives. Some longtime resi-dents of Wasco County wonder if the sannyasins themselves could return to another one of the big ranches in the area. A handful of old-timers mull over the lurid recent past with surprising fondness, recalling the com-mune with utter amazement, still speculating about those folks in red and imagining their nightly orgies.

While doing research at Rajneeshpuram, I had been both fascinated by Bhagwan Shree Rajneesh and his sannyasins and also deeply troubled by the armed guards and the ominous surveillance penetrating every corner of Rancho Rajneesh. My distasteful memories of totalitarian organization blend with recollections of spirited individuals who were trying to fash-ion new ways of being. They were eager to transform themselves and change the world, at whatever cost necessary to themselves and to any-body who seemed to stand in their way.

On one of my last trips up the road to Rajneeshpuram, before the land transfer to Young Life, I briefly trespassed on the old boardwalk of Deva-teerth Mall and discovered some discarded objects, half-buried in the dusty earth underneath the boards. I found a broken red plastic barrette, a rusted Perrier bottle cap, and a rune. A rune is a small round stone stamped with a fortuitous symbol derived from ancient Norse mythology. The one that I held meant "journey." Those three urban artifacts brought me back to that brief time when Rajneeshpuram seemed to be a cosmopolitan community on the edge of a new world.

Later I will look closely at three women who believed they could change the course of their own lives, and of history itself, by following Bhagwan Shree Rajneesh. This first chapter will introduce readers to the sannyasins, to Bhagwan Shree Rajneesh, to the short-lived but amazing history of Rajneeshpuram, and to my own travels to the communal city.

Social Contexts and Personal Choices

Rajneeshpuram was grounded in fifteen preceding years of social movements peopled by baby boomers. An unprecedented array of innovative spiritual groups emerged in the United States during the 1960s and 1970s. The climate of youthful cultural experimentation during the post-JFK period reflected two underlying historical trends. There was a thriving, highly visible free market in religion that incorporated both psychology and politics within spiritual frameworks. That free market flourished because of Americans' surprising affluence in the wake of World War II.

When contemporary cults like the Moonies, Scientology, and the Jesus People first became widely visible in the early 1970s, sympathetic observers often believed that these groups were simply way stations for young adults on the road to full maturity and social responsibility (Levine 1984). On the other hand, hostile critics developed more complicated, sinister explanations involving brainwashing or intentional manipulation of neural function. Neither perspective, however, adequately explained the Rajneeshees or Bhagwan's attraction for capable, accomplished adults, who flocked to his Pune Ashram from the United States and Western Europe in the mid-1970s.

Most sannyasins who lived at Rajneeshpuram in the early 1980s were more than thirty years old, and less than 5 percent were people of color. Two-thirds reported that they had college degrees, in contrast to members of most other new religions (Latkin, Hagan, Littman, and Sundberg 1987). There was no evidence that their intellectual ability had been impaired by psychological manipulation or other causes, and they scored well within normal ranges on a number of standardized psychological tests (Latkin 1987). A substantial proportion of the sannyasins represented the best and brightest of the baby boom generation. They had excelled in college and in their careers, yet they had rejected seemingly limitless possibilities.

The residents of Rajneeshpuram presented one further problem to scholars trying to understand them. The majority (54 percent) were women, while most of the young seekers who passed through cults in the 1960s and 1970s were men. The women of Rajneeshpuram, moreover, stood apart from the men. They were not only more visible in Bhagwan Shree Rajneesh's inner circle, but they were also more physically attractive, more articulate, and more assertive than their somewhat limp consorts.

Many male devotees were compelling human beings, but most sannyasins, outsiders, and even Bhagwan himself agreed that the women of Rajneeshpuram were the stars of the movement. Men had more choices within the larger society, and those who became seekers often rejected conventional models of masculinity. Most male sannyasins were at odds with social definitions of machismo, including competitiveness, athleticism, and toughness. On the other hand, the women justly prided themselves on their appearances and their interpersonal skills, traditionally feminine attributes that they had never shed, although many had caught the second wave of American feminism.

The women sannyasins whom I came to know had all lived through the rewards and failures of the many social movements that swept over the United States in the wake of the war in Vietnam. Sexual and gender "revolutions" changed their lives, but all of the women critiqued the Women's Movement and its ideals. Disappointment with their mothers' lives and their own choices led them to and then away from feminism, and those disappointments eventually brought them to Bhagwan Shree Rajneesh. These sannyasins, like so many other advocates of social change in the 1960s, combined outstanding personal gifts with extraordinary idealism that had been supported by the assumption that failure was impossible for them. The women fought to develop and define their own unique identities through intimate relationships, education, and careers. Eventually, they came to believe that their self-actualization required heart-to-heart connection and merger with Bhagwan. The women of Rajneeshpuram, and the men as well, had unique personal histories, but their identities had been fundamentally shaped by powerful historical forces. The free market in religion, the social validation of personal change, and America's vast wealth and cultural domination combined to produce a unique era in which affluent individuals could search for spiritual fulfillment in an international marketplace.

Free Markets and Free Spirits

Although many of them came from Western Europe, the sannyasins were a quintessentially American group. Bhagwan could not have attracted so many young Westerners without a vital free market in religion in which old faiths changed and new groups sprang up. In the United States religious affiliation is a matter of individual preferences and decisions. Religions rise and fall in influence, and hundreds of new and established faiths compete for adherents within the religious marketplace.

Americans take spiritual pluralism for granted, because there is no established state religion and because the market economy influences every sphere of social life (Finke and Stark 1992). Different faiths vie to attract active members and their financial resources. Upstart groups can grow dramatically, while established ones stagnate or fall. For example, between 1776 and 1850 the Methodists and Baptists rose at the expense of Congregationalists and Episcopalians. Then, between 1985 and 1990, the once flourishing United Methodists declined dramatically, while the Mormons, Southern Baptists, and Assemblies of God expanded (Finke and Stark 1992, 54–108). There is an endless cycle of growth and eventual secularization of large, established denominations. They lose spirit and community over time, as they lighten their requirements in order to please and attract potential members (Iannaccone 1995).

Members of secularized religions turn away from their old churches and frequently affiliate with different religions that are more rewarding to them. While some people drop out of the religious marketplace altogether and give up, most become religious consumers, seeking out sustaining religious commitments (Hoge, Johnson, and Luidens 1994).

Because Americans choose their religions, new groups may enter the competition with relative ease, as the free market supports religious innovation and vitality.

The religious movement that developed around Bhagwan Shree Rajneesh reflected three decades of change in America's mainstream religions. From the late 1960s through the 1980s vast numbers of American Protestants moved away from established liberal mainline faiths—such as Methodism, Lutheranism, Presbyterianism, and Congregationalism—into new, stricter ones (Finke and Stark 1992, 246–49). Many Roman Catholics also left the church or diminished their involvement. While Catholic membership rolls grew modestly during those decades, because of relatively high birth rates along with immigration, regular attendance at Mass declined dramatically across the United States (Finke and Stark 1992, 255–63). There was also a steep drop in seminary enrollments and the number of women entering religious orders (Schoenherr and Greeley 1974; Ebaugh 1977). Some Roman Catholics retained their formal affiliation and shifted their commitment to the spirit-filled world of charismatic renewal within the church (McGuire 1982; Neitz 1987). Others joined strict, conservative Protestant faiths, along with former liberal Protestants. Relatively small numbers searched for spirituality and community in either Christian cults or other novel religions (Neitz 1987, 4–7).

Conservative and reform Jewish congregations confronted the same losses as liberal Protestants and Roman Catholics. In the 1970s and 1980s Jewish leaders worried that they might give up their treasured next generation, as pressures for assimilation and intermarriage diminished their congregations (Galanter 1989, 22–25). Some converted to Christianity when they married, but many Jews simply dropped out (Finke and Stark 1992, 12). Jews joined cults at roughly the same rates as their Roman Catholic and liberal Protestant counterparts, but they appeared to be more numerous, because they were concentrated in a smaller segment of non-Christian faiths, such as Hare Krishna's, Sufi movements, and Bhagwan Shree Rajneesh's sannyasins (Melton and Moore 1982).

Individuals became sannyasins in response to the general weakening of secularized liberal denominations and the growth of more rewarding, strict faiths. Religious change and choice in a free market contextualized individual's decisions to follow Bhagwan Shree Rajneesh, just as they contextualized others' more mundane decisions to change affiliations. Most sannyasins were raised in families affiliated with mainstream religions, as were other Americans who switched religious affiliations during the 1970s and 1980s (Latkin, Hagan, Littman, and Sundberg 1987). Sannyasins responded to attractive alternatives in the same ways as hundreds of thousands of other Americans, but they selected a cult rather than a more moderate group that would require less and offer them fewer explicit rewards.

I deliberately define Bhagwan Shree Rajneesh's sannyasins as a cult, in order to apply a precise, elegant description to the movement. Cults supply cultural innovations for their members, and they also hold the potential to change their host societies (Bainbridge 1997, 23–24; Stark 1996a, 33–35, 44–47). They are independent of established denominations and frequently attract privileged individuals with resources to engage in social experimentation, support their new faith, and protect their cult from stifling social constraints (Stark 1996a).

In terms of their growth and social influence, the Mormons have been the most successful American cult. Another well-known Western faith, Christianity, began its dramatic rise in first-century Europe as a tiny, marginal Roman cult (Stark 1996a). Historically, cults have been defined as a small, cohesive religious groups in high tension with the surrounding society (Stark and Bainbridge 1985, 171–207). The term *cult* took on negative connotations in the 1970s, however, when paid experts and sensationalistic media used the word to criticize unconventional faiths and imply that they were guilty of mind control and sexual exploitation.

Because of these negative connotations, scholars frequently substitute *novel religion* or *new religious movement* for *cult,* although the latter is the least cumbersome, most accurate term. For that reason some sociologists of religion have started to use it once again. I hope that readers will rethink the stigma associated with *cult* and consider it to be a neutral and useful term.

Dozens of new groups start each year in the United States, although only a very few cults thrive and become major religions. The Rajneesh movement has never expanded to more than about twenty-five thousand active members around the world, but it continues to exert cultural influence well beyond its numbers. Sannyasins have personal and financial resources supporting international technology and publicity networks, linking them to one another and reaching out to casual seekers. The movement is now known as Friends of Osho (Rajneesh), serving both committed members and thousands of consumers of eclectic spiritual goods and services.

American values support the moderate consumption of religion and spirituality. Few people think twice if someone reads a book by Bhagwan Shree Rajneesh or takes a class in personal growth. Intense commitment to personal change through becoming a sannyasin or profound involvement in any other religion, however, forces people to live in tension with American culture in general, because they must sacrifice time and money toward spiritual ends. There are strong social norms against any form of extreme commitment—religious, political, or interpersonal. Dedication to a spiritual master like Bhagwan Shree Rajneesh is particularly problematic because most Americans do not organize their deepest values and daily projects around a charismatic leader's religious imperatives.

There is a fundamental contradiction between Americans' mistrust of intense religious commitment and our equally important, religiously grounded ideal of limitless individual possibilities. Our contemporary searches for self-actualization and personal growth are founded in the nineteenth-century Protestant New Light philosophy of free will. Methodists, Presbyterians, and other faiths repudiated Calvinist predestination doctrine and stated that anyone could be redeemed by accepting Jesus as a personal savior. They could be reborn and take on a new self-identity at any time.

This religious doctrine has been expanded to the point that Americans affirm limitless possibilities for personal changes that move people into the cultural mainstream. We praise people who leave behind drugs and become reborn by means of rehabilitation and support programs (Haaken 1993). Seemingly new selves emerge every day through evangelical churches, psychotherapy, aerobic exercise, diet, plastic surgery, or other means. These are often costly, and, like becoming a sannyasin, they are part of a long continuum of voluntary groups and products embodying infinite possibilities for Americans' self-improvement and symbolic rebirth. Even advertisements for new clothes, cars, or hair colors imply that personal change is or should be part of everyone's life. In this context becoming a sannyasin is certainly extreme, but it is also part of a belief system that is woven into our social fabric.

Spiritual and psychological growth movements reflect the democratic value entitling everyone to happiness. The affirmation of individual happiness as a fundamental, universal right is relatively new, although it builds on the tradition of religious rebirth. This system of values is known as psychological gentrification (Skolnick 1991).

Throughout most modern Western history, only the affluent classes with leisure time to spare indulged in a seemingly endless search for self-understanding and self-improvement (Wolfe 1976). The 1960s and early 1970s marked a turning point, when personal growth became a watchword for American adults, transcending divisions of race, social class, or gender. And it was during those years that the Rajneesh movement began to attract American seekers. It was the era sometimes called the "Me" decade.

America's political and economic declines were not yet visible. New communication and transportation technologies and the industrialization of Asia contributed to mass access to an array of items and ideas that had not been available to previous generations of middle-class Americans. In the early 1970s the baby boomers experienced substantial material entitlements. It sometimes seemed as if all the workers on earth were laboring for the benefit of America's entitled youth. Ignoring possible material limitations, they envisaged ever-growing numbers of choices from the far corners of the world.

On any day in almost any affluent American city on the East or West Coasts, people could choose among hundreds of international foods. They could buy clothing suitable for a French movie director, a Tibetan yak herder, or a space traveler. In Berkeley, California, the ultimate university town, a single block on Ashby Avenue had shops selling rugs from the Silk Road in central Asia located near American Indian traders, across the street from African drum vendors, who stood in front of Italian clothing boutiques.

Bookstores overflowed with similar ranges of choices. A small, reasonably stocked urban store would display works by Baba Ram Dass, Lao Tzu, L. Ron Hubbard, Rajneesh, and dozens of other trailblazers in the jungles of self-actualization. The new spiritual marketplace also featured packaged tours for seekers to visit holy men in Asia, sacred sites in New Mexico, or personal growth meccas such as the Esalen Institute in Big Sur.

As the twentieth century closes, young adults no longer travel the costly roads to self-actualization in such great numbers. The generations born after the end of the Vietnam War have less discretionary time and money than their parents had at the same age. They are reluctant to step out of the labor force to embark on spiritual quests, uncertain that they will be welcomed back to well-paying jobs. The ideology of psychological gentrification, however, still appears to have almost indestructible roots. While communal experiments, expensive sojourns to India or Oregon, or costly psychotherapy may be out of the question for almost everyone, there are many inexpensive alternatives.

Currently, Oprah Winfrey provides millions of network television viewers with insights, empowerment, and possibilities for self-transformation, while aspiring charismatic leaders hawk their seminars and tapes on cable-channel infomercials. Chain bookstores sell paraliterature that combines spirituality and personal growth, and shopping malls offer products ranging from crystal angel jewelry to aromatherapy to horoscopes for cats. Competing spiritual perspectives vie for space on the Internet. Twelve-step programs, support groups, and personal growth seminars spread through political organizations, schools, private corporations, and also established mainstream churches. In the midst of this lavish spiritual economy, members of Generations X and Y join their parents on the never-ending road to self-realization.

Continuity and Change

The youngest sannyasins who talked with me are now in their early forties; the oldest are over sixty. As they approach the final stages of their lives, the individuals who tasted the revolutionary fruit of the 1960s seek new ways of aging and coming to terms with the inevitability of death. A surprising number of former Jesus People who evangelized in youth communes and later returned to the mainstream would like to live collectively in their final years (Goldman 1995a). Similarly, some of those who lived at Rajneeshpuram have already returned or would like to return to some spiritual community oriented around their master's spirit.

The vibrant religious marketplace and a culture advocating self-transformation were the basic social preconditions that opened the road to Rajneeshpuram to hundreds of Americans and Western Europeans, and those social preconditions continue to influence American culture. Although relatively few people bought one-way tickets to enlightenment, the common impulse for self-transformation was a major reason why the central Oregon commune became a national media event. Outsiders discovered exaggerated versions of their own desires for a better life in the seemingly bizarre utopian experiment.

The astonishing communal city in the Northwest was more closely linked to ordinary social patterns than many Americans would like to think (Durkheim 1958; Erikson 1966). The sannyasins provoked hostility because of outrageous comments and dangerous acts, but their public reputation as accomplished dropouts also touched a deep nerve among many outsiders. Some envied the affluence that the sannyasins had willingly set aside. Others pondered change themselves. The women and men of Rajneeshpuram embodied central social contradictions between personal change and obligations to others. Their extreme case was an extension of the omnipresent tension between individuality and collectivity that underlies American society.

Personal flexibility is a highly valued American trait because of the vast cultural and economic forces that have repeatedly transformed the United States over the past two centuries, but change is also difficult for everyone involved. When individuals suddenly take on new names, careers, sexual orientations, or personal priorities, everyone close to them has to adjust. There are often unpleasant surprises.

The dangers of change and the challenge that self-transformation posed to those left behind were constant themes in Rajneesh philosophy and folklore. Sannyasins told me various versions of this change tale, each one swearing its truth. It had happened to them or to a friend or a lover. Michael Rockland (1989) presents a similar story in his wonderful novel about the Rajneeshees, *A Bliss Case.*

This apocryphal story lays out the central elements in these tales: After stormy years on the student barricades of the 1960s, Che Hecht changed his name back to Gus, went straight, excelled in law school, and eventually became a partner in a top Northwest law firm. But Che/Gus felt empty. Around 1979 he began a quest for self-actualization that led him to the Shree Rajneesh Ashram in Pune, where he became a sannyasin.

Back in Seattle, after he turned into Swami Marcellus, Gus wore Bhagwan's picture in a locket around his neck and dyed his Armani suits deep
maroon. A year or so later, he commuted between Seattle and Rajneeshpuram, where he directed the mounting number of civil lawsuits filed by
and against the Rajneeshees. Meanwhile, his old colleagues were angry,
puzzled, and concerned. Despite the swami's continuing record as a top
litigator, Che/Gus/Marcellus's law firm tried to fire him on the grounds
that they had voted a partnership to Gus Hecht, and Swami Marcellus, by
his own admission, was a new and entirely different person.

The tale's outcome varied with the teller. Marcellus either walked out
and never looked back or successfully bargained for a huge golden para-
chute or was still tied up in litigation with his former partners. Variations
presented the hero as a tenured professor, a well-known proctologist, a
corporate accountant, or some other successful professional bound to
others through organizational commitments. Aside from being amusing,
however, the tale signified the difficulties associated with fundamental
personal change and the obvious material risks change presented to those
who had invested in professional success and then wanted to try something else.

Many Americans fantasize about change or actually take modest risks
like changing a nickname or enrolling in a few personal growth seminars.
But a relatively small number of us embark on long-term quests for spiritual or psychological truths. And far fewer, no more than 5 or 6 percent,
actually join spiritual groups like Bhagwan Shree Rajneesh's. Yet those
movements remain vital to the religious marketplace and to the wider
culture.

Bhagwan Shree Rajneesh and His Philosophies

Rajneesh's own life story took as many twists and turns as the fictional life
of Swami Marcellus (Carter 1990, 32–42). Satya Bharti Franklin, a
Rajneesh apostate, believed that he was a combination of a madman, a
savior, a charlatan, and a saint (Franklin 1992). His various biographies
and autobiographical assertions can support any of these characterizations, yet there is surprisingly widespread agreement about the basic outlines of Rajneesh's own story.

He was born to a Jain family in Kuchawada, India, in 1931 and named Mohan Chandra Rajneesh. Jainism is an independent South Indian faith, closely related to Buddhism. Thus, Rajneesh was raised outside the dominant Hindu religion, in a tradition that synthesized different philosophies much as his own would three decades later.

Rajneesh became accustomed to the nickname Raja, which means king. It was bestowed upon him by his mother's wealthy father. After his grandfather died, he lived with his parents in nearby Gadawara. Then Rajneesh moved in with cousins in Jabalpur in the northern part of the country, while briefly attending Hitkarini College and then D. N. Jain College, where he earned his undergraduate degree in philosophy in 1955. He received an M.A. degree in philosophy from Saugar University and immediately took a job at Raipur Sanskrit College (Sanskrit Mahavidyalaya).

His lectures created so much controversy that Rajneesh transferred to another university the next year and then received a promotion to professor in 1960. When college was not in session, he traveled around India lecturing about both politics and spirituality. Rajneesh was an insightful, charismatic lecturer who soon gained a loyal following that included a number of wealthy merchants and businessmen. These clients gave Rajneesh donations for individual consultations about their spiritual development and daily life.

These were commonplace, for throughout India, people seek guidance from learned or holy individuals in the same ways as Americans might consult a psychologist or pastoral counselor, and Rajneesh's private practice was not unusual in itself (Mehta 1979). The rapid growth of his clientele, however, was somewhat out of the ordinary, suggesting that he was an unusually talented spiritual therapist. By 1964 a group of wealthy backers had set up an educational trust to support Rajneesh and the occasional rural meditation retreats he led. Like many professionals whose client base grows quickly, Rajneesh acquired a business manager around this time. She was Laxmi, an upper-class, politically well-connected woman who became his personal secretary and organizational chief.

At the request of university officials, Rajneesh resigned his post at the University of Jabalpur in 1966 and started to use the name Acharya Rajneesh, denoting his primary role as a spiritual teacher. He supported himself by lecturing, offering meditation camps, and individually counseling affluent Indian clients. Rajneesh critiqued established politics and religions and advocated more open, liberated sexuality. Building from the work of the Western philosopher Gurdjieff, he also developed active meditation exercises facilitating individuals' ability to observe their own physical, mental, and emotional processes.

Word of mouth and occasional published references to his gifts brought Westerners to the Mt. Abu meditation camps that Acharya Rajneesh directed in the late 1960s and early 1970s. *I Am the Gate* (1977) was the first of Rajneesh's many books to be published in English. It was eagerly received by young adults in England and the United States, many of whom had discovered Eastern spirituality through the Beatles' brief devotion to Maharish Mahesh Yoga. Because of the Immigration Act of 1965, dozens of other Asian spiritual teachers could now come to the United States to cultivate the burgeoning market for new religions and encourage the recent generation of seekers.

A steady stream of visitors from the West sought out Rajneesh in the airy Bombay apartment he acquired late in 1969. He sent a number of these first visitors back home to start an international network of meditation centers. In 1971, as his following grew and diversified, Rajneesh exchanged the title *Acharya,* which means "teacher," for the more expansive *Bhagwan,* meaning "enlightened or awakened one." For the first time Bhagwan acknowledged that he had experienced, almost twenty years earlier, on March 21, 1953, the profound nothingness of true satori, or enlightenment.

The first Westerners who came to Bhagwan with financial gifts and personal talents formed a rapidly growing core of devotees. Visitors did meditations on a nearby beach and developed close-knit support networks and living groups. They attended his meditation camps, and Bhagwan began to lecture in both English and Hindi at different times.

As the movement grew in the early 1970s, an official organizational structure emerged (Carter 1990, 70). Devotees received new names, often those of revered Hindu gods and goddesses, signifying their psychological and spiritual rebirth through taking sannyas, opening themselves to Bhagwan, and renouncing their pasts.

Women immediately used the prefix *Ma,* meaning "mother." Men immediately adopted the prefix *Swami,* indicating that they were holy men. Around this time, in Bombay, Bhagwan also asked all of his followers to wear saffron orange clothing, a traditional color of holy men in India. The names and clothes signifying instant holiness, coupled with Bhagwan's freewheeling political and sexual philosophy, deeply offended the local population. These devices, however, charmed Westerners, who began to outnumber the Indians visiting Bhagwan's quarters and attending meditation camps.

In 1974 Bhagwan relocated his headquarters to Pune, one hundred miles southeast of Bombay. With considerable Western backing and some support from longtime Indian devotees, Bhagwan moved to a six-acre enclave and acquired adjoining real estate in Koregaon Park, an elite Pune suburb. Over the next five years the Shree Rajneesh Ashram grew to include a meditation hall, where Bhagwan could lecture to several thousand people, a smaller auditorium, facilities for a multitude of human potential therapy groups, a medical clinic, cottage industries, restaurants, shops, classrooms, and housing for sannyasins who lived year round at the ashram. The movement was clearly stratified, with affluent and talented sannyasins receiving the most access to Bhagwan.

Some of Bhagwan's discourses were translated by well-known publishers such as Routledge & Kegan Paul and Harper & Row. At the movement's peak, around 1976, close to thirty thousand Westerners visited the Shree Rajneesh Ashram yearly, and the worldwide movement included around twenty-five thousand sannyasins (Milne 1987, 23; Carter 1990, 59–60). Bhagwan wooed, but did not necessarily win, celebrities like Diana Ross, James Coburn, and Werner Erhard, founder of est, an astonishingly popular personal growth movement of the era. After 1976 or 1977 recruitment stagnated. There was greater competition in the American spiritual and self-actualization marketplaces, Western economies were constricting, and some influential figures in the human potential movement publicly denounced violence in the Rajneesh therapy groups.

The Western press criticized the Shree Rajneesh Ashram because of the therapy groups and drew parallels to the Jonestown tragedies. There were also political difficulties in India, stemming from Bhagwan's public lectures against the powerful Janata Party. Bhagwan talked to his devotees about the Buddhafield, a spiritual community built around him and his teachings, but none of the regional governments in India were willing to permit the commune.

Ma Anand Sheela, who would become infamous a few years later, advocated establishing a communal settlement in the United Sates. Her promotion of international relocation was part of Sheela's successful strategy to supplant Bhagwan's original personal secretary, Ma Yoga Laxmi. She courted personal support among affluent Americans, she flattered Bhagwan, and she encouraged extravagant donations to his luxury watch collection. Sheela was also willing to implement his wishes by any means necessary. By 1981 she was the most powerful person in Rajneesh's inner circle, and she would soon take on the formal role of his private secretary, making policies that endangered the movement and Bhagwan himself.

In Pune sannyasins spread reports of death threats to Bhagwan by members of various Indian sects, accompanied by terrifying descriptions of his growing emotional stress and his declining health. There were also rumors of violent incidents between sannyasins and Indian opponents of the Shree Rajneesh Ashram. The Indian government investigated allegations of Rajneesh-sanctioned prostitution, international drug trafficking, gold smuggling, money laundering, and tax evasion. Sannyasins have always denied most of these charges, but the criminal investigations created many difficulties for the movement and its leaders. In June 1981 Rajneesh and his inner circle flew to New Jersey. The Shree Rajneesh Ashram began to shut down, except for a small remaining crew of resident caretakers.

On July 10, 1981, Bhagwan's representatives purchased the 64,229-acre Big Muddy Ranch in central Oregon for $5.9 million, and they started building the Buddhafield at Rajneeshpuram. Rumor had it that the decision to move to Oregon reflected the relatively inexpensive price of the ranch and Sheela's misplaced assumption that all of Oregon was peopled by tolerant liberals who smoked marijuana and let their neighbors alone.

Wasco County proved to be far less laid back than she had expected. During the next four years the ranch became the site of considerable accomplishment and also considerable intrigue and crime. Debates still rage within and outside the movement about who did what to whom and why. One of the central questions is whether or not Bhagwan knew about a whole array of Ma Anand Sheela's plots and criminal activities at Rancho Rajneesh.[2] There are no definitive answers, and it is still a matter of obsessive speculation among many sannyasins who once lived at Rajneeshpuram.

The communal city's rise and fall held historic meaning for all those who had lived there and also for all of the Oregonians whose lives changed because of Rajneeshpuram. To understand that meaning and experience of the commune, it is necessary to consider Bhagwan Shree Rajneesh and his philosophies as a context for the world the sannyasins created and the political intrigues that destroyed it.

Bhagwan's Philosophies

Rajneeshpuram was built on shifting philosophical foundations and, more important, on Bhagwan Shree Rajneesh's presence. Since 1974 in Pune almost every word Bhagwan uttered had been faithfully recorded and published or filmed. He was fond of asserting that there were 108 beads on the *malas* that his devotees wore to suspend their lockets with his photograph, and there were likewise 108 paths to travel toward enlightenment. In more than four hundred books, which were transcriptions of his lectures, initiation talks, and pithy sayings, almost every major religious and philosophical tradition received Bhagwan's attention. He lectured about Buddhism, Christianity, Hassidism, Sufism, the Upanishads, Yoga, and Zen, as well as Marx, Freud, and Henry Ford.

These traditions were not always well understood by Rajneesh's sannyasins, but they melded together in an interesting, palatable spiritual stew that was dominated by Zen Buddhism. Bhagwan asserted that the many internal contradictions and paradoxes in his philosophy were essential to his sannyasins' spiritual development. They could choose to accept or reject any part of his philosophical discourses. It was up to individuals, so long as they remained connected to Bhagwan and accepted him as the ultimate master. In spite of changes, elaboration, and advocacy of individual choice, the two most important themes in Bhagwan's philosophy remained surprisingly clear and consistent. They were, first, ego surrender to Bhagwan and, second, integration of the individual's material and spiritual selves.

Free choice was the essence of Bhagwan's philosophy, but the ultimate freedom of enlightenment was emotional surrender to him. As with almost everything else in the movement, there was considerable latitude for individuals to construct their own meanings of surrender.

Being a sannyasin made it possible to become a new person and achieve enlightenment someday. Every sannyasin had to follow a slightly different spiritual path, but all of their personal quests absolutely required an invisible line reaching directly from Bhagwan and his teachings to each devotee's heart. Uncritical belief in Bhagwan and his extraordinary powers was fundamental to being a devotee.

Bhagwan Shree Rajneesh returned again and again to his vision of a new man who synthesized the worldly and the godly. His ideal was "Zorba the Buddha," a consummate being who combined the spiritual focus of the Indian mystic with the life-embracing traits of the materialistic Westerner. Zen, Tantra tradition, and Reverend Ike's message came together in Rajneesh's vision. Bhagwan obviously relished this ideal, which may have been his personal goal, as well. He stated:

> A new human being is needed on earth, a new human being who accepts both, who is scientific and mystic. Who is all for matter and all for spirit. Only then will we be able to create a humanity which is rich on both sides. I teach you the richness of body, richness of soul, richness of this world and that world. To me that is true religiousness. (Rajneesh 1983, 14)

Bhagwan's enthusiastic embrace of materialism generated media feeding frenzies, and most outsiders still remember his collection of more than ninety Rolls-Royces above any other characteristic of Rajneeshpuram. The extravagant cars symbolized both Bhagwan's embrace of the corporeal world and his tweaking of Americans' automobile worship. He owned his first Rolls in Pune, where there was a tradition of the car's association with royalty that dated back to the British Raj. His collection, however, only reached epic proportions after he settled in the United States. Sannyasins appreciated the humor behind the swarm of Rolls-Royces. They also rejoiced in their masters' luxurious appointments in the same ways that devout members of many other groups appreciate their leaders' splendor.

If Calvin and Luther tolerated worldly achievement, then Rajneesh positively revered it. He asserted that material comfort was a precondition for enlightenment, and his communal policies favored the rich. The most conservative economists might blush at Rajneesh's emphasis on achievement and affluence as indicators of human worth:

> Capitalism is pure freedom. Of course everybody is not capable of creating wealth, hence it creates jealousy. But we should not be dominated by jealousy. We should not be dominated by those who are uncreative, by the jealous, then we will destroy all the talented people—and they are the real people, they are the people who raise humanity to higher levels. (1983, 378)

The successful women and men who joined Rajneesh welcomed his approval of talent and worldly success. That approval affirmed their earlier choices to invest themselves in education and careers. His affirmation of success also encouraged them to continue to invest themselves once they became sannyasins.

Those who chronicled Rajneesh have often made too much of the ways in which he forced skilled professionals to break down their egos by doing menial work. There were indeed temporary reassignments of sannyasins with essential skills, when their therapists or supervisors believed they were too independent or when overpopulation by devotees possessing degrees in the social sciences and humanities brought some former professors into their first direct contact with chain saws. When individuals possessed expertise that was useful to the Rajneesh organization, however, they soon resumed their old lines of labor.

At Rajneeshpuram all but one of the women in the composites were prized for the specific, carefully cultivated abilities that they carried from the outside. Attorneys practiced law, social scientists contributed to long-range planning, psychologists did therapy, and managers supervised others and made deals within the larger economy. The many other men and women with whom I had long conversations also fit this pattern. Despite tales of skilled professionals relegated to dishwashing or road grading, radical job changes were seldom permanent, unless there was a surplus of sannyasins with similar expertise. Essential professional skills, particularly medicine, law, and management, were so important to sustain Rajneeshpuram that they could not be discounted for ideological considerations or for the sannyasins' own benefit.

For the first time ever the women I interviewed received not only status and material advantages but also love and gratitude for their work. They were "having it all": combining career and community at their fullest. This was an almost unrealizable ideal, but the imaginary superwomen of the early 1970s were a possibility at Rajneeshpuram.

Rajneesh encouraged his sannyasins to strive their hardest and immerse themselves in their work as a means of surrendering to him. He sanctified work as worship, and various departments were called temples. So someone could say quite sincerely, "I worship at the recycling temple." Work became a means to transform oneself and to build utopia simultaneously, and even the most self-centered focus on achievement took on a collective moral authority (Tipton 1982). Most of the women worked at least ten to twelve hours daily. Even during tense periods, when deadlines and pressures to increase productivity mounted, however, long tea breaks, Rajneesh's afternoon Drive-Bys, and meals in the cafeterias or restaurants regularly tempered their labors.

Intense discussions about personal problems or collegial difficulties were also part of the sannyasins' work lives, cushioning their long hours and strengthening bonds within the group. Women in Rajneeshpuram's managerial and professional sector discovered an integration of labor and love, of work and community, that they had sought unsuccessfully for many years. Their achievements were recognized and praised as much as, if not more than, men's. The Rajneesh way offered material and emotional rewards grounded in some of the same assumptions as the feminist solutions that had once disappointed them.

Bhagwan called for transcendence of traditional gender roles. Women and men alike were encouraged to merge their own female and male sides and to strive for flexibility in every aspect of their lives (Goldman 1995b). The ideal sannyasin was neither overtly male nor stereotypically female, but Rajneesh placed the highest value on traditionally feminine traits like intuition, expressiveness, emotionalism, self-awareness, and sensitivity. Men were admonished to nurture their own feminine traits, and women were lauded when they acted assertively. Sannyasins were exhorted to move toward androgyny, without forsaking their gender identity (Latkin 1987).

The breaking down of traditional gender roles also involved deconstruction of most relationships that were remotely reminiscent of middle-class American and Western European families of the 1950s. Until AIDS became an issue in 1984 and Bhagwan supported monogamy as a step toward ultimate celibacy, women were encouraged to explore their sexuality through a number of intimate relationships with men and sometimes with other women as well.

There was rampant sexual experimentation in therapy groups, casual contacts, and temporary liaisons. At his Shree Rajneesh Ashram, Bhagwan defined sexual license as a step toward enlightenment. Desire would fall away when sannyasins transcended it and focused on higher forms of meditation. Sex was a first step but by no means the last (Clarke 1985). Few sannyasins appeared to be sexually satiated, until the anti-AIDS campaigns of 1984 limited sexual expression, and even after those rules were laid down many continued to lead active sex lives.

Hugs, strokes, nuzzles, and playful grabs remained the coin of casual friendship at the ranch. Sensuality fairly cracked in the air, even while Rajneeshpuram disintegrated and Bhagwan prepared to flee.

Love of Bhagwan was the moving emotional force in sannyasins' lives. Close, intimate relationships were also important, and casual sex was simply a side benefit. Sannyasins relished gossip about recent couplings and their own sensuality. There were much-told stories like those about Pune therapy groups, in which women were coaxed to multiple orgasms by near strangers. Yet, while casual sex was a welcome diversion and source for potential growth, sannyasins reserved their true love for their spiritual master. They invested their deepest emotions in Bhagwan and secondarily in other sannyasins.[3]

Most of the sannyasins who had been in Pune welcomed the collective pressures for men to have vasectomies, for women to consider sterilization, and for everyone to guard against pregnancy. In Oregon Bhagwan continued to encourage people to think of themselves and their own actualization first, and those who already had children were usually informed that their offspring would be a drain on the collective and thus should be left with someone outside the commune.[4] A handful of sannyasins had children during their years in Pune, and a small number of others brought their offspring to live at the ranch, but there were very few children in relationship to the number of residents who were of child-bearing age.

Since housework was collectivized by sannyasins who worked in cooking, cleaning, or clothes-washing temples, and few women had children to care for, traditional household units were hardly necessary. So there was a practical structure sustaining gender equality. The community's social organization supported parity because both kinship and household work were relatively unimportant. Gender segregation continued in some jobs, such as room cleaning, but in most instances gender roles were so balanced that equality itself became something of an issue after Sheela fled from the ranch.

During the commune's final six months Rajneesh laughed at his male sannyasins' passivity and told women that they had become too strong and too articulate because the men were not aggressive enough. The master asserted: "Here there is no need for women's liberation. Here the situation is totally opposite, the men are afraid of the women" (*Rajneesh Times,* August 16, 1985). After Sheela and her entourage fled, he condemned the corrupt female hierarchy dominated by his personal secretary and chief executive officer. Nevertheless, when the movement reorganized and Rajneesh returned to Pune in the late 1980s, women continued to be among the key leaders, and flexible gender roles remained central to both theory and practice.

Sannyasins did not have to reject their earlier personal and political commitments. They could reinterpret them as way stations on the road to enlightenment. And at Rajneeshpuram they could receive tremendous recognition for their achievements without having to break away from the group's collective norms. Love and work were not mutually exclusive choices. To work devotedly and professionally was to show love for others, most of all for Bhagwan. Labor and love came together in the communal context as it seldom had earlier in the women's lives.

Under Bhagwan's omnipotent gaze his sannyasins briefly created a world that offered high-achieving adults, especially women, more of what they wanted and needed than they could find anywhere else. Their spiritual connection with Bhagwan and his promise of complete rebirth and self-transformation immeasurably amplified the daily gratification of living at Rajneeshpuram.

Becoming a Sannyasin

Taking sannyas had been fairly easy for the women and men I came to know at Rajneeshpuram. Some people became sannyasins and then lived at the Shree Rajneesh Ashram for several years. Others joined the movement somewhat precipitously, on short visits to Pune, during stays at Rajneeshpuram, or in brief ceremonies at one of the urban Rajneesh centers that flourished until 1982. In the late 1970s many sannyasins simply sent a card to the central office in Pune, requested sannyas, and received new names and a *mala*.

Becoming a sannyasin was so simple that a number of individuals constructed their own kinds of affiliation. Some sannyasins, who never lived at Rajneeshpuram, registered, adopted new names, and then ceased to have formal contact with the central organization. Other spiritual seekers shared the sannyasins' intense heart-to-heart relationship with Bhagwan, meditated daily, and dressed in sunrise colors, but never officially took sannyas. To be a full participant at Rajneeshpuram, however, it was necessary, although not always sufficient, for an individual to register as a sannyasin in good standing with the central organization.

All initiates received sannyasin names. In the early 1970s and mid-1980s prospective devotees checked a box on their application forms to note whether they wanted to keep their old first name, which would now be prefaced with Ma or Swami followed by a brief name such as Anand (Love), or whether they wished to receive an entirely different, Hindu-style name inspired, if not actually bestowed, by Bhagwan. After taking sannyas, people were supposed to meditate at least once daily, don sunrise colors (which included a whole spectrum of red-based shades by the early 1980s), wear a *mala* with the locket housing Bhagwan's likeness, and become vegetarian. Along with these practices, sannyasins had to acknowledge their heart-to-heart connection and ego surrender to Bhagwan.

Most of these simple rules were flexible, because free choice was such a crucial element in Rajneesh's philosophy. Residents of Rajneeshpuram had to comply with the regulations about clothes and a visible *mala,* until fall of 1985, but many of them skipped daily meditation and occasionally ate nonvegetarian meals if they traveled away from the ranch.

The essence of being a sannyasin involved a deep, heartfelt relationship with Bhagwan. Devotion was grounded in surrender and spiritual merger with him. For some residents of Rajneeshpuram, surrender involved uncritical acceptance of their spiritual master's guidance about every aspect of their lives (Carter 1990, 226–27). Most of the sannyasins I talked with, however, interpreted surrender as a deeply personal acknowledgment that Bhagwan watched over them, but they usually evaluated his assertions in terms of their own experiences and individual truths. These sannyasins submitted to Bhagwan's higher power and directly experienced a personal tie with him in much the same way that evangelical fundamentalists experience highly individual, emotional relationships with Jesus.

Although there were variations in the meanings of their connection with Bhagwan, once sannyasins regularly participated in Rajneesh therapy groups, spent many weeks at Pune or Rajneeshpuram, or moved to a Rajneesh house, the ashram, or the ranch, everything in their lives changed. Surrender to Bhagwan became life itself.

Sacrifice and Reward at Rajneeshpuram

The communal world around Bhagwan Shree Rajneesh offered very explicit benefits: luxury, fun, connection to others, professional advancement, and, above all, seemingly unconditional love. The high-achieving women sannyasins were well aware of these compensations, and they believed that their choice to live in central Oregon had derived from rational calculations of personal costs and rewards.

In forging their commitment, sannyasins organized communities in which they felt at home. In Pune and later in Oregon they designed attractive, sophisticated, and sensual marketplaces with a spiritual twist. They could purchase attractive New Age goods, try out recently developed personal growth therapies, and enjoy services such as massage and hairstyling that were infused with spiritual significance.

In a walk down the two short commercial blocks in Rajneeshpuram,

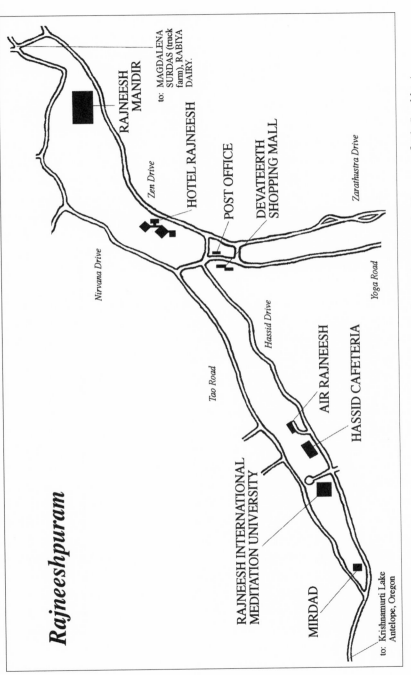

The city of Rajneeshpuram was located on the ten-square-mile Rancho Rajneesh. (Courtesy of Vik Gumbhir.)

one could easily imagine the most cosmopolitan American university communities of ten years earlier. Sometimes sannyasins referred to a time warp that transported them back to their college years. The ambiance on Devateerth Mall combined the joyful spiritual dedication of Hassidic Brooklyn with the countercultural optimism of a Boulder or Berkeley. Videos and print advertisements aimed at spiritual travelers portrayed the ranch as a gorgeous resort for aging boomers, who dressed in the latest casual styles, so long as they were in the color range from deep purple to claret to bright orange.

Rajneeshpuram was the Ruby City, a veritable Oz springing out of the Big Muddy Ranch amid the dry hills and pungent sage. Except for winter snowstorms and occasional spring and autumn rains, brilliant blue skies enhanced the commune's visible attractions: an elegant, marble-faced reception and public relations building, a comfortable small hotel, A-frame cabins for more budget-conscious guests, and the restaurants, boutiques, and the huge bookstore along the mall.

The most elegant restaurant at Rajneeshpuram, Zorba the Buddha, served vintage champagne, brie and artichoke combinations, and multi-layered French pastries. Ordinary devotees ate simple meals in two different vegetarian cafeterias that featured everything that could possibly be cooked with lentils or sprouts. Magdalena and Hassid Cafeterias were located in the ranch's private areas, along with many prefab administration buildings, the intercommunal bus terminal, and the Rajneesh International Meditation University, a one-story building housing therapists' offices and personal growth and meditation groups. Sannyasins lived in A-frames, trailers, prefabricated townhouses, and the few remaining buildings from the old Big Muddy Ranch. All of this was surrounded by the high desert ranch land that the Rajneeshees were trying to turn into experimental truck farms and dairy pastures.

The community, residents and visitors alike, revolved around Bhagwan's somewhat restrained presence. Rajneeshpuram's ultimate purpose was to provide a context in which sannyasins could merge their spirits with their master's. He lived with his companion, Vivek, and his personal favorites in a compound called Lao Tzu Grove, as his Pune household had also been named. From 1981 through mid-1985 Bhagwan was silent in public, communing with his devotees through daily mid-afternoon Drive-Bys, when he slowly steered one of his Rolls between the lines of the faithful who fanned out along Rajneeshpuram's main road.

Rajneesh Mandir, a huge, hangarlike lecture hall, was the ranch's spiritual center. On special days followers convened there to glory in Bhagwan's silent presence and to view him on video and, in the summer of 1985, again in person. Even the ordinary sannyasins who had only ten dollars monthly for spending beyond free room, board, and health care, enjoyed the ultimate luxury of daily proximity to Bhagwan.

Many sannyasins, however, had much more to spend. Their families sent them money, administrators regularly forwarded secured trust fund checks, outside consulting provided discretionary support, or grateful community administrators slipped them extra monthly stipends. They could afford gourmet dinners, soft rose velour shirts, or a brief course of therapy about their past lives. The sannyasins with extra money were often generous with their less affluent friends, buying them small presents like scarves or hats, taking them to dinner, or treating them to a therapy session.

The well-heeled, well-traveled sannyasins appreciated the international atmosphere where, despite American dominance, one could hear Dutch, French, Japanese, German, and Hindi spoken at the same dinner table. Affluent sannyasins had replaced their old communities with a new one that provided the same daily comforts and indulgences that they appreciated. It was organized around a comprehensive philosophy providing them with a sense of unique importance.

Even in blistering heat or in near blizzard conditions, sannyasins worked frantically to erect buildings in order to outpace court decisions that could limit the communal city's growth. Despite the exhausting pace, the conversations, and the laughter, there were also powerful, profound silences. During the first years, before music and singing enlivened Bhagwan's Drive-Bys, sannyasins bowed in quiet reverence to their master and to the divinity within themselves. Leaders and group participants shared deep silences during the later phases of strenuous meditations. And very early in the morning, after Bhagwan began to lecture to everyone once again, the wooden bridge to Rajneesh Mandir was crowded with pilgrims who clasped each other's hands and wordlessly breathed in each new day. Those special times called forth an intense spirit of collective solidarity and something akin to mystic solitude.

At other times the ranch reverberated with sounds of hammering and blasting. The old, reconditioned school busses that provided most of the intracommunity transportation farted up and down the winding roads. Sannyasins shouted out greetings and exclamations throughout the day.

The noise and the quiet together sometimes created an uncanny synthesis of materialism and spirituality, allowing devotees to sense briefly the elusive spirit of Bhagwan's ideal, Zorba the Buddha. In the context of this spiritual community and Bhagwan's presence, every detail of life took on added meaning. People crafted ritual and spirituality in terms of their own daily experiences, and in late-twentieth-century Oregon there was a surprisingly feudal community. It had a king, aristocrats, and serfs, all of whom shared a spiritual quest.

Sheela Silverman and the Politics of Rajneeshpuram

Religious quest and its articulation, not political realities, are central to my discussion of Rajneesh and his organization, and there are already extended accounts of the ranch's bizarre political history (Carter 1990). Some general outlines of the community's history and relationships to the wider society, however, provide necessary background for understanding daily life at Rajneeshpuram.

When the Rajneesh organization purchased the Big Muddy, the movement was in the midst of declining membership and accumulating debt. It had developed a worldwide network of centers, but many of those consisted of only a handful of sannyasins, struggling together to send money to Rajneeshpuram or finance their own trips to the summer festivals in central Oregon.

Ma Anand Sheela, formerly Sheela Silverman, superseded Ma Yoga Laxmi as Bhagwan Shree Rajneesh's personal secretary around 1980 (Carter 1990, 79–80). Her skill at political intrigue facilitated her rise to power, but beautiful Sheela consolidated her position by vowing to strengthen the international movement and establish a communal city in the United States (Strelley 1987).

Sheela was president of the Rajneesh Foundation International, personal secretary and spokeswoman for Bhagwan, and capricious empress of Rajneeshpuram (Fitz Gerald 1986, 278–81). Everything in the communal city revolved around Sheela's intuitions and decisions. She set internal policies and also functioned as the group's spokeswoman to the media and the outside world.

Sheela could change instantly from charming and flirtatious to abrasive and vicious, because she inevitably sought adulation and approval, and became furious when she did not receive them. She governed the community without any previous experience, and she grew increasingly irrational during her four years in Oregon, as litigation and financial overextension threatened not only Rajneeshpuram but also the entire Rajneesh movement.

Only thirty years old when she seized the spotlight, Sheela had been raised in Gujarat Province in India, the spoiled darling of a middle-class family with six children. At seventeen she joined two brothers and a sister who had immigrated to the United States, enrolling as a fine arts major at Montclair State College in New Jersey (Fitz Gerald 1986, 278–81). She met and married an affluent American student, Marc Silverman. The young couple traveled to India, where they both took sannyas and eventually moved to the Shree Rajneesh Ashram.

When Sheela's young husband died of Hodgkins lymphoma, in the late 1970s, she married another sannyasin, who had been a New York banker (Carter 1990, 80). Her marriages to privileged Americans helped cement Sheela's power in the movement, as did her good looks and her well-honed ability to ingratiate herself with other sannyasins who had internal political influence or financial resources. Sannyasins viewed Sheela with mixed emotions, depending on their personal encounters with her or her inner circle, but no one publicly spoke against her until she fled Rajneeshpuram with her entourage on September 14, 1985.

Sheela was deeply implicated in all of the major plots and crimes that guaranteed that Rajneeshpuram would collapse. The central areas of conflict with the outside world involved disputes over land use, constitutional violations, immigration issues, election abuses, physical intimidation and attempted murders, as well as verbal confrontations and harassment. After she decamped, Sheela was also accused of wiretapping, intimidation, conspiracy, and attempted murder of sannyasins living at Rajneeshpuram.

Sheela and other community leaders initially tried to generate citizen support for their communal city, by cultivating influential officials, speak-

ing to local chapters of the American Civil Liberties Union, courting
sympathetic reporters, providing tours and speakers to curious groups,
and organizing a sophisticated public relations staff. Diplomatic efforts
turned into futile exertions, however, because of Sheela's own abrasive
statements and the callous treatment of outsiders who stood in the way of
her many plans.

The Big Muddy had been zoned as restricted farmland, and until the
community disbanded there were public charges made by environmental
groups such as 1,000 Friends of Oregon, as well as civil lawsuits, government investigations, and fines levied for land-use and building code violations. The Oregon attorney general, David Frohnmayer, challenged the
incorporation of Rajneeshpuram itself as an unconstitutional merger of
church and state. In December 1985, after Rancho Rajneesh was already
up for sale, the Federal District Court enjoined the City of Rajneeshpuram from exercising governmental power, because there was no effective
church-state separation.

Along with land-use and legal questions there were also disputes about
who was using the land. The Federal Immigration and Naturalization Service (INS) closely investigated Bhagwan Shree Rajneesh's immigration
status from the very beginning. He had come to the United States to seek
medical treatment requiring a stay of less than a year and later requested
extensions of his visa because of his work as a religious teacher. After legal
disputes with Rajneesh attorneys, the INS rescinded its earlier deportation order (Carter 1990, 161–65). Nevertheless, federal agencies continued to investigate sannyasins who were foreign nationals and had
recently married U.S. citizens (Carter 1990, 150–52). After Rajneeshpuram collapsed, some of those marriages proved to be founded on deep
emotional ties, but the majority were probably arranged for immigration
purposes.

State and local elections also generated tension with outsiders. Shortly
after sannyasins purchased the Big Muddy, they began buying real estate
in the tiny hamlet of Antelope, the town closest to Rajneeshpuram. By
spring of 1982 the forty or so longtime residents feared that they would
be overrun by sannyasins unless they voted to disincorporate. The disin-
corporation election failed because of new Rajneesh voters, whose representatives soon controlled both Antelope's city council and its school
board. The townspeople's varied battles against the newcomers, who

eventually changed *Antelope* to *City of Rajneesh,* drew widespread public attention and generated a number of lawsuits.

More national attention turned toward central Oregon in the autumn of 1984, when Sheela and her inner circle developed a plan to bus in several thousand homeless individuals, mostly men, recruited in cities across the United States. They were to be rehabilitated in the Buddhafield, and, not coincidentally, they could also vote in the November election in which sannyasins were candidates for seats on the Wasco County Commission. Massive negative publicity, state monitoring of voter registration, and legal opposition doomed the plan. At the last minute Sheela instructed everyone at Rajneeshpuram to boycott the polls.

By the end of 1984 almost all of the homeless visitors had left. Before the election, however, information about the conflict and impending debacle spurred Bhagwan to abandon his vow of silence and begin speaking to a small group, the Chosen Few. While control of Rajneeshpuram shifted, state and federal officials continued investigations of Sheela, her entourage, other sannyasins, and Bhagwan himself.

The following year, a handful of influential sannyasins who had been there since the Pune days defected and began to talk with authorities. On September 14, 1985, Ma Anand Sheela and members of her inner circle fled Rajneeshpuram for Europe. Bhagwan accused them of a wide variety of crimes against sannyasins, the public, and the state of Oregon.

The crimes included attempted murder of state and federal officials who were investigating the ranch, attempted murder of Bhagwan's personal physician, and mass salmonella poisoning of 750 individuals in almost a dozen restaurant salad bars located in the county seat of The Dalles. This was the largest known incident of germ warfare in the United States, and Sheela had designed it as a test run for a more massive effort that could temporarily incapacitate large numbers of anti-Rajneesh voters on the upcoming election day (Carter 1990, 224–26). Rajneesh also charged his former personal secretary and her circle with drugging sannyasins, wiretapping, arson, and embezzlement of Rajneesh movement funds.

Police, FBI agents, and more than one hundred reporters were welcomed to the ranch as Bhagwan and his new personal secretary, Ma Prem Hasya, pledged that they would create a clean slate. They blamed Sheela and her intimates for every crime. In the wake of the investigations dozens of sannyasins received subpoenas to testify before the county grand jury, and Bhagwan himself was served on October 6, 1985. There were also rumors that warrants were being prepared for his arrest.

Less than two weeks later federal agents in Charlotte, North Carolina, captured Bhagwan, when two Lear jets carrying him and a handful of sannyasins stopped to refuel en route to Bermuda. His personal physician, Devaraj, and the devotees who accompanied him watched helplessly as agents led their spiritual master off to prison. Bhagwan was taken from North Carolina to Oklahoma and back to Oregon, where his attorneys posted bond so he could return to Rajneeshpuram. He left the United States less than two weeks later, after filing no-contest pleas to two counts of immigration fraud and paying fines and prosecution costs of $400,000 (McCormack 1985, 116).

Sheela was apprehended and returned to the United States, where she pled guilty to one attempted-murder charge, the salmonella poisonings in The Dalles, other poisonings at Rajneeshpuram, and various conspiracy charges. She served close to three years in federal medium-security prison, paid about $500,000 in fines, and then departed for Europe (Carter 1990, 237–38; Fitz Gerald 1986, 374). Eventually, a number of her confederates also paid fines and served jail sentences for their part in Sheela's schemes.

My formal interviews ended when Bhagwan attempted to flee, and sannyasins' faith in the communal city and in their spiritual master had been badly shaken. The week after Bhagwan negotiated his plea, it was announced that Rancho Rajneesh would be on the market, but during the winter months sannyasins stayed on in the cold and snow in order to sell communal assets and consider their next steps.

Bhagwan and his new staff traveled all over the world seeking asylum and meeting rejection from a number of countries. Eventually, his representatives bargained with the Indian government and resettled in Pune. A number of longtime sannyasins began to return to the Shree Rajneesh Ashram. They quietly refurbished each building and cultivated the magnificent Zen gardens. Pune was once again Bhagwan's home, and it was a destination for spiritual therapy and personal growth.

In 1989 Rajneesh decided that Bhagwan was no longer an appropriate title for him because too many people understood it to mean "God." He tried out the name Buddha and then simply Shree Rajneesh. He finally settled on Osho, a name that varied sources have explained differently.

The Friends of Osho trace the derivation to William James's word *oceanic,* which implies dissolving into the whole of human existence—in other words, being at one with everything there is. They note that *Osho* also carries the meaning of "The Blessed One on Whom the Sky Showers Flowers" (Osho Commune International Press Release 1991). Others write that Osho comes from the Japanese language, implying great grati-tude and respect for one who expands consciousness (Palmer and Sharma 1993). Like almost everything else about Osho Rajneesh, his name itself creates controversy, but it could be interpreted broadly to mean a revered teacher of meditation (Palmer and Sharma 1993, 54).

The movement continued after Osho died on January 19, 1990, as sannyasins heeded his message that his spirit was with them and he had merely left his body.

As the twenty-first century nears, none of Bhagwan's predictions of apocalypse or transformation have reshaped the material world. The commune in Koregaon Park still throbs with music, new meditations, a mystery school, and personal growth groups. Although the Indian gov-ernment has renamed Poona as Pune in order to delegitimate colonial history, the city is much as it was twenty years ago, when the Ashram was at its peak and Bhagwan lectured daily.

Osho left twenty-one members of his inner circle in charge of the organization, and several of them have emerged as leaders. The small, international movement keeps attracting affluent seekers from the Amer-icas, Europe, and especially Japan. When they are not visiting Pune, sann-yasins keep in touch by means of their sophisticated electronic network of group and individual home pages on the World Wide Web. Through stays at the commune, personal contacts, and a number of small, active Osho centers, sannyasins, old and recent, continue the work of transforming themselves and creating a new consciousness that synthesizes spirituality and material pleasure.

The communal sojourn in Oregon will always hold a significant place in the participants' memories. Even those who had never visited Rajneeshpuram mourned when Bhagwan's hillside compound burned in the 1996 summer wildfires. Sannyasins who lived through Sheela's reign of terror still argue among themselves about the reasons for Rajneeshpuram's fall, but most of them believe that their years at the ranch engendered invaluable lessons.

Secrets and Serendipity

The voices of sannyasins presented in later chapters add new dimensions to Rajneeshpuram's collective history and to the continuing debates surrounding it. Bhagwan's presence, Sheela's nefarious plots, and the mixture of desperate secrecy and fierce self-disclosure that pervaded life at Rajneeshpuram shaped this book. These influences created the unique research situation that I will describe in the next chapter.

The many levels of political intrigue at the ranch were beyond my understanding. Multiple secrets masked the power struggles, deceptions, legal battles, and reconfigurations of Bhagwan's inner circle. Sannyasins were eager to reveal themselves in many intense and intimate conversations, but they still kept some secrets, which they believed protected Bhagwan or sustained his communal dream.

Until my last visits to Rajneeshpuram, I had little understanding of the destructive potential emanating from Sheela and her inner circle, although I recognized that the intimate questions I asked sannyasins were far *less* threatening to them than questions about Bhagwan or Sheela or the legal and political conflicts within Rajneeshpuram and between the ranch and the outside world. Gradually, I ceased to address political issues. At the same time, I began to realize that sannyasins welcomed highly personal questions, and they did not mind just passing time together. In fact, the possibilities of overcoming the dark forces at Rajneeshpuram motivated sannyasins to talk with me.

Even though we shared a great deal, the fact that I could not or would not fall in love with their master set me apart from the women I encountered at Rajneeshpuram, creating a lasting invisible boundary between us. While I listened carefully to them describing their complicated spiritual relationships with their spiritual master, I had no desire for a deep, charismatic relationship with Bhagwan. Some of the Rajneesh paths to personal and spiritual growth seemed useful and true to me, but I was never caught up in the heart-to-heart connection that is at the core of devotion.

My own lack of full connection to Bhagwan became clear during an early encounter, when a sannyasin and I drove through Portland's crowded, rain-soaked downtown, searching for a place to park. When a space suddenly opened up, this accomplished professional solemnly clasped her hands together, bowed her head, and said, "Thank you, Bhagwan!" She added that the parking space was a sign that my research was OK with Him, and she soon introduced me to several other women and let them know that Bhagwan had sent a sign favoring my presence.

This parking place "miracle" may seem strange, but most Americans search for signs and signals from some higher power. My companion in Portland and the other women of Rajneeshpuram chased contentment by renouncing their past goals and attempting to create new identities. It was the fervor of their pursuit, not the search itself, that marked them as deviant in others' eyes. And the paths of their seekership are what shape this book.

Chapter 2

REVISING VOICES:
THE RESEARCH PROCESS

I spent years grappling with transcripts, field notes, documentary materials, and first and second chapter drafts, because of the almost insurmountable tensions between confidentiality and authenticity. The many personal and legal conflicts associated with Rajneeshpuram made it essential to conceal the women's identities, but it was equally important to convey the complexities and many dimensions of sannyasins' lives, how those different facets fit together, and how each of them constructed and reconstructed their personal worlds.

I chose composite life histories because they anchored sannyasins' own voices in lived experiences that were almost, but not quite, identical to their own biographies. This form is grounded in postmodern approaches that move beyond the confining structures of traditional ethnographic narratives (Denzin and Lincoln 1994, 575–86). I wrote about three composite sannyasins in order to represent the heart of eleven women's life journeys. Readers may become impatient, wanting to know what really took place and what did not. The answers are not simple. The quotations are all taken directly from the respondents, and everything I describe actually happened to them in one way or another. I changed some details, however, in order to protect their anonymity.

As I wrote, the three composite women assumed lives of their own. My descriptions are physically vivid because the respondents' appearances and their overall presences were equally striking. Intellectual, emotional, and spiritual qualities were important to all nine women, but these sannyasins also delighted in the material world. I developed descriptions reflecting what was important to the women themselves while cloaking their actual identities. Thus, for example, all three women who constitute Shanto actually had unique physical characteristics that brought them both joy and ambivalence, although none had long copper-colored curls like those of the woman in chapter 3.

The sannyasins were intelligent, articulate women who described parts of their lives in minute detail. When they did so, I sometimes had to change specifics—for example, transplanting them from other midwestern cities to Chicago, placing a lover in the legal profession when he was actually a corporate executive, or transferring them from the University of British Columbia to the University of Washington. When they provided animated descriptions of people and places, I developed equally colorful images that were very close to their own.

Because my approach reflects recent, somewhat controversial developments in qualitative sociology, I provide an intricate map of what I did and how I did it. This discussion focuses on the specific, concrete aspects of my research, rather than its philosophical foundations in the continuing debate over postmodernism.

The three following chapters present the composite women, Shanto, Dara, and Tanmaya. As their life histories unfold, I will suspend most interpretation in order to emphasize the women's own voices and to allow readers themselves to discern key themes in their life histories. My own voice, decisions, and responses, however, are central to this chapter, because I must disclose something about myself in order to describe the research process. I have pushed against sociological conventions in order to present sannyasins' stories as accurately as possible, but I used widely accepted empirical methods to learn about their lives.

My combination of fairly standard qualitative data with innovative composites anchored by the sannyasins' own words will raise a number of questions about my research, the women I interviewed, our relationships, what I asked them, how they came together into composites, and whether this case study of sannyasins is generalizable to other kinds of people. These issues are central themes in this chapter, and they shaped my own history as a different kind of sojourner in the Buddhafield.

Questions, Answers, and Questions

Composite life histories are most suited to well-researched settings like Rajneeshpuram. Few participants in contemporary social movements have been as publicly visible or historically self-conscious as Bhagwan's sannyasins (Goldman and Whalen 1990). It was fortunate and unusual that such a large variety of unpublished and published resources were available, so that I could focus on individuals' personal accounts.

In order to understand the complicated, multiple realities of life at Rajneeshpuram, I collected hundreds of unpublished Rajneesh documents, ranging from press releases to personal letters. These framed my questions and helped me weigh sannyasins' answers. Throughout my research I read every issue of the *Rajneesh Times,* the community's newspaper, published weekly or biweekly between 1983 and the end of 1985. I could not be so sure of the validity of my approach, however, without many other sources.

I had access to myriad publications by Bhagwan/Osho Rajneesh, his loyal sannyasins, his critical apostates, and outspoken opponents.[1] A few comprehensive books, particularly Lewis Carter's (1990), were also enormously helpful and informative in grounding the women's stories in the larger history of Rajneesh, his communal city, and its aftermath. Without this academic research and the personal accounts published after Rajneeshpuram collapsed, many aspects of the community and its intricate politics would still mystify me.[2]

Because of these resources, I could focus on two dozen high achievers, who resembled the highest-achieving quartile of sannyasins in terms of their ages, education, occupations, and incomes (Latkin 1987). I collected material from eleven female and thirteen male sannyasins, in research conversations lasting from three to more than twenty hours, and met with all of the women at least twice before collapse seemed to be imminent, a time when most sannyasins could no longer sustain their dreams of a Buddhafield.[3]

After the commune disintegrated in December 1985 and January 1986, I sent out short questionnaires to about thirty sannyasins who had talked with me earlier. In the winter of 1997, either in person or on the telephone, I interviewed twenty women who are or who had been sannyasins. I talked with nine of the original eleven women central to this book and, in order to continue to preserve their anonymity, interviewed eleven women who were also high achievers who had become sannyasins. In February 1998 I toured the Big Muddy and talked with members of Young Life, who were in the process of transforming the remains of Rajneeshpuram into a summer camp for Christian youth.

In the course of this research I also interviewed individuals who

resembled the sannyasins but who had never joined a new religious movement. Shortly after Rajneeshpuram collapsed, three colleagues and I
developed a comparison sample of nonsannyasins matched with the
group of twenty-four sannyasins in terms of their occupations, gender,
ages, and education (Sundberg, Goldman, Rotter, and Smythe 1992). All
of the members of the comparison group knew about Rajneesh and his
philosophies, but they never became sannyasins. We were interested in
discovering what, if anything, about the sannyasins differed from their
comparators, in terms of their life histories and the organization of their
personalities, as measured by a widely used projective test, the Thematic
Apperception Test (TAT).

In the middle of our first and second research conversations I asked
sannyasins to invent stories in response to six cards from the Thematic
Apperception Test.[4] The TAT is a collection of ambiguous pictures that
cue people to invent relatively long stories, which can reveal central
emotional issues, such as their desires for affiliation, intimacy, power,
achievement, or transcendence (Murray 1943). The sannyasins enjoyed
devising elaborate tales, and they all scored well within normative ranges
on every variable while also demonstrating their considerable intelligence and imagination (Sundberg, Goldman, Rotter, and Smythe 1992).

One TAT card measures achievement motivation, portraying a boy
gazing at a violin that sits in its case on the table before him. A sannyasin
who is part of the composite Tanmaya told a long story about this card
that demonstrated both the general kinds of descriptions the cards
prompt and also the sannyasins' storytelling talents. She began:

> There was this child, and his name was Tony. He had been told many
> things in life about what could happen to him when he got older and
> what was possible when he became "somebody." One of the things
> that they advised him, to round out his personality and to help him
> become what he would like to become, and what his parents and
> society would like, was music. . . . He chose a violin because it was
> smaller. He could put it in a case, and he could carry it around with
> him. He could also go into a room away from his parents. He didn't
> have to be out in a big room like with a piano.

She went on to describe Tony's many difficulties learning to play and to
overcome his awkwardness. He often felt discouraged. But at last some-

thing in him awakened, so that Tony could contemplate the beauty of the music and the beauty of his own possibilities. He sometimes sneaked out to play baseball when he should have been practicing, but he continued to play the violin regularly and to grow because of it. She concluded, "He will be able to communicate and love people more deeply and have more understanding, because he did allow the music to grow within him."

This story resembled those of other sannyasins in its detail and imagination, but it was far richer than the usual responses to the card. The TAT manifestly offered information about sannyasins' cognitive and emotional functioning, but it also provided me with a way to understand some of the unique creativity, self-awareness, and emotional expressiveness that the women in this book compelled me to record.

I broke almost every unwritten methodological rule by distilling down from forty-six male and female sannyasins and their comparators to twenty-four male and female sannyasins, to eleven women sannyasins, and finally, to only three women. First I focused on women, then only on Rajneesh women, and finally captured those women in the three composites in order to present their rich outer and inner lives.

Even forty-six, the amount of interviews with which I began, is a minuscule number for conventional sociologists, who often consider a thousand people to be only a tolerably representative sample. Innovative sociologists, however, are increasingly drawn to a small number of cases, or even a single individual, in order to examine the full range of intricate interactions of personal choices and structural forces (Romero 1995). Because my research questions focused on sannyasins' life histories and their personal and spiritual development, I diminished the quantity of respondents to facilitate deeper understandings. As we talked over the months and sometimes years, the women revealed many dimensions of their biographies, although their candor and the richness of their accounts also presented unexpected challenges.

Boundaries

At the Rancho Rajneesh I moved back and forth along a continuum between being an observer and a full participant. I was more than just a visitor, but in most cases I was less than a friend (Becker 1967; Neitz 1998; Reinharz 1992). My own identity as a middle-class, achieving baby boomer created wordless understandings and assumed commonalities between me and many sannyasins. At some point in their lives most of the women had resided in or near the three big West Coast cities, which I knew very well, so we could become acquainted while chatting about colleges, neighborhoods, restaurants, bookstores, and boutiques. We also discovered a surprising number of mutual friends and acquaintances from our pasts, and talking about them allowed us to be more open to one another.

The sannyasins, as they themselves often noted, were possibly the most interesting single group ever to settle in Oregon. One of my major identifications with them was as an urban outsider, caught in a relatively bland state that seemed to be peopled by individuals of Northern European descent who told me things like, "I've never met anyone Jewish before. Do you mind if I stare at your nose?" If I was unusual, the sannyasins were positively inexplicable in this homogeneous social landscape.

My most important identification, however, was with the women who had scaled down or given up exciting careers for something more meaningful to them. Like many of the sannyasins I met, I had grown up expecting to make marriage and children my profession. When the second wave of American feminism opened new possibilities to women, I was at the front of the line, struggling through those recently unlocked doors. But over a decade of work I had learned that occupational mobility didn't provide everything I needed. I had two children in my mid-thirties, and I had begun to rethink the priorities in my life.

In the early 1980s thousands of women my age were also reflecting on their decisions (Gallese 1985). The women who talked with me had already reordered their priorities, often leaving behind hard-won educational credentials, lucrative careers, lovers, husbands, and children in order to create meaningful, integrated lives. Their extreme choices could allow me and other women to examine those that we made.

We could consider why we continued to cast family and love in stark opposition to occupational achievement. At Rajneeshpuram accomplished women appeared to have developed a synthesis of love and work. Was that synthesis possible elsewhere? How and why had the sannyasins made their choices? What did those choices mean for them?

Although we resembled one another in so many ways, sannyasins rec-

ognized my distance from them far more readily than my academic colleagues did. Since I was so enthusiastically interested in each devotee, in
their communal city, and in Bhagwan and his philosophy, a number of
other sociologists became suspicious. They asked me about joining,
remarking: "Did you go native? What's 'it' like?" My last major book was
about prostitution, and I'd heard those sorts of questions before. Same
tone, slightly different leer.

The phrase *going native* signifies contempt for positive identification
with an individual or group that is part of research, and it also carries
Eurocentric undertones about white anthropologists and tribal peoples.
While the phrase has passed from serious ethnographers' vocabularies, it
is still part of many sociologists' casual conversations. Often, *going native*
is now used with humor, masking continuing assumptions that different
social groups are somehow less evolved than contemporary American
academia. Nevertheless, despite its obvious condescension and narrow-
ness, the pejorative *going native* raised underlying issues about myself.

I shared many similarities with the women of Rajneeshpuram, but I
differed from them in fundamental ways. At times our dissimilarities star-
tled us, because we seemed to share so much, and it was very difficult for
us to be open to one another in the moments after we discovered some of
our many differences. Not surprisingly, the greatest distances involved
the fact that I did not develop a charismatic connection with Bhagwan
Shree Rajneesh. I certainly "went native" in terms of empathy with sannyasins and recognition of our mutuality. Yet our unique relationships to
one another were bounded by continual surprises about our differences
(Neitz 1987, 14–20).

Boundaries shifted again and again, as we came to know one another in
the process of extensive research conversations. Emotional and intellectual connections with many sannyasins came easily for me, but I never
truly considered the complete identification of becoming a sannyasin
myself. Because I could not fully share their daily experiences or subjec-
tive realities, the women themselves had to supply the thick descriptions
that illuminate the process of living as a devotee (Geertz 1973). Their
own voices were essential to their unfolding stories.

Some sannyasins who only met me casually also assumed that I was a
"native" because I was a frequent visitor, and I picked up the community's
argot fairly quickly. Without thinking about it, I began to use words like

juicy for *full of life* or *conditioning* to signify past socialization. My language was not a careful research strategy, but it was instead a natural adaptation to conversations in a bounded social group (Richardson, Stewart, and Simmonds 1978). In writing this book, I also use the language I heard at Rajneeshpuram, so I usually call the spiritual master Bhagwan, rather than Rajneesh or Osho.

One instance of mistaken membership occurred shortly after new leaders announced that Rajneeshpuram would be closed. A young woman sat down companionably at my table at Magdalena Cafeteria and asked, "What, are you still here?" She believed that I would be one of the early departers, because I had a car at the ranch. Although I never dressed entirely in sunrise colors or wore a *mala,* she had failed to register those differences because she had seen me so many times.

Our brief conversation took place less than two years after my first visit, when I came along with two University of Oregon psychology professors and their graduate students. They had already collected demographic information and administered the California Personality Inventory to sannyasins, with the support of key staff and Ma Anand Sheela's tacit approval. When they invited me to visit Rajneeshpuram with them in spring of 1984, the psychologists planned to report to the Rajneesh Humanities Trust about their progress with data analysis, hoping to receive permission to conduct more research

It was an unusually cold and damp May, and mud clogged Rajneeshpuram's unpaved streets. Everyone else was dressed sensibly in jeans, sweaters, and warm jackets. I wore a professional-looking blue blazer, gray flannel skirt, and, inconceivably, polished black pumps. The shoes represented my misguided attempt to communicate that I was a serious sociologist who was not trying to pass as a Rajneeshee or otherwise ingratiate myself. Much later I learned that some sannyasins wondered who on earth I was and why was I dressed in such a "weird costume." On subsequent visits to Rajneeshpuram and with sannyasins in other places, I dressed more casually, but I remained careful not to wear any red-based sunrise colors. Boundaries had to be clear, I reasoned.

I became aware of the full implications of my choice during the following winter, January 1985. It was freezing in central Oregon, so I pulled on a warm rose-colored sweater as I prepared to join a group of

sannyasins for a festive dinner at Zorba the Buddha Restaurant on Devateerth Mall. One of our party was a casual acquaintance. When she saw
my sweater, she gasped, "You *do* like us after all!"

At the time I simply laughed. But later that night I realized some additional symbolism of my insistence on separation. Red was fast becoming
an almost forbidden color in Oregon, and Nordstroms, the state's major
upscale department store, had racks and racks of red garments that could
not be unloaded at any price (McCormack 1985, 51). I communicated
mistrust, not professionalism, by never wearing any red-based colors.
From that evening on I tried to wear at least one garment in a sunrise
shade.

Later that spring I understood the significance of color even better
when I drove my mud-covered Volvo home and stopped for gas at
Madras, the largest town in the vicinity of the ranch. My Rajneeshpuram
parking permit was visible on the dashboard. I wore a red flannel shirt
with ordinary Levis. The attendant refused to serve me. This was a common kind of occurrence, as mutual political hostility escalated in Oregon, and sannyasins and outsiders became increasingly suspicious of each
other.

Dangers and Disguises

Perhaps my research would have worked out differently if I had worn
something in a sunrise color on my first visit to the ranch. I submitted a
two-page request to research gender roles in the communal city, before
seeing the ranch with a public relations hostess, sometimes called a
"Twinkie" (a reference to Hostess cupcakes). After the tour we had lunch
at Magdalena Cafeteria, and I conversed with some other influential sannyasins, who were clearly checking me out. The verdict was split, and late
that afternoon one of Sheela's representatives told me that the board of
the Rajneesh Humanities Trust would not approve my research plan. I had
no authorized access to sannyasins or formal communal support of any
kind. Sheela's representative sneered that I really didn't understand the
sannyasins at all and that it would be best if I came to live at Rajneeshpuram to "be with us." I was still welcome to visit, however. And there was

one other small opening in the wall as well. In keeping with Bhagwan's teachings, if people wanted to talk with me, they could. The swami hissed, "It is up to the individual."

That evening the psychologists, their students, and I ate a Marseilles-style pizza on Devateerth Mall, and the two sannyasins who joined our table seemed interested in my ideas. Over the coming months I became acquainted with another devotee based on the outside, who introduced me to a number of sannyasins living both at Rajneeshpuram and else-where in Oregon. They were the first sannyasins I got to know, and through our discussions I gradually developed a list of questions that became the framework for all of the semistructured research conversa-tions. I continued to visit the communal city, taping a handful of inter-views with residents whom I had originally met outside the narrow canyon walls.

During my third stay at the ranch, early in 1985, doors opened. As I gulped an espresso at the Eurostyle coffee bar in the Hotel Rajneesh lobby, waiting to catch an old school bus to Rajneesh Meditation Univer-sity for a Nataraj dance meditation, an attractive swami started a conver-sation. We sipped our coffee and chatted about current events, life on the outside, the ranch, and my research. He made some insightful sugges-tions and described some sannyasins who would probably enjoy partici-pating in the research. When I returned from meditation, I made several appointments for that visit and the next one. Somehow people seemed generally friendlier, the public relations staff was more encouraging, and my research progressed.

Much later I learned that the man I encountered was one of the sann-yasins who quietly and consistently challenged Sheela and her policies. A few months earlier, after the public debacle of Sheela's Share-a-Home project, he had been selected as part of the small group in attendance at Bhagwan's private discourses with the Chosen Few. The balance of power at Rajneeshpuram was slowly shifting, and the increased acceptance of me and my work reflected that shift.

I long considered the meeting at the coffee bar to be a matter of sheer chance. For years afterward I believed that the happy combination of my persistence in the face of initial rejection and lucky coincidence gener-ated the fateful conversation with someone who immediately seemed like an old friend. He reminded me of the guys I had grown up with, who had been longtime confidants since high school. Now I'm not so sure about the role of chance. As more and more material emerged about Rajneesh-puram, the wiretapping, bugged rooms, plots and counterplots, I think it quite possible that our meeting was carefully orchestrated. I saw my contact from time to time over the following year, and he was always friendly, never overly inquisitive or controlling. Nevertheless, I wonder if I was not an insignificant, easily manipulated part of the schemes and artifice that defined the politics around Bhagwan. People with influence may have advocated making Rajneeshpuram more open to me.

Throughout the year following that cup of espresso there was always the possibility that access could be denied as quickly as it had been facilitated. During the July 1985 Summer Festival I enlisted the help of two visiting sannyasins, who held doctorates in psychology. They formally interviewed nine of the thirteen male sannyasins after Sheela left and most informed outsiders believed that Rajneeshpuram would collapse. I wanted to catch sannyasins at the height of their commitment, when they still could believe that Rajneeshpuram was a utopia that could last forever and even Sheela's misdeeds could be overcome. When Bhagwan was arrested in flight from the United States, most of the residents knew the Buddhafield was doomed, although there was short-lived optimism that he could return to Oregon. Sannyasins hoped that new leadership could convince detractors of the rank and file's peacefulness, sincerity, and potential economic contributions to the state.

In order to find out answers to the questions that were most interesting to me, I, too, had to keep many secrets. In retrospect, perhaps the greatest secret was denying my own fear during most visits to the ranch. I was barely aware of how afraid I had been, until shortly after Bhagwan had left the United States. When sannyasins were still trying to keep Rajneeshpuram afloat in the master's absence, I drove up the winding gravel road past empty guardhouses. The armed security personnel and their walkie-talkies had vanished, and, despite bad weather and the threat of snowfall, the drive had never felt so relaxing.

This was a startling contrast to most of my other visits. From spring 1985 through fall 1986 security appeared to tighten weekly. Each successive time I visited, more guards noted cars on the winding road to Rancho Rajneesh, more patrols checked identification to enter the private residential and farming areas, bigger, more powerful weapons were visible, and the armed protection surrounding Bhagwan expanded. I accepted the formal explanations for these changes, and I shrugged them off as necessary responses to growing negative publicity and rising external hostility. These justifications also grounded my rationalizations for greater and greater invasions of my own privacy, most obviously searches of my car, luggage, and eventually my person.

On my first trip to Rajneeshpuram registration was a brief formality. By October 1984, however, visitors had to sign lengthy statements absolving the Rajneesh Corporation of any liabilities, stipulating that they did not use or carry any street drugs or weapons and agreeing to abide by the many rules set forth by Rajneesh Foundation International. I automatically signed those conditions of registration many times, and I also allowed my car, luggage, briefcase, and purse to be searched by hand and sniffed by dogs. On two later visits a somewhat abashed swami gently frisked me.

These incursions did not occur suddenly or all at once. At Mirdad Reception Center polite rationalizations and embarrassed humor accompanied each new violation. I submitted to them because they were gradual and cumulative, and everyone around me also complied with the rules for disclosure. In an isolated situation it is easy to suspend judgment and follow the rules, especially when refusal seems both inappropriate and impolitic (Milgrim 1972; Browning 1992). No one threatened me with punishment for noncompliance, but I understood that, if I refused to be searched, my precarious entrée into the community could vanish, possibly forever.

With each visit I had also invested more time and thought into understanding the sannyasins and the world they had created. I did not want to lose my investment or affront the people who had already befriended me. If, by protecting my privacy, I were ejected from the community, some of the sannyasins who talked with me would probably fall under suspicion. All of these considerations crossed my mind in response to each new security measure, but I never paused to consider them seriously. I kept telling myself that my discomfort didn't really matter, and I suppressed my chilling doubts. At the time I rationalized and complied in many of the same ways that sannyasins did.

Later, as I thought about my own responses to various physical risks, I could better comprehend why so many people acquiesced to Sheela's reign of terror. They wanted to stay near Bhagwan at Rajneeshpuram, so they seized on every possible rationalization to neutralize their discomfort. Sannyasins failed to respond to their own fears or to others' distress because they were able to believe that they did not understand the full meaning of each situation. They disassociated their experiences of risk from the tapestry of danger that spread across Rajneeshpuram.

Over the years since the communal city collapsed in 1985, I have learned, through published information and personal conversations, that my hotel rooms had been bugged, my telephone conversations monitored, many mailed transcriptions had never reached the respondents who wanted to review our discussions, and I had been followed while walking around Rajneeshpuram. Sheela's confederates had even taped a few research conversations. By the spring of 1985 some sannyasins arranged the location of our discussions outdoors, where there was little possibility of monitoring.

I suspected many of these occurrences, and for the most part I went out of my way to talk myself out of my fears. Yet a dozen years later, after I returned to tour Sheela's secret passages and laboratories, I realized that I had been at remote, albeit real, physical risk (Goldman 2000). It is doubtful that I would have been physically harmed, because Sheela and her inner circle viewed me as an annoyance rather than a threat. Nevertheless, danger influenced my selection of topics and the ways in which sannyasins responded to me (Ferrell and Hamm 1998).

I was trained to jump into formidable communities, armed only with a paper, pencil, and portable tape recorder. This is the approach to fieldwork developed in the University of Chicago's Department of Sociology shortly after World War I (Park 1925; Ragin and Becker 1992). Chicago School approaches to qualitative research exhort sociologists to become immersed in exciting social worlds, trusting that their academic training and good intentions will keep them safe from harm.

Those of us who follow the Chicago School tradition of fieldwork walk in the footsteps of holy clowns found in many faiths, ranging from Buddhist to Christian to Zuni (Krueger 1996). Holy clowns and ethnographers share a common disregard for conventional wisdom, so that we may perceive larger truths. Ethnographers pursue questions that are of personal and theoretical interest, often disregarding emotional and physical dangers. We unintentionally appropriate power because we believe that we are safe and that we will ultimately make discoveries explaining different social worlds to both our subjects and also the wider society (Dunier 1992).

From the beginning of my research I was wary and occasionally even melodramatically suspicious, but I never considered realistic possibilities of harm. Unfounded anxiety marked my first visit because of the sharp memory of Jonestown six years earlier. Rajneeshpuram's isolation from the outside world called up associations with that other doomed community. I should have worried about ruining my shoes, but instead I feared that the spicy lentil stew served at Magdalena Cafeteria might be doped with some kind of feel-good drug like Ecstasy. That wasn't true, but I later learned that selected sannyasins' food was routinely laced with tranquilizers or mildly debilitating poisons.

Even in the spring of 1984, before large-scale spying developed, I was occasionally afraid of being monitored. Phoning home, I spoke tersely, somehow sure that the public telephones were tapped. I later learned that they were indeed one of the first areas of covert surveillance.

Sheela also installed listening devices in all twenty-four rooms of the Rajneesh Hotel at the ranch. I usually shared quarters with a visiting sannyasin whom I knew or with a graduate student, and when we talked in the room I tried to applaud everything and everyone connected with Rajneeshpuram. Occasionally, I attempted to quiet my fears of monitoring by candid, somewhat negative comments indicating assurance that the room was not wired. In one case I made negative remarks about a swami who had eagerly shared part of his life story but later on refused to meet with me again. He was always cold after that weekend, probably because my exaggerated criticisms had been relayed to him.

On another day, alone in the hotel room, I was moved to read aloud from the social theorist Max Weber's classic discussions of charismatic leadership. These translations from nineteenth-century German sociology can be stupifyingly dull, and I have no idea what my unseen listeners thought or how they presented this material to their superiors. This was hardly rational behavior on my part. It was a gauntlet of sorts thrown before someone who I wasn't even sure existed. At that moment, however, I sensed that someone was listening. I was powerless, but I wanted to discover if my fears were true.

Sometimes I was sure that operatives watched my every move, and at other times I dismissed my suspicions as unwarranted paranoia. I was alternatively wary and blatant, suspicious and naive. All of my responses seemed to be intense, mirroring the intensity of the communal city itself.

As a young mother and committed college teacher, I had no need to embark on this adventure. I now realize that my scholarly curiosity might have led to injury or professional embarrassment. I trusted, however, that I would be safe, and I recognized that curiosity can generate new understandings. Yet, when I consider the basic question "Why did you do it?" I can only answer, "Because Rajneeshpuram was there in Oregon."

Physical dangers accompany fieldwork more often than sociologists like to admit (Ferrell and Hamm 1998). Some researchers, however, are aware that they study closed and dangerous groups. Some, like Maurice Punch (1985) and Jerome Skolnick (1966), explore important, powerful organizations such as the urban police. Others focus on dangerous fringe groups such as the Synanon movement or the survivalist Right (Mitchell 1993; Ofshe 1980). Sociologists have been frightened, threatened, and physically assaulted as they pursued intrinsically important questions.

When I began research, I did not believe that the Rajneeshees were particularly powerful, threatening, or violent. Instead, I was fascinated by their potential to provide some answers to fundamental questions about women and personal change. The extreme case of the sannyasins could reveal something more general about the ways in which contemporary American women come to terms with work and love.

Conversations

Research conversation or *extended discussion* describes my interactions with the respondents far more accurately than the term *interview*. *Interview* implies formality, hierarchy, and structure, all of which were notably absent as I recorded sannyasins' life histories. I developed a list of questions from academic sources and from my early discussions with sannyasins, and these provided rough guidelines for our conversations. Although I introduced some topics and sometimes requested clarifications, our discussions were usually mutual and reciprocal.

Conventional sociologists are sometimes troubled by blurred distinctions between subject and researcher. The ambiguity in our roles, however, generated trust and encouraged disclosure. The sannyasins who talked with me shared my curiosity and also many of my concerns. I recorded my own feelings during the research, because emotions are part of the creation of knowledge (Reinharz 1992). Ignorance of one's own assumptions and responses distorts the research process itself and the analysis and presentation of information.

The sannyasins and I began our long talks with the first question from the list guiding all of my focused conversations with the eleven women. I asked, "Tell me about the day you took sannyas." This usually prompted an elaborate description and ensuing discussion, providing preliminary answers to some other questions. From that point I occasionally steered the conversations back to a topic that was on my list, but usually I let them flow.

Although I recorded interviews with the sannyasins' informed consent, my tape recorder broke down occasionally. So, just in case, I took enough notes to insure that specific answers would not get lost. After every interview I checked our conversations against my list in order to make sure that each sannyasin was addressing the same questions and also to make sure that I followed up issues the women had introduced.

I imposed structure in only three places: at the end of our first research conversation and in the middle of the first and second conversations. At the end of our first conversation each sannyasin and I went over demographic information about things like her year of birth and number of sisters and brothers. In the middle of the first and second discussions I asked sannyasins to make up stories in response to cues from the six TAT cards.

The sannyasins revealed themselves during the interviews, through the TATs, and when we simply hung out together. Our casual encounters often provided as much information as our formal conversations. Fortuitous interactions, shared meals, and even my occasional faux pas substantially supplemented our scheduled discussions. When I spilled coffee on her prized antique oriental rug, I learned about a sannyasin's grace and tact, as well as the luxurious life she led before finding Bhagwan. On another occasion a pile of velvet I assumed to be drapery material actually turned out to be cloth for Bhagwan's robes. How and why two women glossed over my tactlessness showed me about the ways in which sannyasins revered and guarded their spiritual master.

Throughout every part of the research we learned about one another and also about ourselves. Our focus on personal life histories and the length of our acquaintance made it unlikely that sannyasins would deliberately lie to me. Nevertheless, the frantic secrecy and quiet desperation that lay just below the surface of life at Rajneeshpuram undoubtedly influenced our encounters.

Keeping Secrets and Speaking Truth

In the context of Rajneeshpuram ordinary, formal guidelines for the protection of human subjects had to be expanded. Like my navy blazer and gray flannel skirt, they didn't fit the situation. I informed each participant about the broad outlines of the project, the protection of respondents' anonymity, and any risks that I believed sannyasins might face through participation.

In most research contexts participants sign a form indicating that they have been informed about those issues. Because of their unspoken knowledge of internal surveillance and the continuing investigations and lawsuits by state and federal agencies, some sannyasins suggested that I take unusual precautions to protect them. I guaranteed complete anonymity, consistently substituted pseudonyms on tapes and transcripts, and gave every respondent a statement documenting their rights. Both of us signed and dated two copies of an agreement, and I kept a copy signed with only their nonsannyas name.

Federal human subjects guidelines require both informed consent and also special sensitivity to topics involving sex, drugs, or crime. Once again established guidelines did not fit research at Rajneeshpuram. Because of Bhagwan's support of open communication about intimate matters, the sannyasins, to a woman and to a man, took pride in the ways in which they had come to terms with their own sexuality. I offered to turn the tape recorder off during florid descriptions that sometimes made me blush, but they laughed and made comments like "No, you *must* hear this!"

Sannyasins also offered candid discussions about their consumption of street drugs *before* finding Bhagwan, possibly exaggerating their use in order to affirm the positive effects of spirituality. Some admitted that they still used recreational drugs on occasion, and those conversations went unrecorded.

Until Sheela was deposed, sannyasins were cautious about their slips of criticism against her or her entourage, and they shied away from any topic touching on the internal or external politics of Rajneeshpuram. After Sheela and her inner circle fled, some sannyasins talked at length about how they had felt while she was ascendant, often blaming themselves for their tacit compliance with her arrogance and impulsive decisions. A few women briefly described their complicity in minor crimes, and I immediately forgot the details of those conversations.

Although I had sent early respondents transcripts of our interviews, most did not reach them. I discontinued mailing copies to Rajneeshpuram in June 1985 and then resumed in September of that year. This interchange was an important part of mutuality in research. The sannyasins who returned transcripts to me usually corrected grammar and spelling and amplified their comments. Only one sannyasin deleted our substantive discussions, taking out references to a convenient marriage to a foreign national and to personal financial arrangements for supplementary income. She was unusually protective, and other respondents described similar marital and financial arrangements without reservation.

One of the women, who returned her transcripts after she had left Rajneeshpuram, voiced a positive response shared by other respondents. She wrote: "Thank you for sending the huge transcript. It has helped me to read about my life in this time of transition."

Each conversation provided a framework for both of us to understand more. Sannyasins engaged in explaining their decisions to themselves as well as to me. In our research conversations they witnessed to the meaning of their commitment and affirmed the choices they had made. Our talks became vehicles for self-definition, and women sometimes gained sudden insights into specific relationships between past and present. All of them talked with me after Sheela left the ranch, and the interview process was a useful forum to discuss their enduring devotion to Bhagwan in the face of so many negative revelations.

None of the women whom I asked to take part in the research refused. Some sannyasins even sought me out during the month before Rajneeshpuram finally collapsed. Positive word had spread about the interview process itself.

The success of the interviews reflected the therapeutic sensibility characteristic of the Rajneesh movement. Introspection, reflection, and self-disclosure were essential parts of sannyasins' paths to actualization and enlightenment. Most of the women respondents had partaken of some forms of psychotherapy before becoming sannyasins, and almost all of the men had as well. Sannyasins saw our discussions as a novel opportunity to explore their feelings, often discussing the meanings of their stories in subsequent conversations (Runyan 1982).

The intrinsic value of our meetings, however, was only one reason why people spent time with me. Some sannyasins with strong social science backgrounds were interested in research on gender and spirituality. Two who stood at the edge of Sheela's inner circle kept a watchful eye on me and my project and tried to present positive information about Rajneeshpuram. Others saw our discussions as reasonable acts of rebellion against the current regime. All of the women I interviewed were motivated by mixed combinations of these three reasons, along with more personal, idiosyncratic desires. For the most part, however, the sannyasins' motives did not detract from their merciless truthfulness about their lives.

I still trust each woman's overall honesty, in the face of some general reasons to doubt it. Authorities in relatively small, closed communities like Rajneeshpuram sometimes encourage members to present the same viewpoint or even instruct them explicitly in a common rhetoric. Certainly, honesty was not the order of the day at Rancho Rajneesh. This would not have been the first time that Sheela tried to control information and orchestrate responses (Fitz Gerald 1986, 354; Carter 1990, 274–75, 284).

Deception, however, was more likely to have skewed some of the answers to anonymous questionnaires given to hundreds of sannyasins rather than the highly individual, extended personal interviews that were central to my research. I selected respondents because of their documented educational credentials or high personal incomes. They spoke for themselves and did not represent the whole commune. They told their own life stories and not the story of Rajneeshpuram, so Sheela or her subordinates could not easily orchestrate systematic distortion.

The questions I asked encouraged veracity, as did my written assurances of confidentiality. Few of the women interviewed discussed any of my questions with one another. Most important, however, was the fact that I talked with each of them a number of times, over many months, and with each meeting they disclosed more. In most cases we came to know one another beyond the interview situation, although our mutual respect did not completely compensate for the official ambivalence toward the project, which lasted until Sheela left.

The ambivalence was more than Sheela's personal whim or her attempt to safeguard her own secrets. Ambivalence toward academic scholarship was also embedded in Bhagwan's philosophy. On the one hand, the movement attracted professionals and intellectuals, who became acquainted with Bhagwan through his writings. On the other hand, Bhagwan asserted that formal education created *unconsciousness*. Becoming a sannyasin was the only true way to acquire knowledge of the world and to develop self-knowledge (Clarke 1985, 40–41).

Despite their mistrust of intellectuals, however, movement executives courted academic legitimation in order to enhance the community's public image. The Rajneesh Humanities Trust bestowed formal research access on those scholars who appeared to be both favorable and also useful to their goals. At times the sannyasins' self-interestedness led them to overestimate academics' status and power. For example, some sannyasins on the board of the Trust were naively disappointed and even angry when University of Oregon researchers could not bring large research grants to share jointly with them.

As my research progressed, I was pressured to write letters to editors and to state agencies supporting the sannyasins' efforts to construct buildings in the face of land-use restrictions. I finally wrote in favor of a request for special permission to build a proposed Academy of Rajneeshism housing comprehensive archives that would be available to outside scholars. Less than a week after I mailed the letter to the Wasco County Planning Commission and sent a copy to the Rajneesh public relations temple, I received a thank you note from Shanti Bhadra, one of Sheela's closest associates, who was arrested with her less than a year later in West Germany and who was later convicted of attempted murder in Oregon. The inner circle watched and measured my actions, and that letter served as an important indication of my sincerity and goodwill.

Because of the many pressures on them, sannyasins would not have talked so openly with me unless their anonymity were protected from Sheela's scrutiny, other sannyasins' curiosity, and outsiders' ability to identify them. Although Sheela's displeasure is no longer an issue, and almost all of the criminal charges involving sannyasins have been settled, anonymity remains a problem. Sannyasins did not want to hurt their families, friends, comrades, or lovers, but they wanted to discuss those relationships openly and honestly. Anonymity also became important in the aftermath of Rajneeshpuram, as some people had to patch together new resumes, and some are still in the process of creating different kinds of new selves.

I responded to their diverse concerns as best I could. My explicit promise to guard respondents' identities was in tension with my implicit pledge to present the women's life histories as clearly and accurately as possible. I had to conceal identities without diminishing the full impact of the devotees' life histories, so I developed anchored composites. The composites I constructed present three women whose lives resemble the respondents'. The details I created are frameworks supporting the central ideas and actual voices from our recorded research conversations.

Composites' Logic

My construction of composites is a disputed form of data presentation. Recent criticisms of composites in news reporting have been particularly bitter. Janet Cooke returned her 1981 Pulitzer Prize for feature writing after confessing that she had entirely contrived a six-year-old heroin addict. In 1998 Phillip Glass, a rising star in journalism, confessed he had made up numerous individuals and incidents in stories published in magazines ranging from the *New Republic* to *Rolling Stone* (Bissinger 1998).

Although sociologists Richard Sennett and Jonathon Cobb (1972) created composites grounded in actual interviews and observations, they received some criticisms that were as harsh as those leveled at the journalists who passed off imaginary characters as real composites. Sociologists usually pull together quotations from a number of individuals to illustrate a particular point. Thus, in order to illustrate the fact that the sannyasins had difficulties with their mothers, I might make a statement about those tensions and present two or three quotations to illustrate the point. This type of organization sustains respondents' anonymity, but it does not illustrate the ways in which personal visions are inevitably enmeshed in changing life stories.

I believe that this standard method of presentation is neither more nor less accurate than responsible composites. Quotations drawn out of the context of people's life histories are constructions that distort their voices. I have used composites in order to present all of the women's voices in terms of life histories very similar to their own. I changed some aspects of the women's histories so they could not be identified, but no major event such as marriage, divorce, or childbirth was recorded unless it was shared by the majority of sannyasins in a group.

Because of journalists' fabrications and the many questions raised about composites in academic work, I must present my strategy in some detail, so that readers can evaluate both my general approach and also the specific ways in which the composites were grounded in actual life histories. Some of my strategies for constructing composites are recounted in this chapter, but, in order to avoid tedious descriptions, I have included the full list of my decision rules in appendix B.

Composites built on actual life histories and accurate quotations permit people to speak in their own ways. When sannyasins talked with me, they were organizing and reorganizing their experiences in the same fashion that sociologists examine and classify respondents' accounts. Almost everyone considers and categorizes, trying to learn from the past, consider the present, and anticipate the future. We configure and reconfigure our lives as the construction of social meaning becomes a daily project. In qualitative sociology the search for theoretical meaning is embedded in the research process itself, but it becomes most important when transcripts and ethnographic materials are finally analyzed, organized, and presented.

Qualitative sociology such as this book is an endless spiral of research and reflection in which analysis and writing are as important, possibly more important, than data collection (Becker 1986; Geertz 1988). Narrative inevitably reflects writers' own language and perceptions. Composites offer solutions to some of these distortions by providing readers with access to actors' own voices, while anchoring each voice in a collective biography.

Since I had interviewed such a small number of women sannyasins, I finally decided that the composite approach was the best way to introduce them as multidimensional actors engaged in the process of shaping their experience. I am committed to allowing readers to hear the sannyasins' own voices and appreciate and understand their lives.[5] The composites are true to the women's words, making it possible to reflect on the intricate processes of seekership and surrender.

What sannyasins said and how they said it shaped the three collective biographies in this book. Composites allowed me to shape and prune their stories while still remaining true to the central issues the women themselves raised. Verbatim, unedited transcripts would reveal too much about their identities and too little about the important sociological themes.

As I read and reread transcripts, clear themes emerged. These themes were central to the biographical material and the organization of sannyasins' accounts. I almost memorized most of their interviews in the process of discovering those themes. All of the quotations attributed to the women are gleaned from our recorded research conversations, although there are some minor editorial revisions.

The details in their stories capture the essential experiences of each group of women. Each of the eleven respondents was part of only one composite, and it was the *single* composite most emblematic of her life. Thus, each composite is separate and unique.

Appendix C specifies actual demographic and biographical details in frequency distributions for all of the sannyasins, along with the comparison group, so that readers concerned with specifics can follow the integration of individual biographies into the composite life histories.

In constructing the three women, I borrowed from Karen McCarthy Brown's methodology in *Mama Lola* (1991), a brilliant book about a Haitian *vodou* priestess living in Brooklyn, New York. As she describes Alourdes Margaux and the people surrounding her, Brown relies on Alourdes's own voice while at the same time creating evocative stories with invented details and imagined supporting characters. I have circumscribed my invention, grounding each major life history theme in explicit biographical information.

It was surprising how much the women in each of the three groups sounded like one another, using the same words and articulating similar concerns, even compared to women in the other two composites. They used language and images that reflected when and how they had come of age, and even a few years could create marked differences (Whittier 1995). Historical circumstance was the underlying element bridging individuality and making it possible to join the women together in composites.

The great sociologist C. Wright Mills (1959) perceived sociology as the intersection of personal biography and historical forces. This is precisely what I found in searching for commonalities on which composites could be based. The oldest and youngest women interviewed came of age in quite different historical eras, although they were separated by less than two decades. The women in each cohort resembled their times, even more than they resembled their parents (Bloch 1953, 157).

Historic experience washed away most of the social class differences within each group of the women. The most notable contrasts in social class were among the five individuals who comprise Dara. Three were working-class, one was upper-middle-class, and one was born to the new American aristocracy, but their lives were all remarkably similar. Relative economic security and the availability of student subsidies smoothed class distinctions in their educational experiences and their youthful hopes. Both the daughters of workers and the child of a successful capitalist studied abroad during high school, graduated from outstanding universities, earned professional degrees, and anticipated limitless possibilities in useful, meaningful careers and satisfying egalitarian marriages.

The number of respondents is so small that many patterns within each generational group may be matters of chance. It is probably chance that all of the Shantos were Jewish, four of five women who became Dara were raised as Roman Catholics, and two of three Tanmayas had mild liberal Protestant affiliations when they were growing up. The women were bound together, however, by something far deeper than their original religions. Their similarities cut across their parents' social class, their ethnic backgrounds, or their own educational or occupational histories. Generational experience ultimately defined each of the three composite sannyasins. American women's worlds changed so fundamentally between 1950 and 1980 that the sannyasins' ages during those times defined the range of their life chances.

No single year absolutely marked transitions from one generation to

the other. The three cohorts do not fit precisely within conventional generational parameters because those boundaries are somewhat elastic. It is
implausible to assert that one year or another absolutely demarcated a
new generation, so the three composite groups flowed from sannyasins'
life histories rather than their specific years of birth. Nevertheless, there
was an oldest, middle, and youngest composite, and none of the three
groups' birth years overlapped. The three oldest women were all born
before the United States entered World War II, and the three youngest
were born in the early 1950s. The early baby boomers were the most
uneven, with two born during the war, two born between 1946 and
1948, and one, who skipped ahead in school, born early in 1951. They
shared a common historical experience, however, as did the oldest and
youngest groups.

In fall of 1985, at the time of our last conversations at Rajneeshpuram,
the oldest sannyasin was forty-nine and the youngest was thirty-three.
Only sixteen years separated them, yet those sixteen years represented a
vast cultural gulf. The three oldest women grew up in the shadow of the
Great Depression, and their early biographies were connected more
closely to the past century than to the next one. They matured to become
wives and mothers, having been taught that marriage was a goal that was
morally and materially superior to any other career for a woman.

The five early baby boomers had a very different experience. While
they were growing up, they shared the spreading national affluence and
optimism that marked the 1950s. Their mothers were housewives who
wanted their daughters to do well in school before they became home-
makers themselves. But the 1960s changed the young women's lives, as
they questioned their old assumptions and redirected their energies
toward changing the world.

The final three women were only slightly younger than the earlier
boomers. From the time they were in elementary school, however, they
expected to work outside the home just as their mothers did. They were
of high school age when feminism claimed the covers of all of the national
news magazines, and by the time they were twenty-one these sannyasins
took the issue of women's equality for granted. They were interested in
personal, not social, change. Some of their old friends became yuppies.
They became sannyasins.

Even with a much larger number of respondents, the three different generational categories would remain important defining classifications. There would be marked discontinuity between the lives of women born at the end of the Great Depression and those born during and after World War II. Yet, since the historical changes in the 1950s unfolded unevenly, some women born in the early 1950s would belong to the early boomer cohort, while others would lead the lives of late boomers, depending on their mother's labor force participation and their own experiences as young adults.

I doubt that additional information from many more sannyasins would have added much to the understandings that these eleven cases provide. Both the interviews themselves and the composite presentations made it possible to penetrate surfaces and come to know the sannyasins. The composite women represent the best way of presenting extensive, intensely personal conversations.

Sannyasins often provided the information I sought without my asking, and they also raised unexpected issues that forced me to rethink the theoretical assumptions that originally grounded my research. This possibility for sociological surprises is a major strength of the life history approach in qualitative research. Once social reality and theory meet, both are modified and enriched.

The direction of my questions and the number and nature of respondents defined my research. Once again, the warning: This is not a conclusive history of Rajneeshpuram. I have no definitive answers about the movement's demographics or about the educational attainments of most sannyasins. Instead, the composite approach provides insights into why and how high-achieving women turned their back on affluence and social recognition as they sought to redefine themselves. The women of Rajneeshpuram add to our knowledge of the general process of spiritual seekership and the dynamics of creating and recreating new selves that are embedded in the American spirit.

Common Sense and Case Studies

Case studies like this one are designed to further understanding of some general social processes and also uncover specific information about particular kinds of peoples, places, and times. My research is part of a theoretical tradition that postulates that most behavior that looks different or deviant is, after all, not so far removed from the larger culture.

Deviance is not inherent in any person or action but is, instead, tied to social definitions. To be sure, all societies have rules, but they vary dramatically depending upon what is culturally important (Erikson 1966). The sannyasins appeared to strike at the heart of American values by setting aside achievement and affluence in order to search for personal fulfillment. But their quests for actualization were merely extensions of even more cherished beliefs surrounding the pursuit of happiness.

Some of the most important social-psychological understandings of why and how people change have developed from case studies of a dozen or so believers like the sannyasins. In the late 1950s three University of Michigan social psychologists studied a small group who eagerly expected extraterrestrial visitors to appear and usher in the millennium on a particular date in their near future. The guests from outer space failed to materialize, but members kept their faith and redoubled their efforts to convince others. While they never welcomed in a new planetary order, the group paved the way for the concept of cognitive dissonance (Festinger, Reicken, and Schachter 1956).

Their atypical experience illuminated how people in a variety of circumstances cling to their beliefs in the face of overwhelming empirical disconfirmation. The smitten young man who refuses to acknowledge his lover's growing disinterest or the CEO who continues to invest time and money in a bankrupt business are balancing cognitive dissonance in the same ways as members of the original UFO group.

In another case study a sociologist, John Lofland, spent several years with a tiny group of social misfits in the San Francisco Bay area who formed one of the first cells of the Unification Church, or Moonies, in the United States (Lofland 1981). His research generated a basic model of the social processes leading people to join and work for intense, marginal faiths. The model involved a number of sequential steps, most important of which were diminished contact with individuals who did not believe and increasing interaction with people who shared the faith. Although Lofland's model has been critiqued and modified, it continues to help explain processes like joining a fraternity, getting married, or becoming a political activist.

Extreme cases like the saucer group, the Moonies, or the sannyasins illuminate more common but related social interactions. Because the sannyasins had to give up much in order to harvest the rewards that Bhagwan offered, they were often acutely aware of their own calculations of costs and benefits. They could articulate their choices because they had thought them through and explained their reasons to themselves and to the friends and family they left behind. Thus, the sannyasins' stories reveal other, more pervasive patterns of seekership and commitment that involve less sacrifice and stigma.

Comparisons and further applications of theoretical explanations derived from the sannyasins will indicate whether their situation is actually an extension of more common processes or if it is astonishingly unique and isolated, without wider applicability. At this point it is most likely that the sannyasins can tell us a great deal about ourselves.

Rodney Stark (1996b), sociologist and historian of religion, recently criticized case study approaches. He urged colleagues to stop investigating small, unimportant groups and consider religions with widespread influence and growing membership. Why study groups like a tiny coven of witches or a Rajneesh center in Seattle, Stark asks, when the Jehovah's Witnesses are fast becoming a significant world religion? Yet studies of both large and very small, apparently insignificant groups are important.

Small numbers and extreme cases make it possible to understand fully how and why groups like Jehovah's Witnesses or Mormons have been so influential in recent decades. In-depth research on small groups illuminates processes of recruitment, conversion, and commitment that may be obscured by the size and societal influence of larger groups. When behavior and groups are close to the mainstream, we may accept them without asking necessary questions. When they are at the margins, like the sannyasins, we pay more attention. One central purpose of my research is to better understand the ways women seek connections and spiritual meaning.

The three chapters following this one are about the intimate lives of Shanto, Dara, and Tanmaya. They are composite characters built entirely around the real life histories of eleven women sannyasins whom I interviewed at length, came to know well, and, in some cases, have continued to see regularly. This composite approach allows the women of Rajneeshpuram to read their collective biographies and recognize themselves, while making it very difficult for anyone else to identify them. The women can speak in their own voices while sustaining maximum confidentiality.

The sannyasins allow us to better understand general themes about how women's choices are limited and our desires are socially shaped throughout our lives. Why is it that so many talented women are disappointed with their earlier commitments and seek something different at midlife? How and why do American women go through the life cycle expecting to become fundamentally different at different stages? As you read about Shanto and the other two composite sannyasins, consider the similar themes in all of their life histories. Imagine each one holding up a mirror to millions of other American women who also long to fuse love and work and to create new selves.

Chapter 3

A BORROWED LIFE:
SEEKING AUTHENTICITY

The first time I saw Shanto tiny snowflakes swirled around her upturned collar as she jumped up on the wooden sidewalk that spanned one side of Devateerth Mall in order to avoid a bike rider who was speeding through the crowded street while balancing a huge cake box on his handlebars. Everything about her was exquisite. Tiny and slim, she was dressed in a handwoven, rust- and rose-colored tunic and matching velour stretch pants. From a distance she looked two decades younger than her forty-eight years. One of her housemates, an attractive, somewhat younger man, joined her, and they went inside the general store. They laughed as they stood in the Wine Corner, gently bickering over which vintage would go best with that evening's meal.

I noticed her bright, warm smile and the way Shanto's amazing, flirta-tious blue eyes stood out against her deep olive skin. I also took a good look at her little brown, square-toed alligator boots. They were the kind of boot featured in *Vogue,* probably *French Vogue.* When I see shoes like that on a pedestal in the window of Barneys New York or some other exclu-sive store and then see the $600 price tag, it's easy to go and buy a box of overpriced European chocolates in order to obliterate the passionate, ridiculous desire to own those boots.

Shanto seemed to be unaware of her exquisite clothes or the sidelong glances a number of other sannyasins threw her way, but she was undeni-ably posing as she tossed her shoulder-length mane of curly auburn hair whenever she laughed. For as long as Shanto could remember, that magnificent hair had been her blessing and her bane. Its red sheen prompted her father to nickname her "Copper Penny" during the years she grew up as Penny Bernstein.

Penny's mother used to nag her every night to brush it 100 strokes when she could barely get the bristles through a single time. Her little sister tried to persuade Penny to cut it short so she could be perky like Debbie Reynolds. Her brother, almost twenty years younger, pulled it mercilessly when he was a toddler. When she was little, strangers stopped Penny on the street and commented about her curls. Her fierce Russian grandmother poured out Yiddish curses on her hair, asking rhetorically whether anyone would believe that she wasn't a *shiksa*.

As a girl, Shanto was called Penina or Penny. And she didn't know what to think about her startling hair or beautiful eyes. For years she wished she were blond like the most popular girls in her class. She felt that her hair—in fact, all of her attractive features—seemed to belong to someone else. She was a different person in different contexts, and she was never quite sure whether she was real. At school she was called Penny by her friends and Penelope by teachers who had no knowledge of Jewish tradition. At home she was usually Penny, occasionally Copper, and sometimes Penina, her name from the Torah, honoring her mother's dead father, Pincus.

All her life Penny knew that her looks could be useful in getting what she wanted, but she didn't like it at all. Remembering what she was like when she was eight, Shanto said: "Well, I must admit that I was quite adorable. The type of child people tend to fall in love with. The price is heavy. But it gives you a sense of belonging I guess." Penny also thought of herself as very sharp and precocious. She was a child whom adults loved and other children respected and enjoyed but did not necessarily want as a best friend. And not every adult loved Shanto/Penny unconditionally. She never understood why her grandmother spent hours raging at her.

The Women of the House

Penny's grandmother, Anna Bernstein, was truly terrifying. A tall, fierce woman, she told stories about how she took her ten-year-old son, Penny's father, and walked and bartered and bribed her way from Stalingrad to Riga so that she could spend her last money on tickets. In 1923 they went by ship to New York City. From there they took a train to live with cousins in Chicago. Sometimes, with tears rolling down her cheeks,

Anna used halting English to describe the confiscations, conscriptions, and pogroms that had driven her from Russia. On Friday nights, after a glass of schnapps, she might recall happier memories of her own father, who had once owned factories, or her grandfather, who brought back a silver samovar from his rug- and tobacco-trading expeditions in Central Asia. But she never mentioned her husband or the two grown sons she had left behind.

Anna's son Norman revered her. When he became a successful entrepreneur and moved his family to a big-frame house on Chicago's North Shore, Norman renovated a suite of rooms on the third floor and insisted that Anna move in. Norman was rarely home. He was absorbed in his business and his investments and the board of his orthodox synagogue, so Anna ruled and terrorized his house.

She raised her grandchildren, imperiously ignored her daughter-in-law, and supervised a series of disgruntled African-American domestics. Until Penny was married, she had no idea that *schvartze* was a pejorative term for African American. To her it simply meant Negro, and Anna's stage-whispered phrase "Shh! Not in front of the *schvartze*" was an integral part of private conversations. Her grandmother spent hours cuddling Penny until she was almost three years old. Then Anna lavished her love and attention on Candace, the new fair-skinned granddaughter who had resembled her grandmother from birth. As soon as Candace was born, Penny felt that Anna turned against her: "She didn't speak English and I learned every curse in Yiddish there was, because she laid it on my head. Maybe I wasn't an easy child to be with. I was rough and tumble. I answered everything she said. I didn't like her either, so we were constantly at each other. She would kind of look at me and yell and scream."

Penny's mother, Evie, refused to interfere. She was shamefully relieved that someone else was receiving the curses that Anna had so often aimed at her. Her own father was a gambler and an entrepreneur, sometimes making money and sometimes so broke that he couldn't afford to feed his family. "When she found security, she thought that was the greatest thing that could ever happen."

Anna ruled the house with an iron hand, giving orders to everyone. But by the time Candace was born, there was hardly any housework for Evie to do anyway, because Norman insisted that his family—or "harem," as he sometimes joked—should live like queens.

Evie wanted to be close to Penny, especially after it became clear that she would not bring Norman the son he so desperately wanted. But it never quite worked, and Penny wondered why. "I somehow always felt that she didn't much like me, I guess." Penny tried to be the dependable, intelligent sort of human being that Evie could be proud of. Evie tried also, imparting her dreams that Penny would grow up to be a housewife married to a wealthy man who would treat her like royalty—preferably a man whose mother lived elsewhere.

She was a good mother, arranging piano, ballet, and tennis for both of her daughters, ferrying them back and forth along the road between Wilmette and Winnetka. She took them into Chicago to the best Michigan Avenue specialty shops, pointing out hand-finished buttonholes, deep hems, and other nuances of high-quality clothing. And for eight long years she made sure that Penny and Candy both attended Hebrew school, although orthodox law prevented women from fully participating in religious life or studying for a coming-of-age ceremony comparable to boys' Bar Mitzvah.

Evie drove out of her way to market at the kosher butcher and dairy store. She taught her domestics to separate milk from meat dishes, washing each different set of plates by hand in a separate sink. When Penny was nine the family got not one but two dishwashers—one for meat, the other for dairy—and everything everywhere was always sparkling clean.

The highest compliments Evie bestowed on other women centered around their ability to keep good, steady domestic help or maintain spotless kitchens. She worried about cleanliness all the time. In fact, Evie worried out loud about every small possibility of danger to her family. Shanto laughed, "Worry is her middle name."

When she visited Shanto at Rajneeshpuram, Evie chattered about how tidy everything was. She raved about the AIDS precautions, which required frequent hand washing and ubiquitous bottles of alcohol to be sprayed on sinks, telephones, and toilet seats. It was just like Israel but cleaner!

Evie did not go in for designer clothes, fancy country clubs, entertaining, or social climbing. Instead, she stayed around the house, avoiding her mother-in-law and reaching out for contact with her two young daughters. Penny believed that Evie was incredibly content. "My mother would clean a drawer all day, and then tell me, 'Oh Penny, I just cleaned my drawers.' How that could bring satisfaction to anybody was out of my realm."

"She adored the house, and the home, and cooking, and cleaning. To her, to have a beautiful meal in a nice restaurant and drive a new car and have a beautiful home and go to a good movie and laugh and play cards, your life is fulfilled. I mean you have made it. I didn't respect or admire most of the way she was. She was a very deeply unintelligent, uncultured person.

"I made a decision early on in my life that I would never be like my mother. She was not imprisoned. She loved being able to sit at home and wait for the man. And he got to have all the fun! He went out and played cards and fished and did everything. And she tended to him and loved it. But I thought I'd never sit home and be like that."

Norman preferred to stay away from the house, and business and synagogue affairs provided convenient ways to maintain distance from all of the women in his family. He avoided his mother's acid tongue and his wife's passivity. He was the good provider who expected a hot dinner at 10:00 P.M., when he got home from work. Norman insisted that the family keep kosher and honor the promise that he had made to his father when he was a small boy. The only weeknight he was home for dinner with his family was Friday, when he and Evie would recite the blessings to usher in Shabbat. On Saturday he got up very early to read over business papers, before going to services for three or four hours.

Most Sundays Norman left the women at home once again and joined his buddies to go fishing or take in a baseball or football game. Norman was an avid Bears and White Sox fan. When he and his friends attended games, they forgot kosher law. Norman and the other Jewish men all savored bratwurst and plump, pork-filled hot dogs. After Anna died from a brief illness, around the time that Penny was a junior in high school, Evie continued to obey orthodox Jewish dietary laws in her home. But once in a while Norman would sneak a package of Swift's bratwurst into the house, preparing them himself late at night in a special pan.

His wife and daughters were not supposed to know about Norman's illicit sausages. Norman told his family that Jews were the only people they could really trust. Christians were dangerous, and they could turn on you in a minute. Negroes, he believed, were inferior.

Although Norman rarely stayed around the house, Penny felt that he

paid special attention to her. She said, "My father wanted a son, and I was
it." Yet he never encouraged her to think of a career. In fact, he absolutely
discouraged it. When she was at New Trier High School, Penny decided
that she wanted to be a doctor. Her father counseled her to forget it. And
later on, when she was dating a medical student, Norman tried to talk her
out of the relationship, saying, "Doctors' wives don't live happy lives."

Norman willed only the best for his wife and daughters. The best for a
daughter meant a fine Jewish husband to support her in style and father
many children. A grandson or two in the group wouldn't hurt either.

"My parents never had a success orientation. My Dad had such a queen
syndrome. It was beyond Jewish princess. It was like my queen, my
princess, my women, my girls. Women are just totally women. You don't
ever think of making A's in school. That's for *goyim*."

Being Jewish

Norman, Evie, and their daughters were acutely sensitive to the boundaries between Jews and the rest of American society. The *goyim,* the
schvartzes, the others. Norman had experienced the terrors of anti-Semitism in revolutionary Russia. It was not so overt in the United States, but
Jews were by no means welcome everywhere. He had to be careful to
lower his voice in public and wear conservative suits so outsiders wouldn't
label him a "flashy Jew." He was cautious about haggling over prices or
appearing too sharp in his business dealings, so that his behavior would not
support anti-Semitic stereotypes.

Norman arrived with his mother just as the gates to America were
closing for Eastern Europeans. The National Origins Act of 1924 reflected widespread popular desires to place restrictions on the safe pas-
sage of people who were not Anglo-Saxon Protestants (Lipstadt 1993).
When President Roosevelt considered bringing the United States into
the European conflict against Hitler, he was accused of pandering to Jewish interests. In the 1930s Norman had forced himself to join along with
the millions of Americans who listened to Father Coughlin's anti-Semitic
diatribes on CBS Radio. Millions also agreed with Henry Ford's accusations about international Jewish conspiracies.

When Penny was born, in 1937, there was considerable isolationist sentiment to keep America out of the "Jews' war." Norman and Evie discussed the plight of the European Jews at home. Over and over again Anna reminded everyone that it could have been them. Her grandchildren were immeasurably fortunate to have escaped the fate of other little ones trapped in Europe. At temple the rabbi said the mourner's kaddish to honor the friends, the relatives, the unknown dead killed by Hitler's soldiers. Evie and her girls lit *yarseit* candles in memory of the departed Jews in Europe.

Even after the war was over many Americans did not sympathize with the Jews. They did not understand how horrible it had been. Chicago's own *Tribune* entreated the French not to treat captured Nazi war criminals like "Moroccan savages" (Lipstadt 1993, 44). And Robert Maynard Hutchins, esteemed president of the University of Chicago, begged for sympathy for the German people, arguing that "the wildest atrocity stories" did not alter the "simple truth" that "no men are beasts" (45–46).

Norman was not surprised. He angrily assumed that his family lived in a culture in which most people believed that Jews were Christ killers. He felt certain that influential Christians saw Jews as canny and avaricious conspirators who wanted to weaken America and take it over. He was sure that it would be best if his daughters stayed among their own kind. It was his job to protect them from the injuries of anti-Semitism. Part of the reason why Norman worked so hard to build his fortune was his certainty that a wall of comfort would cushion the blows of prejudice.

Penny felt it was her father and mother, not others, who were the prejudiced ones. "I was forbidden to associate with non-Jews, which I thought was stupid. I never rebelled against it, but I always said to myself that I would never do that to my children."

Jews had their own clubs, their own restaurants and shops, their own neighborhoods. Norman thought, "Why go farther?" After all, he had been invited to join the Standard Club, Chicago's elite Jewish social institution. That membership brought connections and advantages for his women. Evie wholeheartedly agreed, except she wanted to do her part to help make Penny a social success, which, in America, translated into being "not too Jewish." So Evie was willing to compromise, just a little. But just one small compromise proved to be devastating.

When Penny was twelve, Evie enrolled her in Cotillion, the most prestigious social dancing class on the North Shore. Disgruntled sixth-grade

boys pushed anxious girls around the polished wooden floor on two after-
noons a week from January to June. They came back in the fall and were
"presented" to their parents and friends at a festive holiday dance. At
Cotillion students learned manners and ballroom dancing. Most of all,
they learned which other preteens were well connected and affluent
enough to be their companions when real dating began in high school.

Alice Jean Forrest, the formidable head teacher, had an open mind.
After the horrible war it was time to be more charitable toward Jews. She
was delighted to meet with the lovely blue-eyed girl and her skittish
mother. For many years a handful of Roman Catholic children from good
families had enrolled in her predominantly Protestant classes, including
the nascent sixth-grade group, so she could easily assure Evie that the
class was religiously mixed and her daughter would be welcome. Miss
Forrest did not mention that almost all of her students lived in Kennilworth, an exclusive suburb with graceful houses and imposing mansions,
where Jews were entirely locked out of the housing market. Nor did she
tell Evie that Penny would be the only Jew ever to attend Cotillion—
something of a first, like Jackie Robinson and the Brooklyn Dodgers.

Penny loved the music and dancing. She was graceful, vivacious, and
immensely popular with the boys. The girls seemed to like her too. Penny
hardly knew anyone. Many of the others went to private schools, and the
few kids from her public school were part of a different social set. No one
offered to car-pool or asked for a ride, although it was clear to their
mothers that Evie was eagerly available to drive to or from every class.

Gradually, Penny realized that she was the only Jew. She kept quiet and
did not tell her parents. Throughout the fall she became edgier and more
withdrawn. Evie was oblivious. She was thrilled with Cotillion, with Miss
Forrest's reports of her daughter's success, and with anticipation of seeing Penny shine at the final holiday dance.

Part of the holiday tradition called for everyone to bring two Christmas gifts for the giant Cotillion tree that always graced the celebration. It
stood straight and green, reaching toward the ten-foot ceiling of Miss
Forest's front hall. One gift was to be a small remembrance for another
girl or boy in the class. Names were drawn from a hat, and the "secret
Santas" were never identified. The other gift was for some less fortunate
child, and Miss Forrest and her assistants would donate them to the Salvation Army.

Although some of her Jewish friends displayed holiday trees, often decorated with blue-and-white ornaments and lights, Penny had grown up lighting Hanukkah candles. Norman insulated his family from trees and Santa Claus and Christmas. Penny wasn't sure why, but she felt queasy about giving Christmas presents. Finally, two weeks before the big dance, she could contain herself no more.

Penny put her trust in Miss Forrest's pretty assistant, a sweet young Kennilworth matron who had been a Cotillion girl herself. Penny confessed that she could not give Christmas gifts because she was Jewish, did not believe in Christ, and celebrated only Hanukkah. The young woman put her arm around Penny and told her not to worry and that everything would be all right.

At the next class everyone was dressed in the new outfits they planned to wear to the dance. Penny shone in her delicate white dress, but none of the other kids would speak to her. No one asked her to dance the first dance. The hidden anti-Semitism was now out in the open. Whatever their private feelings, everyone else in the class went along with the ones who were the most prejudiced. Someone whispered, "You're a Jew." Penny bolted from the room, telling Miss Forrest that she felt sick and that she would phone her mother from the front hall so that she could be picked up. But she was too embarrassed to telephone her mother. She was afraid that her father would find out and be angry at both of them. So Penny ran outside on the icy November afternoon and shivered until she saw her mother's big Lincoln arrive the usual ten minutes early.

Penny sobbed all the way home. As soon as she got inside her front door, she went upstairs, took a long, hot bath, ate dinner from a tray her mother brought to her, and went to bed. The next day her white dress and the headband of artificial white roses disappeared from her room while she was at school, and so did all of her Cotillion invitations. No one spoke of dancing class again. Norman had been right.

Penny did not believe that her parents were truly religious, although they celebrated major and minor holidays, went to synagogue weekly, diligently observed Shabbat, kept a kosher home, and wholeheartedly supported Zionist causes. There was an elaborate structure of lip service and ritual erected around an empty space that was devoid of true faith. She described them as being Jewish without understanding the supernatural, spiritual aspects of religiosity. Despite her parents' relatively strict adherence to Jewish custom and law, they were unable to comprehend the true meanings of religiousness (Hoge, Johnson, and Luidens 1994). She said: "They were orthodox in a very strange way. My mother and father both had Judaism as a race. Jewish is Jewish. I don't think they know anything about Judaism. It's just that they are Jewish. And their synagogue is *the* synagogue."

Penny always felt that she wanted more spirituality, and, as she grew older, she read and thought and studied. "My love for fellow man was immense. We are all in essence the same. And to me that was religion. And the more I got into that, the more I realized that I grew up in a very prejudiced home." Nevertheless, she did not rebel against her parents' practices, and she always loved Jewish custom and tradition. Even though she belonged to a Jewish sorority at college, Penny brought stash packs of kosher salami and matzos to see her through the dull menus. And naturally she went home to her parents' house during the High Holidays.

When the time came, she married a nice young man from southern California, who had also been raised in a kosher home. Penny and her husband broke with their orthodox pasts, but they continued to be active in conservative synagogue life, and they were mainstays of Zionist charities such as United Jewish Appeal. They lived in Brentwood, a comfortable, leafy West Los Angeles neighborhood, which reminded Penny of Wilmette. All three of Penny's children attended Jewish day school until they were in their teens, and two of them were B'Mitzvah. Despite the distance, Evie and Norman called often. They fully approved of their daughter's Jewish family life.

For the first years of their marriage Richard took Penny and the kids to his parents' large house overlooking the Pacific for Shabbat dinner every Friday night. They attended synagogue less frequently, however, than Penny had when she was growing up. Aside from the High Holidays, they went to services once a month at most.

Penny wanted to be more flexible than her own parents, and she tried to make sure that her children's Jewish experience differed from hers. "I always taught my kids that being Jewish didn't mean excluding other people as being better than, less than, different than, whatever." When her youngest son turned twelve and balked at any more Hebrew school, she did not try to change his mind. "I just told him that you don't have to be

Bar Mitzvah! Can you imagine my orthodox mother saying that? You go play ball and have a good time! He totally loved me for doing that.

"But the weirdest thing happened. He married the most Jewish girl that you could ever imagine. They keep kosher. He wants to be Bar Mitzvah now! Honest to God. He is so traditional now that you think everything is backwards. I have a feeling that he'll insist that his own son is Bar Mitzvah, even if he hated it!"

Her own falling away from Jewish observances was gradual but seemingly inexorable. Penny's youngest was just six years old when she became aware of slipping. She said, "I never asked for one minute, is this bullshit or is this God? I just was Jewish." But she gradually stopped being active in Jewish religious or community organizations. The family no longer attended her in-laws' Shabbat dinner. "I really didn't drop being Jewish. It just didn't matter anymore."

Wishing and Hoping

After the episode at Miss Forrest's Cotillion, being Jewish mattered deeply to her, but Penny did not dwell on it. Because they were orthodox, Penny and her girlfriends from synagogue did not go through rigorous Hebrew and Torah study or anticipate mountains of Bar Mitzvah gifts the way the boys did. She and other Jewish girls attended about fifteen boys' Bar Mitzvahs, and those were sometimes followed by elaborate evening dinner dances. This was the Jewish alternative to Cotillion.

Norman and Evie were proud of how lovely she looked with her bright hair piled on top of her head, dressed in full-skirted formals that were held up by thin spaghetti straps. Penny loved growing older and earning independence and responsibility. When she was thirteen, independence was being able to go out for sodas after the big dinner dances. Four years later independence meant a new red-and-white Chevy convertible on her seventeenth birthday. Responsibility meant having a large clothes allowance to budget, a puppy to care for, and a flexible curfew for weekend dates.

In high school Penny was part of the popular Jewish social crowd. She gladly accepted the coveted invitation to join the most desirable Jewish high school sorority. Yet she always saw herself as somewhat distant and removed from all that. During endless telephone calls she offered her girlfriends sage advice about how to handle their boyfriends and their parents. Occasionally, she was caught up in the process of being popular. But most of the time Penny felt alone, an observer and not a full participant in teenage rites and rituals. She was separated from the crowd by the same emptiness she brought to her religion.

"I had a total fascination with people and myself. What makes me tick? What makes you tick? Why are we here?

"I just never got off the telephone. When I was a teenager I was always having all my friends call. We're talking boyfriends and girlfriends and I was like the therapist. I was always listening to everybody and mothering them and figuring it out when everybody gathered to talk.

"I started dating when I was very young. When I was thirteen, I was going steady with a person who was a senior in high school. I was always going steady from the time I was thirteen on.

"But I was a loner. I liked being by myself, too. I was also the one that was playing football with the guys. I broke my foot playing football when I was seventeen."

Penny looked incredibly feminine, and boys were attracted to her voluptuous little figure. Still, she saw herself as a tomboy, in part because she sometimes enjoyed annoying and worrying her parents. They were becoming concerned that their lovely daughter might not marry well, because she was too studious. Penny saw it quite differently. Looking back, she felt that she had misplaced her energies on social life in high school, instead of learning all that she wanted to.

"School came easy for me. I didn't do much studying. I didn't have a lot of drive. I made the honor roll and I made a lot of A's, but I noticed that took very little effort. I was smart, but I wasn't a good student. I didn't have good study habits.

"My parents were not educated and not cultured. So I was not motivated by them to achieve in school. I never remember any push or any motivation toward education. It was no big deal.

"I was interested in how things worked. I had a mechanical mind, so I did a lot of that kind of seeking on my own. I had a scientific kind of mind, but not cultural. I didn't like to do a lot of reading. I was always drawn to science and math as a student. I was drawn to medicine."

During her senior year Penny vacillated between attending nearby Northwestern University as a general science major or enrolling in a junior college to become a medical technician. At her parents' urging, she decided on Northwestern. She pledged a Jewish sorority and got top grades first term, smoothly continuing her high school career. But, over Christmas break, she met Richard and dropped out to marry him before she finished her freshman year.

Richard was much older than Penny. Almost thirty, he was a junior partner in his father's thriving construction and real estate investment corporation in California. In the winter of Penny's freshman year at Northwestern, he was in Chicago to negotiate directly with his major steel suppliers, and he dropped in on some old family friends who lived in Wilmette. Penny was over when he stopped by. She was impressed with Richard's good looks and sophistication. She persuaded his friends to introduce them, although they were reluctant. "He was a friend of my neighbors, who thought I was too young even to talk to him." But Richard asked her out.

He made several more trips to Chicago, and business became a pretext for spending time with Penny. Richard gave her his mother's small first diamond in April, and the Kaplans flew out to meet Penny and her family. She dropped out of college almost immediately in order to plan the wedding. While her girlfriends studied for finals, Penny spent her days with Evie, shopping for clothes, linens, china, and almost everything else needed to create a well-run household. Norman gave away his beautiful daughter at a huge orthodox wedding, followed by a dinner dance that night at the Standard Club. Richard and Penny took a plane to Nassau the next afternoon.

The honeymoon was everything Penny had hoped for, although Richard sometimes stayed on the phone for hours, talking business with his father. She saw the ocean for the first time. They drank tall tropical drinks and toasted themselves on the hotel's pristine white-sand beach.

"I was a virgin and marriage was forever and ever. The thought of divorce never even entered my mind. I grew up Victorian sexually. I thought, 'Don't touch me until I sign these papers and we say 'I do.' "

After ten days in the Bahamas they returned directly to Richard's apartment in Westwood, California. Crates of wedding gifts remained in storage, while Penny toured the Westside of Los Angeles with a real estate agent. Beverly Hills was too expensive and pretentious. Westwood was too urban. Malibu too remote. Penny wanted a house and neighborhood just like the place she grew up, only better.

Like the Chicago suburbs, some Los Angeles neighborhoods considered Jews unwelcome. Richard and his father explained that Hancock
Park and Pasadena were not only too distant from the senior Kaplans'
house; they were also closed to Jews. The Westside was where affluent
Jews lived, and it was where Penny hunted for her home.

Los Angeles seemed very far away from the Midwest. It was almost
another planet. The soft summer breezes felt like the Caribbean, not the
United States. The sky was gorgeous. Penny could pick a real lemon off a
tree that grew outside her in-laws' front door. She and Richard sometimes picnicked on the beach or joined friends on their Chris Craft and
headed to Catalina Island. Los Angeles was strange, but it was wonderful.

Penny had seen dozens of movies and TV shows set in LA, but she had
never been there. "My mother didn't know where it was on the map!"

Finding a house was an urgent project, because she became pregnant
on her honeymoon. "When I went into labor a month early, the doctor
said, 'Well, I think you miscounted.' I said I had not miscounted. My oldest son was born eight months to the day we were married."

Penny had an easy pregnancy with little morning sickness or bloating.
And she happily found a four-bedroom Cape Cod doll house just south of
Wilshire Boulevard in Westwood, about two miles from the University of
California at Los Angeles. Richard said that was fine for the time being,
but they would need to buy something much bigger as their family grew.
It was 1956, and there were still a few large open lots in choice neigh-
borhoods, where they might build their perfect house and perfect life.

Even while Penny was settling into Los Angeles, getting to know
Richard's family and buying furniture, she thought about returning to
college after her baby was born. After all, the university was close by, and
she had already hired live-in help. Penny still dreamed of being a doctor.
It would be hard, but maybe she could do it. Richard was appalled. He
sounded just like her father. "He was adamant about that. It was sort of
the Jewish ethic, women were wives and mothers. They weren't doctors."

The Life You Should Live

In 1956 Los Angeles seemed like a promised land, where nothing bad
could happen to Penny. It was clean. The air was pure. People looked

healthy and happy. Everyone had enough money, and even their maid owned her own house. Penny's friends wore bright colors and slacks in the daytime. They dyed their hair improbable shades of blond and red. Men had beautiful tans. Her children could grow up out of doors, without mosquitoes in the summer or chilling winds in the winter. Penny felt blessed.

"When I first got married, I lived the kind of life that I thought you should live. I didn't have a lot to do with it, I just sort of thought this is what I was supposed to do, and I did it. So when you were a Jewish housewife-mother, this is what you did, whether you wanted to do it or not. None of my friends ever thought, 'Do I want to or not want to? Do I even want to be married?' I mean, it was automatic, preordained. That's your life!"

Penny was amazed at how much she loved her infant son, and her love for Richard deepened during the months after Jonathan was born. She was surprised and annoyed when Evie refused to travel west to help her with the new baby. Penny thought about how she couldn't win. She would have hated her mother's interference, but she wanted her there just the same. First, Evie complained that she had to prepare for Candy's wedding to a young Chicago attorney the following June. Then, when the baby was three months old, Evie revealed the real reason. Surprisingly, unexpectedly, and joyously, *she* was pregnant at the ripe old age of forty-one. According to Evie, Norman was thrilled. And Jonny would have an uncle or aunt who could be a playmate too. Penny's new brother would be less than a year younger than her own child.

Penny was literally speechless, but she recovered from the shock and immediately sent piles of presents to her mother and even more when the baby was born. But she did not come back to Wilmette for five years. Norman was overcome with joy, which was only slightly tempered by his sorrow that Anna had not lived to see the birth of her grandson. Joshua Israel was named in honor of Norman's father, and he was a headstrong, spoiled baby who never outgrew his tantrums.

All Penny remembered about baby Josh was his interminable hair-yanking. She responded with outraged screams, and her mother's mediations and excuses only made Penny angrier. She had as little to do with him as possible, avoiding Josh on visits to Chicago or when Norman and Evie brought him to visit her family and see Disneyland with their grand-children.

"I don't know how to talk about Josh. He's a product of the late sixties and early seventies. I don't know much about him. He was a spoiled brat. He was not given a lot of direction. He's an incredibly intelligent person. But he has all of the rebellion that I didn't have, and he's been paying for it. It's sad. He's a waste.

"A while back he got into LSD and went and sat in the desert. He went with Alan Watts and Meher Baba and really got lost in things like that. Then he got really messed up. He took drugs." Josh became extremely ill and entered a rehabilitation program. Penny had always preferred to forget about her little brother and focus on her own children.

Penny's daughter was born two and a half years after her son, and the family prepared to move to a much, much larger house. The Kaplan family owned one of the dozens of small Los Angeles construction companies that had grown during the building boom following World War II. Richard's father was smart enough to follow the trail of the big sharks like Mark Taper, and, when Los Angeles began its massive expansion over the mountains and into the San Fernando Valley, he was there. By the time that Richard had graduated from college and returned from two years in the air force, Kaplan Construction had sold tracts of houses to automobile workers in the Valley, to aircraft assemblers near San Bernardino, and to rising executives down on the Palos Verdes Peninsula. Now Donald Kaplan was investing in the booming Westside and in the reshaping of the downtown business district. By 1960 he had amassed several million dollars, and Donald was delighted to help his only son, Richard, construct his dream.

A Mansion of Boredom

Only someone like Penny's husband or his father or, for that matter, *her* father could think of a four-bedroom house with a maid's room as inadequate for a family of four. People were starving all over the world, while Rich complained that his family was living too far below their means. Nevertheless, Penny wanted an outlet for her creative juices, and she was as excited as Richard when he found an acre lot high on a hill in Brentwood, an exclusive neighborhood three miles northwest of where they now lived. There were big sycamore and yew trees on the property, and Penny set out to work with the architect.

They talked and talked, and, together, Penny and the architect designed a big, old-fashioned family house with wide-planked wood floors and huge windows. After six months of consultation, blueprints for a 6,000 square foot home were complete. Plans included a master suite with his and hers dressing rooms and four additional family bedrooms upstairs, staff quarters near the state-of-the-art kitchen, a swimming pool and pool house entertainment center, and a family room with a big hearth and built-in areas for TV, stereo, and even a movie screen.

Penny was relieved. Her adorable one-year-old daughter was learning to talk already and kept up a steady stream of chatter about dirt and trucks up at the building site. The details of building could be left to the architect, who promised the house would be finished by Annie's second birthday. Now Penny was only involved with one aspect of the dream house, a sound system. She wanted to be sure that there could be music in every room. "Just get me the best sound system and have it piped through the whole house. Once that was all done, I didn't care."

Penny felt great. She was back to a size eight. Her relationship with Richard had never been better. Both kids were thriving with a doting nanny, and Jonny had started nursery school three mornings a week. Penny began thinking about UCLA once again. "I always had this feeling of being inadequate intellectually because I didn't have a college diploma. And everybody would talk about their alma mater, and I would shrink. And then I was afraid that I wasn't real good in English." She talked with Richard about going back to school. He persuaded her to postpone her decision until they settled into the new house.

Amazingly, the house was ready before a year was up. Penny organized the move and worked with a decorator to fill the gaping, empty rooms. She was pregnant again. Penny put aside her dreams of college indefinitely and concentrated on her kids. "I was very attuned to every sound. I would be up there before the Nanny could get to them in time. I would take them out visiting with me, or friends would visit us. They were just so young and so innocent. They were my prize product in the moment." Penny added another son, Kenneth, in March 1962, and she threw herself into the role of affluent suburban housewife.

During the early 1960s Brentwood was not particularly glamorous. Movie stars and other entertainment industry millionaires had not yet swallowed up most of the prime real estate on the Westside. Penny's neighborhood was peopled with very successful businessmen and professionals who had come to California since the end of World War II. Brentwood residents still looked to their suburban roots in the East and Midwest in order to structure their lives. Men earned the money. Women ran their houses, raised their children, and played tennis or golf at the country club.

Penny did her own grocery shopping, and she was active in the Parent-Teacher Association. She generally wore simple outfits of slacks and a silk shirt, but she never took off the five-carat, emerald-cut diamond ring that Richard had given her when Ken was born. Yet, despite her good fortune, Penny was not happy. "I was always terrified of being bored. I don't think I'd ever said, 'I'm bored,' because I'd never even gotten close to where I could say it. I had a thousand escape hatches."

"I always had tons of friends. And lots of activities. I played poker and bridge and golf and tennis. I would never feel like there was a lull in anything.

"Now, I understand it's fear of inner emptiness. It wasn't so much my love of life as it was my fear of boredom.

"This was in the midst of raising three children, and all their activities, and keeping a home. But you should have seen me. When I was watching television, I was also reading and writing letters and doing jigsaw puzzles. I also learned handwriting analysis and astrology. I was an ardent stock market player too. And just on and on. Just to drive from my house to the grocery store without turning the radio on was major for me. I was like a machine. Just 'go, go, go; do, do, do.' My husband was going crazy with me.

"The greatest thing in my life at this time were maids, of course. I couldn't have done anything without them. I couldn't have survived. You just can't believe what I did for these maids, because my whole life was dependent on whether they would show up or not. God forbid that I should do something boring like housework or anything that would be displeasing."

In the midst of her material comfort Penny became ill less than a year after her second son was born. She had painful stomach ulcers, and her doctor hospitalized her briefly. Then her back began to give her trouble. There were physical therapies and injections and finally several operations. After every bout with illness, Penny plunged herself into more activities. Her friends provided a powerful support network during her illnesses, and she came to rely on their knowledge about domestics, caterers, and children. Her friends' delight in being Brentwood wives was at once reassuring and troubling.

"Friends are a wonderful escape from boredom. I surrounded myself with incredibly conventional women who adored the hearth and the family and cooking and cleaning. They were so much my opposite, or something that I was missing. When you miss something so much in yourself, you want to have it around you to be able to relate to the world. And, of course, they felt the same way about me.

"They would say, 'I had the greatest day. I did my child's curls and I cleaned my drawers and I stayed home and I watched soap operas.' And they were so happy that I felt I was missing something. But I couldn't find that contentment or the happiness in the suburbs. When I made friends, we were forever, for years and years. I watched for something. I wondered, 'What is it that you are doing?'

"I've always been around people who are so grounded in the program society has given them. 'This is what we do when we get married. This is how we take care of our houses. We don't ever do that.' They don't ever think about doing anything because they're contented.

"I thought for a long period that I was off and they were on. I was just trying to see how I could get into this program of being so upset when my bed wasn't made or being so organized.

"One of the things that broke me out of this was my next-door neighbor. She was the perfect example of what I thought I should be. Her kids were always starch clean and never had a spot. Her whole house was spotless. Her meals were always on time. Everything ran. My house was always nine million kids. It was like chaos all the time because I didn't care. I loved having people, having fun.

"Then one night she came over in the middle of the night banging on my door. She was drunk, and she was in total despair. She was trying to kill herself and asked me to save her life that night. And then all the story unraveled.

"She did this 'perfect' thing as her cover, so that she could drink all day.

That changed my whole—everything! I had that whole thing that she was perfect. She never has a problem. And she's *not* [perfect].

"I was into a real rut of a boring housewife life, which was playing cards, playing golf—the society kind of life that I thought was so boring that I was choking. And I decided that it wasn't really my life. It was the life that I thought I was supposed to lead. I was really unhappy. And that's when I decided I was going to stop playing cards like canasta or bridge, because it was what my parents did and I hated it!

"I really got to the point where I was having a headache. I had steady games where the boys [husbands] played something and the girls [wives] played something.

"All my friends all had children the same age. So we took turns playing at each other's houses. A lot of us had help that lived in. Then I was just up to my earlobes in it, and I realized. I don't know if it happened one day or it was this rude awakening.

"I looked at my fingernails. I had long, painted fingernails. I went to the beauty shop once a week. I hated it. It was just not me.

"It absolutely wasn't me. I had very long hair that was done up in a French twist or in one of those weird kind of hairdos. And I thought this just isn't me. And so I announced that I wasn't going to play parts any-more. And I decided that I wanted to go to school.

"I kept weaning myself away. I designed and built the greenhouse. And I spent many hours in the greenhouse. And I was doing things that were more and more and more alone. And I just developed more and more and more into hobbies.

"I was always looking for something. There is something more. I knew that I had everything. That's what was so weird. You have a husband and you love each other, and a great sex life. And your mother-in-law adores you. And you have friends and excitement. You're pretty neat. You're sex-ual. You're this and that. You have an airplane and boats and a new car every year. You have a list of all of your goodies that life is about. And you still find yourself in such discontent. The only thing I could do would be to think, 'I'm really sick. I need to go to a therapist. This is *really* sick.'

"To have everything and have this mysterious angst. And no one knows about the spiritual quest. I am talking about the late fifties and early six-ties. You just wonder if you're bonkers.

"It was so weird. The therapist was puzzled. I remember him kind of

making faces. He asked, 'How were your pregnancies?' All of my pregnancies were great. They were fabulous pregnancies.

"Then he asked, 'And your children, and your husband, and your
mother-in-law?' Everything was great, you know. And he never even
probed that maybe I was lying to myself. That maybe things couldn't be so
great. That something had to be a little bit off. I said that everything was
just great. 'Well,' he said, 'You need to play golf.'

"I ardently got into golf. I had to bring in trophies and play every day.
The whole golfing addiction occupied me.

"I'm not apathetic when it comes to things. I used to always say I was a
jack-of-all-trades and a master of none. I had to know how everything
worked. I had to know how to do it. And once I achieved doing it, I could
drop it. I'm an incredible golfer. But once I learned to do it, I had no
desire to be a champion. The competitiveness is inside. I don't care about
beating or winning. I have to know."

At the same time, Penny began to sample the many other kinds of therapies easily available in southern California. "I did a lot of transactional
analysis groups. I wasn't a junky. I just wanted to know. I have this enormous quest to know who I am."

Seeking Herself

Penny continued to play golf, work in her greenhouse, manage her household, and drive her children to their lessons and appointments. The kids
were growing up healthy, tall, and tan in the California sun. All three
went to school for a full day, and Penny had more time to explore therapy and once again think about college.

It was 1968. Richard fussed and fumed about the ingrates in the universities and the traitors marching in the streets against war in Southeast
Asia. Penny gave her household staff the day off so that they could attend
memorial services for Dr. Martin Luther King Jr. She took armfuls of
dresses to be shortened by her dressmaker. She gradually stopped golfing,
and she turned the greenhouse over to the gardeners, who also tended
the lawns. Penny carefully read catalogues of undergraduate offerings by
a half-dozen schools in the Los Angeles area. And she devoted more and
more hours to psychotherapy.

"The one psychiatrist who was a lady was a very tough lady. There was no playing any games. And I wanted a woman who could be tough so that no male-female games could be played. I did not want to be a female knowing how to manipulate a male. I wanted a woman who would know my game and therefore could call me on it immediately.

"She was recommended by an old friend of mine, a psychiatrist actually. I spent a few months with her. In quick summary, she said, 'You experience yourself like a biological accident.'

"I've done everything that my social background—now I call it my conditioning—said. And if I did accomplish X, Y, and Z, I should be happy and therefore there would be meaning to my life. So I did them all. And each time I did another accomplishment, the more meaningless life was becoming. The promise was not being kept. And the more I accomplished, the more I had, the more embarrassed I was."

Penny continued to try out different therapies. But in 1970, with the approval of her current personal growth group, she enrolled in Santa Monica City College. Penny was thirty-three years old, although her slim figure and casual clothes made her indistinguishable from other beautiful California coeds. Medical school was out. She wouldn't be ready until she was almost forty. So Penny took a general science major in order to discover what she wanted to do. She felt unprepared for UCLA, and the excellent community college only twenty minutes away from her house offered students small classes and personal attention.

Going to School

"I decided that rather than put myself out and fail, I would start with junior college. If I could get forty-two credits, I could just transfer. And the very first course I took was international economics. And the very first week, it was such a gift. I was so excited about what I learned that I didn't have to cram for courses. Once I had absorbed it, it was part of my knowledge. It was *mine!* I didn't have to study it again. I realized that when I was being educated before, I didn't care what I was learning. So I never learned. But this stuff was interesting and I loved it and I learned it. And in about a year and a half I had a straight-A average."

Penny transferred to UCLA. She was accepted into an honors program in economics and business. "It was my world. I loved it so much. I loved every aspect about it. I loved studying. I loved learning. I loved everything about it. It was just this vast opportunity to be, to get lost."

Then her family life began to crumble. Richard and the children resented her intense focus. They felt that she was neglecting them. Donald Kaplan, Richard's father, also pressured Penny to quit and suggested that she get involved with the volunteer medical auxiliary at UCLA Medical Center.

After months of prodding from everyone in her family, she dropped out of college. Penny met an attractive young doctor at a party, and they started a torrid affair. It was her first. She filed for divorce in 1973. Richard thought that she had gone crazy. She said, "He couldn't understand why anyone would divorce him."

Richard, however, did not contest the divorce. In the settlement Penny received the house, which was increasing in value daily. She also got ample alimony and support money for Jonny, Annie, and Ken. Richard's attorney crafted a joint-custody arrangement, but the kids only stayed over at his nearby townhouse on weekends. With tears in her eyes Penny followed the approved trial script and testified about Richard's preoccupations with business.

Her parents were grief-stricken. Although Jewish law accepts divorce, this was the first one in either Penny's or Richard's family. Penny's in-laws were shocked. Her sister was not really surprised. Penny felt free. She could turn the sound system up as high as she wanted it. She could finish college. She could explore her own sexuality. She could somehow understand and obliterate her feelings of emptiness.

Terms of Estrangement

Penny did not blame Richard for their failed marriage. The kids missed him, but they were into their own lives. After the divorce she sat on her enormous California king bed or went back into the greenhouse and considered the inevitability of the breakup. She wanted more out of life. She wanted to make her mark on the world. Richard simply desired the obvious—family, money, fun. Still, Penny was not without regrets.

"I knew that I had to make a total break and that part of my life had completed. I was a wife and mother. I was a good wife. I was a good mother. And this husband? I knew from that space that I wasn't going to complete my growth, or whatever you want to call that word, with this man because he didn't speak the same language. I would talk about truth, and he didn't know what that meant.

"I felt like a stranger in a strange land. I was driving my husband nuts.

"He's a capitalist. He's a beautiful, incredible human being. But he's light years away from understanding what I talked about. I knew that my life was going to carry on through a different space. This was it. I knew it.

"I was married to a nonseeker, and he is probably the reason why we couldn't live the rest of our lives together. I still love him. He's the father of my children. I stay in contact. He still has a hard time understanding how I could love him and leave him."

Her children also had a very hard time understanding how Penny could love and still leave. But they learned to enjoy their two houses, and Penny continued to be an indulgent, enthusiastic mother. Despite the difficulties of the divorce, even eleven-year-old Ken returned her affection.

"There were many freak-outs. But it's really funny. I always said that when I grew up, I hoped I would never sit and lament what I did wrong. I just had to pray. I just had to say I intuitively knew deep down. Even if I wasn't what other people thought was the right mother, everything really turned out great. I knew that if I got free and wasn't operating on neurotic behavior, my kids would be free.

"I remember starting out with Richard. I adored my kids. I didn't want them to go to camp or anything. I wanted to hold them. And then there was the double side. It's usually the child who's trying to break from the parent. And here I was the parent who's letting go. And that really hurts. They want to do the breaking while the parent holds. When I let go psychologically, they didn't know where they were going with all of that rope.

"When they were in high school, after the divorce, my two older kids got stoned every day of their lives at their expensive private school. And I knew it. It wasn't anything I was heavy with. I told them it wasn't something you have to run away from or hide from your folks.

"I knew it. It was part of my ability to say, look, I know that I can't stop you from doing something. It's a disadvantage for me to be heavy on you.

I used to say that if you smoke as an escape, then maybe you need help. If smoking pot is a social high, I can't see anything wrong about that. Just be sure that you don't drive when you're whatever. Be careful! But if you are using it as a crutch, you need to look at it and you need help.

"It was a way of telling the kids that I respect who they are. I think that parents really bum out in the case of not trusting the human beings that they call their children. So what happened was that because I was so accepting, everybody turned out great. You know the saying, 'It's 11:00, do you know where your kids are?' I said, 'Yeah! They're in the back den, with about a hundred other kids!' Before and after the divorce, my house was always open and people knew it. That's the way I liked it!"

The older kids reveled in the new freedoms and the interesting treats that came with the divorce. But things were much harder on Ken. First, he quit Hebrew school and refused to be Bar Mitzvah. He reasoned that Penny only thought about herself, so he would stop doing what she wanted. Just after Richard moved out, Ken refused to shower or bathe for several weeks, and his room got messier and messier. It was so bad that Penny put a large note on his bedroom door asking the maid not to step inside. Finally, she told Kenny *not* to clean up! *Not* to make his bed! Penny told him to go out and play, and she rumpled his bed even more. She said: "Something great may be happening. You can make it when you get back."

"It's good to make your bed, but not to have your bed be master over you. You can still make it through the day, and then you can make your bed! You have a choice." Kenny responded, and over the coming months his room returned to a normal level of confusion and clutter.

This recent wisdom came from Penny's own experience with "shoulds," and from her seminars and groups about personal growth and the expansion of self-awareness. Her classes, self-improvement projects, and sudden lively, almost hectic social life made Penny increasingly inaccessible to her kids. They slowly pulled away. All three of them spent more time at their friends' houses and with their grandparents.

Two years after the divorce Richard offered Penny a large cash settlement and regular payments in exchange for the Brentwood house. It was a house that symbolized his personal definition of family life, and she gladly accepted, moving to a much smaller, three-bedroom "divorcée residence" in Benedict Canyon above the Beverly Hills Hotel. The kids stayed at the house, spending occasional weekends with Penny. Once they were settled with Richard, all three of them began to confide in her again. They learned to count on their mother less, and they became more affectionate toward her as they let go of their expectations. Annie and Ken even called Penny once in a while to talk about their problems, seek her advice, and arrange to spend time with her individually.

Soon after he moved back into the big house in Brentwood, Richard remarried. His wife was a slim California blond fifteen years younger than Penny. Laurie had graduated from UCLA in sociology and worked as a secretary in a talent agency for two years. She was anxious to take care of Richard's children and to begin her own large family. Penny congratulated him, and Richard promised always to be there for the mother of his three oldest children.

Over the decade following their divorce Penny has tried to convince Richard that he was missing something important. "I've told him he deserves more! Our divorce had nothing to do with the fact that I don't still love him. It was the frustration of trying to talk a language that I knew he didn't relate to in any way, shape, or form. I realized that there are lots of people in the world who are just nonseekers. They don't know what seeking means. They don't ask, 'Who am I?' That basic, basic question. For me, it's not what I do. It's who I am."

Searching

"Who am I?" was the question Penny asked as she embarked on a series of related searches. It was the early 1970s, a time filled with disco, drugs, sexual experimentation, and a candy store of groups and teachers promising self-actualization. Penny sampled everything, grabbing on to new knowledge and sensations with the same energy she had given her golf and her greenhouses. Somehow everything, even the most contradictory experiences, were related. She became interested in men, in feminism, and, most of all, in personal growth. She thought about completing college and then set that goal aside. A brief marriage to a glamorous arbitrageur intervened, and in a short two years she quadrupled her considerable financial assets. This is how Penny described what she laughingly called her personal "decade of liberation":

"I was beautiful and I was young and I had children. I was divorced and then I had lovers and I had more and more. Before I had all these things and relationships, there was something to go forward to. But once it was all accomplished, it was, 'Oh, my God, now what?'"

Penny dipped into a bewildering variety of traditional psychotherapies, encounter groups, and New Age therapies, always trying to discover her essence, who she was and the reasons for her existence on earth. She was reborn, reprogrammed, realigned, redirected, and ultimately frustrated. The panaceas of the "Me" decade grew frustrating to her.

"My therapists knew less than I knew. But I could not admit to myself that I was seeking, because it may have been something like seeking God. I started with analysis and then I went into other therapies. I even went to a psychopharmacological doctor because I felt that if I could unlock my childhood memories, I would really get to the truth of who I was. There was something in me that knew there would be a place to go, but I had no idea what it was or where or how."

She continued her search in the wake of her divorce from Steve Glassman, one of the wonder investors of the mid-1970s. Penny married Steve, in part, because she became anxious about what she saw as her out-of-control year of dating and experimentation. She also found him to be uncommonly attractive. He was the first man who could laugh her out of her intense moods. They fell madly in love with each other. He was tall and dark, but what she liked best was his amazing sense of humor. He was also a terrific salesman, who talked Penny into getting married again.

Through her contacts from the old Brentwood neighborhood and country club Penny opened doors for Steve. In turn, he took her with him to Europe, where he was gathering information and contacts for his investments. In 1974 he borrowed from banks, cajoled investors, and persuaded Penny to take everything she had or she could borrow and buy Swiss francs. Late that year the franc began an incredible ascent, and within six years she was truly wealthy. Her personal assets soon were in the low eight figures. In the time she lived with Steve, Penny had learned a lot about international investment, but her marriage was over in less than two years.

Part of Steve's charm was his endless enthusiasm for financial schemes. He loved deals. Penny felt that their marriage was just another one of those, and once Steve had closed it he was off chasing some other deal. The divorce was straightforward and businesslike. They parted as good friends. Penny's kids had hardly noticed either the marriage or the divorce. And Penny began to search again. This time she was more careful with her personal life and more focused on seeking a deeper truth about herself.

Penny went to Martindales in Beverly Hills and once again bought books on self-actualization and meditation and on something relatively new to her: feminism. She saw more therapists, joined transpersonal psychology groups with spaced-out ex-hippies, and took every turn on the road to self-transformation.

While Penny dipped into the New Age, she also became interested in the Women's Movement. She shrank away from the bra-burning, strident feminists she saw on magazine covers and the nightly news. They were ugly. What they said was ugly! But she found herself attracted to the softer edges of feminism.

She bought books, signed up for a women's studies class and then canceled, and she attended a few women's meetings and consciousness-raising groups in the Beverly Hills home of an old friend who had recently divorced her own contractor-husband.

"Steve used to call me a feminist, and it used to offend me because it was true that I believed in rights, but I believed in people's rights. I thought men were as put down as women, so, to me, I wasn't a feminist. I really believed in the rights of human beings.

"Then I went to a woman's workshop on sexuality. One film was the most beautiful film I have ever seen of two women making love. And then afterwards we broke into little groups. And each group had a gay woman lead. The most courageous gay women you have ever seen. I mean stunning, bright, sexual, loving. Just the kind of women you kind of fall into, like you can't believe they're real.

"You have women who want to change the world, which a lot of women do. And you have a power that's not overt. It's very underground. There is no power like underground power! It's been very quietly seeping into people who are asleep without knowing their desperation."

Penny was enormously attracted to the gentle, cultural messages of these feminists, and she was sexually drawn to some of the women who joined the feminist discussion group she attended for six months in a bohemian Venice beach-front duplex. But, before she could become fully involved in the growing Westside lesbian community, she met another man. He was a decade younger than she. Tim was a tall man with a long blond braid who had a deep recognition of his feminine side. He taught a seminar based on Bhagwan Shree Rajneesh's *Book of Secrets*. Penny felt that it had been written just for her. "I thought it was one of the most incredible things I had read. There was someone reading my personal mail."

Looking back on the class and the relationship, Penny is still not at all sure whether she first fell in love with the teacher or with Bhagwan—the real Teacher. But in the late 1970s Penny was certain that Tim was the true object of her affection. "I never wanted religion, period. I wanted to be happy, and, for me, happiness and a man were all mixed up together.

"As our relationship was moving on and on, we planned to take a trip around the world. It was a romantic trip with a man. I was looking for expansion, a broader understanding. But certainly nothing connected with spirituality.

"I was very psychologically oriented. While we were traveling, we got into some terrible fights. And I did one of my dramatic stands and said, 'Well, I'm leaving. I'm going back!'

"And he just said, 'Please don't do anything. Wait until we get to Bhagwan, and I'll put out our whole situation before him. Whatever he says, I'll take his wisdom.'

"And again, I went crazy. I was screaming, 'What has this Indian got to do with my relationship with you?' But somehow, something in me was moving forward, so by the time that I arrived there, it was a 'yes' without knowing what or why or how."

Before leaving California, Penny had arranged to rent a former British diplomat's verandahed mansion, close to the Poona ashram. A smiling staff of four greeted her and Tim. Her new personal maid unpacked their belongings, while they slept for twelve hours after the exhausting journey. Then they set out for the Shree Rajneesh Ashram, which would soon become the center of her life.

Penny Becomes Shanto

Because Penny had a cold and could not approach the master, it was almost two weeks before she took sannyas in Chang Tzu Auditorium. While she lay on her verandah sipping tea and blowing her nose into carefully ironed linen handkerchiefs, Penny's mind was like a butterfly. One minute she was absolutely sure that she wanted to become a sannyasin; the next she wanted to buy plane tickets and take the fastest possible route to Monte Carlo. But Tim, whose new sannyas name was Samira, meaning "love's breeze," supported her decision to stay and commit herself to Bhagwan. "It was sort of a state of being in an unknown situation," Shanto recalled. "Not knowing what I was getting into or why or whether I wanted to. And yet something in me was driving forward, going on with that."

"I had very little understanding of the master-disciple relationship and what that entails. I came from an understanding of commitments being something sacred, and being responsible for my commitments. There was a fear of how I could maintain my commitment to something which I didn't understand. 'What is it I am committing to?' I had to be able to accept the fact that there was no commitment. It was my own idea of how I enter situations."

But once she had completely recovered, Penny made an appointment with the office staff to become one of Bhagwan's sannyasins. Dressed in a magnificent orange silk sari threaded with gold, she heard her name called and moved to approach Bhagwan on the raised dais, escorted by his longtime companion Vivek. She knelt in front of several hundred people and trembled as Bhagwan touched her shoulder. Penny was reborn as "Shanto" early in 1978. She kept her eyes closed tightly as her master pressed the invisible third eye in the middle of her forehead and spoke in a soft voice: "This will be your new name. Ma Deva Shanto. Deva means divine, Shanto means silence, peace, serenity. All that is needed is the knack of falling into spontaneous silence" (Rajneesh 1981, 170–72).

More than seven years later Shanto is breathless when she recalls her intense emotions on her initial sannyas birthday. She was elated, but she was also furious. As soon as Bhagwan finished discussing the full meaning of her new name and she was led back to her prized seat on the floor in the front row, he began his audience with another sannyasin. Shanto bolted outside into the velvet Indian evening.

"I somehow went crazy right after Bhagwan spoke to me and gave me my name. I took life very seriously. I considered my life to be very intense and somewhat strategic. And basically his message for me was peace and serenity.

"From having been serious, intense, and responsible to being named serenity and silence. I literally went crazy afterwards! I decided he was making fun of me. He was a chauvinist. My boyfriend came out so over-whelmed and loving and so happy with my name. He came to embrace me saying, 'He gave you such a beautiful name.'

"And I remember pushing him into a banyan tree outside on the street. I thought, 'Leave me alone, you men!' Today, looking at it in retrospect, Bhagwan was laughing at me. But not from the space that I was imagin-ing. My name became sort of a direction. Whenever I felt myself going into any intensity about my life or my situation or talking too much, I knew I was off track."

For a while Shanto found that slowing down meant speeding up. Guided by Bhagwan's suggestions, Shanto and Samira took more than a dozen Rajneesh growth groups. Sometimes they were together and sometimes apart. There were encounter groups, de-hypnotherapy groups, meditation groups, and tantra groups. Shanto explored her iden-tity and her sexuality, casually partnering with a number of other partic-ipants, both male and female. She investigated her anger and almost broke Samira's arm during a couples' encounter.

While still involved with Samira, Shanto began a warm, long-lasting intimate affair with another woman who resembled an old sorority sister. She rationalized her new affair by reminding herself that her male lover was born Roman Catholic, while the woman in her life was Jewish like herself.

Life at the ashram was dramatic and ever-changing; it was a kaleido-scope of sensations and insights. Every morning Shanto rose at five, and her maid brought steaming café au lait. Then she was driven to the ashram, where she took off her shoes and engaged in strenuous dynamic meditation, devoting 100 percent effort to all four stages: breathing quickly, then strenuously pounding the floor to experience her childhood pain and anger, then jumping up and down shouting the Sufi mantra "hoo, hoo, hoo," and finally lying quietly and experiencing a vast range of sen-sations. On some mornings she went back home to sleep. But on others she quickly showered, slipped on a loose orange Calvin Klein jumpsuit, and attended Bhagwan's morning lecture.

Remembering her first year, Shanto groaned, "I did dynamic for about nine months every single day, and I must admit I never got past disliking it. I just felt I had to release something!"

She enjoyed the softer breathing and humming meditations. Shanto did those to center herself and stand back from her hot-and-cold relationship with the man she had once thought was her one true, ultimate love. Love's Breeze was a good name for Tim, because he could not go near a beautiful young woman without breathing hard. He was more like "Love's Panting."

"I spent my first years with Bhagwan wallowing around in a topsy-turvy relationship and having darshan after darshan in which questions to the master were all about relationships, love, communication, honesty. You know, the little things. But the big insight came later, after the relationship was basically over. When it finally hit me, I felt almost embarrassed about it taking so long to see something so simple. It wasn't until 1981, when Bhagwan came to America, that it finally fell into place for me."

For the three and a half years after her arrival, however, Shanto thought of Koregaon Park as home. Her days were as filled as they had been in Brentwood when she golfed, played bridge, raised her children, and met with therapists. Only things felt much better: "There was an immense sense of belonging and being connected."

The groups brought Shanto great joy. And her public darshans, during which she asked Bhagwan questions, filled her with emotion. But it was the daily schedule of work that pleased her most, particularly since she came to see it as a holy form of worship.

"I like physical work. I have always liked being physical. I was working in the cafeteria as a dishwasher. I just loved that job. Then my body freaked out from standing on my feet for hours, and I was transferred to the book-publishing house, which was affectionately called cripple's corner, and I didn't know it. I was doing sort of nothing really, piddley work like 'go-for.'

"And then one day we got this huge order from B. Dalton and the coordinator asked, 'Who knows how to type?' And I said I did and that was the worst thing I could have said. For the next three months I was typing twelve hours a day and dying.

"I wanted to be outside and be physical. I was typing, and I went through lots of trips. I would complain about it, and I went to everybody. They kept saying, 'Yes, we understand, but. . . .' I was bored out of my skull. But I finally got it when I let go of being attached, really let go of that space of desire. It was a real lesson for me to know that this is existence. That was an incredibly good lesson for me. I was almost grateful for it after awhile. You have to go through it to learn it.

"Then I went to the bookstore. I was in the bookstore and I was with people. I loved it. But I was happiest working with my hands. Next, I went to the jewelry shop. It was the first time I could say I was in total bliss being there. I was working with tools, making models for jewelry, and making wooden *mala* beads with inlay. I'm adept at working with my hands, and so it came quickly."

While she was learning to craft beautiful jewelry, Shanto was also a key consultant for the Rajneesh investment portfolio. She was a trusted advisor on currency trading and the U.S. real estate market. After about a year at the Shree Rajneesh Ashram, Shanto began to have regular weekly chats with decision makers in the top levels of administration at Krishna House. Her shrewd advice facilitated Bhagwan's eventual move to Oregon.

When she decided to stay in India, Shanto turned her stock portfolio and other assets over to a team of financial managers recommended by Steve. They were careful, conservative, and used to dealing with clients far richer than Shanto. Her manager consulted Steve, and together they persuaded Shanto to place most of her assets in living trusts for her three children. She also signed agreements that tied up her capital and only gave her access to interest and dividends. In 1979 her yearly interest alone was almost three-quarters of a million dollars. It was enough to live in style and support Bhagwan's vision as well.

Shanto described her activities at the Shree Rajneesh Ashram. "The things that I was involved in would make me a person. That was my process of discovering who I am. Basically, I discovered that I wasn't." She looked toward merger with Bhagwan, toward connection with the infinite, and transcendence of her ego.

During her first two years at the ashram Shanto made a few unsatisfactory trips back to Los Angeles to see her children. Jon was in his fifth year of college, Annie was a sophomore at Berkeley, and Ken attended the same private high school that his brother and sister had.

All three times she returned to LA, Shanto made every effort to visit with her former in-laws and spend lots of time with her children. Richard's parents were hopelessly suspicious. The kids, however, were

becoming interested in Bhagwan's ideas, and they tried to find out what
had drawn Shanto to him. Finally, Annie even arranged a two-week visit
to the ashram, although she came more as a tourist than as a seeker.

Shanto made up her mind to stay in India and return to the United
States only on Bhagwan's business. Shortly after that decision Shanto's
father was diagnosed with a terminal illness. Her mother and her sister
pleaded with Shanto to come home and help. Torn between her ties to
Bhagwan and her family's claims, Shanto attended a darshan and asked
Bhagwan's advice. He told her to go at once, so that she would be free to
come back and stay forever. Bhagwan produced a delicate wooden box for
Shanto to give to her father as well as the very special gift of one of his own
robes, so that she could continue to experience the heart-to-heart connection that was the core of the relationship between master and disciple.

Rajneesh at once empowered Shanto and also bound her more closely
to him. He reassured her that he would be pulling for her throughout the
ordeal. She reaffirmed her love for Bhagwan. It was the love for her
teacher that would allow Shanto to express deep affection for her father.

Norman lived longer than anyone had expected. After two months in
the United States Shanto went back to Poona for two weeks, and then she
stayed in Wilmette for five more months, as Norman sank into a coma
and died in his own bed. Shanto felt that she was forever indebted to
Bhagwan for the time that she shared with her dying father. "He was an
incredibly prejudiced man," she said, "but I loved him dearly. The last
months made a whole relationship beautiful."

During the period leading up to Norman's death, Evie was distraught.
Josh was an unruly, uncaring teenager. Candy blamed Shanto for somehow not doing enough. None of this really mattered, because Bhagwan
was omnipresent in her life.

After Norman died, Evie decided to stay in the family house, so that
Joshua could remain near his friends and she could stay close to hers.
Shanto lingered for two more weeks after Norman's memorial service,
supporting Evie and visiting with the many distant friends and relatives
who had come to Wilmette to pay their respects. Then she packed her
two bags and included a few things from her childhood room and a pair
of gold cufflinks that her father had given her on his last lucid day. She was
bound for the only true home that she had ever known, the Shree
Rajneesh Ashram.

She came back on a Monday, settled into a different rented mansion, and was ready to kneel before her master at the Wednesday evening darshan. He asked Shanto how long she planned to remain at the ashram. She confidently replied, "Forever." And he responded, "That's what I wanted—for you to be here forever."

At the end of their brief conversation in front of so many other devotees, she whispered almost involuntarily, "I am yours." Bhagwan said, "That's true, so just forget all about yourself—your work is done. Now let me do my work!"

Bhagwan's work with Shanto continued in ways she never dreamed. It was soon clear to her that *forever* did not mean forever at the Poona ashram. A few months after Shanto returned, the ashram community pulsed with rumors about vast changes. There was some talk about moving to a great utopian settlement in rural India, although a small utopian farm at Kailash had failed in 1973. Bhagwan's 1978 booklet *My People: A Community to Provoke God* had announced plans for Rajneeshdham, a proposed commune that would house thousands of sannyasins in the countryside near Poona. They would form a Buddhafield, a utopia in which a new kind of human could develop. But problems with taxes, charges of communal trafficking in women and drugs, and publicity about extreme violence in therapy groups foreclosed the possibility of a utopian commune within any of the regional states in India.

Despite continued rumors of an Indian utopia, those close to the two wielders of bureaucratic power, Ma Anand Sheela and Ma Yoga Laxmi, cautiously whispered about possibilities of buying vast tracts of land in the United States. Commune representatives jetted to Mill Valley, California, where the Rajneesh Geetam growth center was already flourishing, to the fertile Willamette Valley in Oregon, to rural New Mexico, Arizona, and Florida. Nothing was either large enough or cheap enough.

Shanto was among the forty sannyasins who first knew about plans to move to the United States. She was consulted about different possible locations and also about financing for the enormous project. Ma Anand Sheela, who became the central political figure at Rajneeshpuram, discussed a number of issues with Shanto. Knowing that their spiritual master would soon be in the United States, Shanto and a group of friends made arrangements to establish an interim center in California while they waited for the Buddhafield to come into being.

She left India in March 1981, the same month that Bhagwan stated that his health made it necessary for him to stop appearing for morning discourses. In April the ashram's press office announced that he would begin the meditative work of being in silence, and he would no longer speak in public.

Sheela became Bhagwan's personal secretary, entitled to impart his wishes to his followers. She purchased a small mansion in Montclair, New Jersey, where he arrived on June 1, 1981, with a four-month visa to visit the United States for back treatments. The ashram was in an uproar, and devotees were told to await instructions. Many, like Shanto, were temporarily dispersed to Rajneesh centers in Europe and the United States or advised to go "home" for a while. Others stayed in India. Late in the summer of 1981, they learned that the Buddhafield had been located in the Northwest.

Although Shanto was temporarily settled near Santa Barbara, California, Sheela and her advisors consulted her about securing a mortgage through an insurance company. She was instructed to wait with her friends and help raise funds to create utopia somewhere on the Pacific coast.

During her last weeks in India, Shanto met an old acquaintance, the former wife of a wealthy Los Angeles attorney. Her ex was the younger brother of one of Richard's golfing buddies. The two Los Angeles divorcées and another affluent sannyasin from New York combined resources to purchase a huge, gated Spanish-style house overlooking the Pacific from the cliffs of Montecito, a wealthy community adjacent to Santa Barbara. It had a beautiful garden and thick stucco walls. Penny felt comfortable immediately.

Movie stars like Michael Douglas lived nearby, as did people of established wealth associated with steel, railroads, and publishing. But the bulk of visitors to the mansion were newly rich, part of the financial networks to which Steve, Shanto's former second husband, belonged. These men and women came to the new Rajneesh center to work toward insight and self-actualization, just as Penny had tried out different approaches when she was a recent divorcée. They paid thousands of dollars for individual therapy sessions, group work, and evenings that included catered eight-course dinners, Rajneesh videos, and disco afterward. All of their donations were sent to Sheela so that work could continue on Rajneeshpuram.

The small circle of friends living together in the Montecito house became Shanto's new family. "Where you are simply living in a house and applying Bhagwan's teachings in your everyday life. And you kind of grow to where you are finally communal, where you're in an organism that's humming with the teaching. With Bhagwan you just keep moving on and moving on and on.

"We lived together there. It's something to want to break out of the old and find a group to do the same thing together. To create something unknown together, not knowing what it is going to be. And then supporting each other on the path."

At one point as many as twenty people lived in the mansion's ten bedrooms, but the core remained Shanto and the two other Poona veterans. "Sometimes we opened the gates and we had hundreds of people come and share our energy and everything," said Shanto. "At other times we would close the gates and go in. It wasn't time for anybody else. Then we would open the gates and close them. It was kind of a rhythm."

"We would take Bhagwan's audiotapes—hours and hours. Then we would look at different people in the group and what they're looking at and how they're hearing. Bringing clarity. It was intense. And the amazing thing is the subtle change that happens all the time. When you wake up everyday, you're always new and you don't know.

"In the Montecito house, I was always struck with the discovery of something, wanting to teach it or share it or guide people. And having to deal with what they thought they were in for versus what *I* knew they were in for. It was coming from such an overflow of so much stuff that I learned that I needed to pass on."

When she came back to California to wait for the communal city to be built, Shanto briefly became a Rajneesh therapist, a spiritual guide. She embraced the challenges of facilitating insight and understanding. And she was enthusiastic about living in Montecito near the pounding ocean, the endless blue sky, and the jasmine scent at night. The deep closeness she felt with her housemates was most important. But less than two years after they formed their household, she and her new family were summoned to the Buddhafield in central Oregon. They sold the gated mansion at a large profit and raced up to Wasco County.

A year later Rajneesh told all of his sannyasins to forsake the Golden State, because it was doomed to ecological catastrophe from earthquakes and AIDS. Looking back on the distant years as Penny the Brentwood housewife and the recent times as Shanto in Montecito, she was grateful that she and her friends had been called to central Oregon.

"He has told all the sannyasins to get out of California. This was a year and a half ago. But he knows and we know that if you tell somebody something like that, it takes a long time before a person will listen to it. Those who were smart and who trust the master were out in a week. No questions asked, just trust. You know that the master takes care of you, and you just move!

"It could be symbolic that California is going under. When I go to California, and I love California, I feel like I'm diving into a dark hole because the energy there and the people there are in fear. The panic, the greed, the climbing ladders that go nowhere. All of that stuff makes the whole place what it is.

"You just fall, and suddenly you are vibing on a consciousness that everyone agrees on. Everyone now agrees that it's OK to cheat and be greedy."

Rajneeshpuram

Shanto accumulated firsthand knowledge of greed. During the past year she had taken several trips to San Francisco and Los Angeles on Rajneesh matters such as retaining external counsel and negotiating loans with suspicious bankers. She also went regularly to Portland on similar business or to pick out exquisite fabrics for the elaborate flowing robes that Bhagwan now wore. Shanto also learned to do calligraphy, and she worked with her hands in Bhagwan's small decorative garden. She most liked, however, to sit on her deck and witness herself while the surrounding hills changed color as the sun shifted. Each time she traveled away from the ranch, Shanto was happier to return.

Although most sannyasins were crowded three or four to a room in a trailer or clustered townhouse, Shanto and three of her friends enjoyed the relative comfort of two small A-frames joined together by a long hallway and built on a relatively isolated bluff. Shanto's room was a model of spare luxury. A king-size mattress covered with a rose velvet spread dominated the large, white room. Several dozen throw pillows in sunrise shades of a similar velvet spilled from the mattress onto the lush forest-green carpet. There was a desk, a chair, two armoires, a tape deck and tape shelf, and a small bookcase, overflowing with Bhagwan's works, other philosophy books, and a few popular novels by authors such as Danielle Steele. The only picture on the light walls was a large black-and-white photograph of Bhagwan.

Shanto sometimes shared her room with a lover from the ranch or, very infrequently, with a Frenchman whom Sheela had pressured her to marry so that he could avoid immigration hassles. The room clearly belonged to her alone. When I asked her about her personal space, Shanto infused every object with a meaning that made it special in my eyes as well as hers.

"I love my room. The best way that I can describe it is to tell you how it came to be. I lived in a very large house, and when I came to this room, I had to get all of my worldly possessions in one space, so my things are what's most important to me. My music, some of the books I've read and some that I haven't read yet, and my crystal. A lot of the things just have a quality because somebody I really loved gave it to me, and I couldn't part with it. So that is how the things that are around stayed."

The living room and open kitchen with an L-shaped counter were at the other end of the house. Shanto did not cook, but her housemates did. They had special dispensation to go to Madras, Redmond, or Bend for supplies, if the ranch kitchens or general store did not have what was required. Shanto hardly ever ate in the two cafeterias like an ordinary sannyasin. Except for morning espresso, she usually brought take-out from the restaurants lining Devateerth mall or ate at one of them.

For Shanto life at Rajneeshpuram was seldom physically stressful, and the world away from the ranch sustained her interest. But she would have been willing to endure discomfort or even pain, so long as she could remain close to Bhagwan.

On October 30, 1984, Bhagwan partially broke his public silence. The commune was beset by litigation and public charges involving the abortive attempt to bus in hundreds of homeless people. In addition, the movement was falling back in both recruitment and financial support. Somehow, probably through his personal physician, Devaraj, Bhagwan received explicit information about these difficulties. Facing the disintegration of his movement, Bhagwan began a series of evening lectures to several dozen followers designated the Chosen Few. Shanto was among those rich or influential devotees who had been selected to sit before the master. They gathered in his compound, Lao Tzu, but videotapes of these conversations were later shown to everyone who gathered in the evenings in Rajneesh Mandir. Shanto described her reaction to the news that she had been chosen.

"I always had these dreams that I would either be sitting in front of him, and I would hear him speak. I knew it somehow in my being. I was working in the post office last October, and I got a call. She said, 'Your master is starting to speak again.' And I lost it.

"I just got hysterical crying. I mean, I was just out of it. I remember someone's voice saying, 'Oh, she is crying, she fell apart.' And another voice, 'Good for her, let her do it!'

"When she said, "You're going to him,' I really lost it or something. To have a vision and then it is given to you. Soon, I was sitting in close to him and listening to him speak."

Again and again, Shanto affirmed her overwhelming love and gratitude toward Bhagwan. "When you go to Bhagwan actually and in reality and in truth, the search is over. You've come home. But you can't believe how I searched, even after I was a sannyasin. It takes a while. But these days I realize that the home is more home, and more home, and more home."

Shanto continued her private love affairs, but those affairs were both part of and secondary to her complete love for Bhagwan. Everything in her life centered around her heart-filled surrender as a devotee. Her friends, her lovers, and her own self existed because of Bhagwan. She saw all of her most intimate connections as revolving around him.

"You could say we are of like mind. And we are together because our passion and trust toward consciousness, toward Bhagwan, toward the work that he is creating, is so like-minded that the thing that is greater than us draws us together."

Shanto was also involved with a man with a Ph.D. degree in physics who had been a therapist at Gitam, the large Rajneesh center at Mill Valley. "He has definitely been a player with me. I mean, he definitely wanted to play. An incredibly thirsty, very gutsy, beautiful, courageous person. We just met because his thing and my thing were like 'click.' So it was like that. We have an incredible time together. I mean flying, playing with all different aspects of the flight."

While Shanto explored the flights of love, she was still technically married to the French sannyasin. Their relationship was probably one of the many marriages arranged so that devotees who were not American citizens could stay at Rajneeshpuram. Shanto mentioned her legal spouse only once, in response to a direct query about her current marital status. He virtually disappeared from her life after Rajneeshpuram collapsed.

Total and absolute collapse occurred about a year after Shanto was invited to join the Chosen Few. She had been privileged to hear Bhagwan speak almost every night. Yet, because of her independent resources and her inclusion in the Chosen Few without Sheela's endorsement, the manipulative personal secretary had defined Shanto as one of her enemies. Shanto's private telephone conversations were taped, her bedroom was bugged, and she was discretely followed on errands off the ranch. All of this unraveled during her last year at Rajneeshpuram.

As the July 1985 summer festival honoring Bhagwan approached, everyone was excited that, during those few days, the master would once again offer discourses to large audiences of devotees. Shanto was caught up in the excitement. She focused on her master and the many joys of being in his presence, but she was also aware of the political intrigues at Jesus Grove, where Sheela and her entourage lived.

After the summer celebration the communal city itself looked sadly frayed to Shanto. Construction had ceased. Trees planted for the festival were allowed to grow dry and wither. The herd of riding horses and the pet flock of exotic birds disappeared. In September Sheela and her close associates fled Rajneeshpuram and the United States.

Bhagwan appointed a new personal secretary and denounced Sheela and her circle for a long list of crimes, urging authorities to prosecute her. During the following few weeks dozens of sannyasins were subpoenaed to appear before a grand jury. Outsiders believed that the commune could not survive another year. But Shanto, who was once again involved in financial planning at the highest levels, had faith that the Buddhafield could still flourish. She saw Sheela's crimes and manipulations as lessons that would strengthen her and other sannyasins. Bhagwan, she believed, had orchestrated the horrible events of the last years as lessons about power and corruption and as tests of his sannyasins' faith.

"One of the joys of life, in this kind of Buddhafield, is that each day is different. And each moment. He said the other night, like every moment is a surprise. I can't tell you where I'll be tomorrow or the next day. It's very exciting. It's like the razor's edge.

"We don't know what each of us would do faced with the same situation as Sheela. I'm not just saying that from what Bhagwan says. But I really know that it takes some doing to go beyond temptation. To be able to go beyond and to rise above.

"I used to think that I had to leave my mark on humanity to make my life worthwhile. Somehow, somebody had to know that I lived. I had to make a difference to humanity. It was important. Then I took sannyas and realized that wasn't it. It was just looking inside.

"The thing that strikes me the most when I look at people here that have been underneath Sheela's regime is their strength, and the courage, and the dedication to have gone through what we've gone through. And out of that there is just a tremendous fire. And out of that fire, something has been born. A new intensity, a new light, a new spark."

Shanto described a new spark, but in a short time the fire that lit Rajneeshpuram burned itself out. Bhagwan tried to flee the country in a rented private plane. Shanto had been informed in advance, and she was resigned to the necessity of his flight. Yet she was terrified for his health and safety when he was arrested and held in jail. Released on bond, Bhagwan returned briefly to Rajneeshpuram and left the country, after negotiating his plea bargain. On November 22, 1985, the remaining leaders announced that Rajneeshpuram would close. All of its assets would be sold. Shanto facilitated the closing financial arrangements by phone and fax from her new house in Montecito.

That announcement caused stunned disbelief and tears among hundreds of sannyasins, but Shanto, her housemates, and another intimate friend had already left Oregon. Through their usual real estate agent they leased a different ocean-view mansion. This one was a dramatic postmodern edifice, with a pool and two hot tubs.

Shanto was marking time until she could once again join Bhagwan somewhere else in the world. In Montecito she was like a Russian refugee who had fled to the Riviera during the revolution. Like a survivor from the czar's court, Shanto waited for the old society to come back to life. She and her housemates adhered to the same routines that they had at Rajneeshpuram. They got up early to watch the sunrise together, they discussed Bhagwan's writings and tapes, and they meditated. At all hours they talked on the telephone to sannyasins spread throughout the world.

Shanto continued to wear sunrise colors and her *mala*. She knew in her heart that Bhagwan would rebuild the Buddhafield. The spirit of Rajneeshpuram would soon be restored—somewhere.

Chapter 4

REPAIRING THE WORLD:
A WOMAN OF THE SIXTIES

Shanto introduced me to Dara in spring of 1985. On my way into the ranch I stopped to register and get clearance at Mirdad, the reception and visitors' center. The huge room with counters, seating areas, and a small coffee bar looked like an elegant bank with soft couches and rose-colored carpets. My papers were passed along quickly, but I bought some guava juice and a luscious ranch-baked chocolate cookie so I could linger and overhear a tearful German sannyasin plead his case. The lanky, balding man with sweeping sideburns was visiting the ranch for three months of rebalancing courses at Rajneesh International Meditation University. Swami Siegfried was dead broke because his Deutschmark transfer had not yet reached Rajneeshpuram, but his high-gloss burgundy leather jacket and Piaget watch signaled wealth. I had no doubt that policies would be flexible. While the flustered clerk telephoned the coordinators at Jesus Grove, I caught a glimpse of Shanto's unmistakable red hair, and my focus shifted.

She was bent over a book of photographs with two other sannyasins. The three women looked lovely together. There was red-haired Shanto, blond Kira, and brunette Dara. They were animated and enthusiastic as they examined photos in galleys for a forthcoming book about the ranch.

Kira was a very slender sannyasin dressed in a bright-red velour outfit that brought out the lights in her ash-blond hair. She was well-known because of her huge trust fund and her family's highly public attempts to obtain power of attorney in light of her devotion to Rajneesh. The brunette in cerise was Dara, another visible figure, who sometimes spoke to the media about Rajneesh immigration and land-use planning.

Shanto waved me over, introduced me to the other two, and we had a pleasant chat about the forthcoming book. During our brief talk Dara appeared to be very intelligent, very committed, and slightly uncomfortable. She giggled a lot, and at one point she changed the subject with irritating abruptness. She was much taller than Shanto, attractive, but not beautiful. Dara possessed none of Shanto's immediate interpersonal ease, but, as I came to know her, I appreciated her wry sense of humor and her slightly off-center way of seeing the world.

Because she was important to the ranch's public face, Dara was given a stipend for haircuts, cosmetics, and fashionable clothes. She was acutely sensitive to the aesthetic beauty of objects, and she often selected what she wore because of its unique color or fine handwork rather than its appropriateness. Even in an era of huge earrings, Dara's chased-silver circles were outlandish. Her chic purple silk pantsuit from Nordstroms wrinkled across the broad shoulders that her brothers used to call "football pads." The red scarf Dara chose for her third sannyas' birthday was beautifully batiked, but it clashed with all of the outfits she wore. Where Shanto had innate fashion radar, Dara possessed erratic aesthetic sensibilities that were not always in tune with middle-class social cues.

Part of Dara's unique quality, her ability to see things in a different light, reflected her working-class roots. While Shanto took elegant clothes, international travel, fine art, and classical music for granted, Dara was delightfully amazed by them and by smaller luxuries like frothy cappuccino or an extra gold bead to attach to her *mala*. When she occasionally missed her old life before Rajneeshpuram, Dara remembered special treats she had purchased during the years between completing graduate school and taking sannyas.

Sometimes she longed for a glimpse of San Francisco Bay or the sunlight shooting through the antique stained-glass window of her room in the Victorian house she had lived in on Berkeley's North Side. Dara missed her herb garden, the brilliant turquoise ring she always used to wear, and her hand-crafted acoustic guitar. When she was particularly frustrated or exhausted from a string of sixteen-hour workdays, she felt an almost physical longing for her old things. These were part of a self whom she had created. They were utterly foreign to Dara's childhood on the old residential streets of Tacoma, Washington, where she had lived from the day her parents brought her home from the hospital until she journeyed a long forty miles to the University of Washington.

Tacoma was a blue-collar town, built around the Port, where Dara and her friends used to ride their bikes down to the docks to watch giant cranes pluck containers from cargo ships, and Dara dreamed of traveling on the sea someday. If she left Tacoma, Dara could leave the Weyerhaeuser pulp mill that spewed out odors that inevitably permeated her clothes and hair. She would escape the endless grind of caring for kids and working and saving money and making do. She would escape her parents' fate.

Dara's father, Joe Kelly, had worked in the shipyards during World War II. But less than a year after she was born, in January 1945, Joe was laid off from his well-paid, unionized job, and he became an assistant manager of an auto parts store. Then, while Dara was in third grade, he took a job driving a grocery delivery truck. Once again, he was a proud union member with a solid living wage, guaranteed sick days, and a pension plan. Dara's parents had married during the depths of the Great Depression, and they felt fortunate that Joe had always worked.

Theresa, Dara's mother, was a housewife, as her own mother had been. She stayed home and had five babies in the twelve years, between 1933 and 1945. Dara was the last, the second adorable Kelly girl to be dressed in ruffles and shown off at church. She remembered growing up as an only daughter, because her oldest sister, Catherine, married and left home at seventeen, when Dara was only five years old. She became the little mother to her three rowdy older brothers.

As a baby, she shared her sister's room, but, when Catherine started her own family, Dara was alone in the small rosebud-papered room on the top floor of their narrow city house. Her room was always warm, because of the big oil furnace in the basement. At night she could hear the three boys talking and fighting below. Late at night her parents fought too. Dara recalled: "My father would sit and my mother would yell and throw things. It was a very ugly atmosphere. But I think they did have long conversations as well." After they fell asleep she could hear her Dad's snores and her mother's muffled sobs.

The Kelly Family

Dara was christened Dorothy Rose, a beautiful name that Theresa had been saving for a decade. Kevin, her youngest brother, was three years old, and he couldn't pronounce it. By the time she was two, everyone in the family had taken to imitating his lisping pronunciation. And she became known as Dara.

The Kelly's social life revolved around church activities and union celebrations. In the Northwest economic security reached far down into the working class and brought the Kellys a new Ford every five years, driving vacations to the Canadian Rockies or eastern Washington, where Theresa's parents now lived, and restaurant dinners two or three times each month. Joe and Theresa both hoped that all of their children would go to college if they wanted to, especially the boys.

The three oldest Kellys went straight through Catholic school from first grade through high school graduation. Catherine never went to college, marrying at the end of her senior year. James attended Washington State for a year, hoping to become a veterinarian. But money was tight, and he enlisted for a career in the army. It was John, the middle son, who received a science scholarship to the University of Washington and went on to complete medical school. Kevin, the youngest, was a varsity basketball player at St. Ignatius High School. He played for City College, where he took drafting classes before becoming a carpenter and furniture maker.

Dara washed her brothers' clothes and cleaned up after them, but she also compared herself to Kevin. "He always had quite a competition with me because I was always smarter, more competent, more capable. No matter what I did, I did it better. And I was younger, and this was quite painful."

"Now he has a marriage that works and he has a family. He has succeeded and I should be in there being appreciative, come to little family gatherings and play with the kids and admire them.

"I'm not sure where they are at the moment. The last I heard, I think they were in California, but they move around a lot."

Dara always thought that her brothers isolated and ignored her. "I had this strong memory of when I was about eight years old, going to the movie with my brothers. It was a war movie, and I started crying in this movie. Of course, my brothers were so embarrassed, they all moved to another side of the theater. I remember being somehow devastated by the ideas of what people would do to each other. They were my own psychological feelings of devastation."

Dara and Kevin were usually at odds, but they bonded briefly when they were both transferred to public school. Kevin was popular because he was athletic, and Dara survived because she was bright. But they still needed to support each other in the momentous transition from Catholic education.

Kevin's teacher created the conflict. Dara said: "He was very weird. My parents were absolutely right. He was a lay teacher they had hired. I think he only stayed another year or so before they finally got rid of him. It was a big thing for our parents to be that rebellious against the parish."

"We had to go to catechism classes. We weren't going to Catholic school, so we had to go to these classes for Catholic education." Dara continued to believe, but Kevin, like his brothers, stopped going to Mass midway through high school.

Being Catholic, Saving Others

Most of the other kids in the neighborhood were also Roman Catholics. Like Dara's, their grandparents or great grandparents had come over to the United States from Ireland. Dara seldom gave a thought, however, to being Irish American. They celebrated St. Patrick's Day, but it seemed like everyone she knew did. All of her friends' fathers had joined the American war effort. She was an American, and she was a Catholic.

Dara cherished being religious. She admired the nuns in her old school, the Latin Masses, the holy water, the smells of incense and candles. Briefly, in first or second grade she fantasized about becoming pope. But she also wanted to be a nun, and a doctor, and a Catholic missionary. "A missionary, maybe go to Africa. Then I wanted to be a missionary doctor or something. I had many different desires at different points."

Dara was vague about why she wanted to become a nun. "I just thought those habits were beautiful. And it seemed like a really good way to spend your life."

"When I was twelve or thirteen, I was into the lives of saints and all that stuff. Catholic saints were really into self-sacrifice." And during her "Catholic phase," as Dara termed it, she used to sleep on the floor without her blanket for the good of the souls in purgatory.

"I don't think I told my father I wanted to be a nun, because actually he wasn't much of a Catholic. He would have hit the roof. But my mother said, 'Well, just wait.'

"My parents said I couldn't be a doctor because I was a girl. I have never forgiven them for that. Their reasoning was that you can't be a doctor because some morning one of your patients will be in an emergency room and need you. 'What are you going to do about getting your kids off to school and getting them fed?' So I said, 'Oh, OK' You know, I was about twelve at the time."

Dara added ruefully, "If you're a nun, then you're *really* going to have trouble getting your kids off to school." Later on in high school she wanted to be a different kind of helper, although she sustained her desire to save others. "I wanted to be a counselor, psychiatrist, sociologist, or psychologist. Something like that, because I started looking at how miserable people looked. I thought, 'God, there are lots of miserable people around. Maybe I could do something to make them happy.' I thought I had something to offer."

"I'm the kind of person who sees starving children in Ethiopia on television and goes to pieces. I don't do that so much anymore, but I've been that kind of person."

Dara identified the misery of others with her own sadness and frustration at home. In some ways she was two different people. At school she was bright and effective, if a bit shy. She belonged. At home she often felt sad, almost like a stranger in her family.

Life at Home: Battles of the Sexes

Outsiders saw Dara's family as "large and loud." Inside it was quite different. She said: "I have always felt like a stranger in a strange land among my family. Always, since I was a little child."

"We used to sit around and watch television at night. Every night, it was watch television while he [my father] drank a few beers to relax. I couldn't talk to my parents except during commercials. They used to get really upset if I talked to them, if it wasn't during commercials.

"I suppose everyone has some fantasy about being in the wrong family or something. I *really* wondered what I was. I looked physically like them.

But, from as young as I could remember, I couldn't really imagine what I was doing in a family with these people.

"They swear to me that they're it, and I'm sure they are. But on another level, it's like sometimes you're born among people who are strangers.

"All the information in my family went through my mother. In order to maintain her power, she had different techniques of disturbing any conversations that weren't including her. So basically, I grew up not really close to anyone.

"My parents had high school educations, and nobody went on to graduate school or did anything like that. That's another reason why I felt like an alien in the family. I always knew I would do graduate work of some sort or other. It was just an assumption that I made early on that was completely alien.

"I knew what society was like. I felt it since I was very young. My mother used to say to me that girls are supposed to be tactful. I said, 'Well, do boys have to be tactful?' She said that it's different. And I said, 'Well, I don't see where it's different. I don't see why I should have to be?'

"I refused to learn to cook, although I learned later that this was sort of self-defeating. But I just wasn't going to get those housewifely skills.

"She told me once years ago that she always thought she had to please my father, because otherwise he would leave her with five kids, and then what would she do? I was older then, I was talking to her about her life and the way she made her choices.

"My mother was miserable. She hated cooking, and she hated housework. That was all she did. She never did anything else. It was obvious. She let everybody know. She was home, bored and miserable. She let herself go. She let the house go. She wasn't even doing well what she was doing.

"Her lot was a constant amount of housework. And I was determined that my life was not going to be a constant amount of housework. There had to be some adventure, something more of a contribution. She could see that I felt her frustration.

"I knew that I didn't want to be a housewife. That was real clear.

"I can never remember feeling identified with her at all. I just can't remember it. She was an alien creature to me. 'Who is this woman, and what is she doing?'

"I can never remember relating, really feeling connected. Like she was a role model or anything. If I was connected with anyone as far as a role model, it would have been my father.

"He could bring a liveliness. He was mostly tense, but he was very intelligent. Maybe that's why I related to him more. Anyway, he was very sharp. He didn't do much with it."

Joe never tried to intervene between Dara and Theresa. "He was so insecure himself, it would have been hard to see what somebody needed. He was a workaholic."

"The family would do things together on Sunday. That was his day off, Sunday. Later, when he switched to his other job, he had Saturdays off. But he often worked then. That's when he had to do repairs for the house and yard.

"He would putter around his workshop a lot, and make things at home. He was really into making things and just inventing all kinds of stuff.

"But sometimes the family would go out. Which would mean that everybody would go along on a picnic and he would go fishing. There was time in the car.

"He was a very silent, very sensitive man. I never had many real conversations with him. I can actually remember two conversations in my whole life that I had with my father of any importance. I can remember one when I was thirteen about why I wasn't like other kids.

"The conversation that I remember with my father when I was about seventeen was that I really think my mother is crazy. She's just crazy. I really had got into psychology then. He simply said, 'Yes, of course she is.'"

Going to School, Getting Away

Dara excelled at school. But she still felt different, less able to cope than other kids. "I did make friends, a few friends at school. And I would talk to them. I was very shy, very studious. I always found that I could get along with teachers. I wanted desperately to please."

"We wore uniforms. Everybody wore uniforms, and that kind of deleted clothes from the equation of status. There was a fast crowd. There were guys who hung out at Bob's at lunchtime. But, of course, I always brought my lunch."

Both at home and at school there were strict rules and regulations. She had three good friends, and until she was fifteen they all had pajama parties at one of the other girls' houses. Then, when she was fifteen, both school and parents forbade it, just in case boys would be there. Dara was outraged, although there was nothing she could do.

"We were always supervised. It was not like Sue's parents were not going to be there. And they were all Catholic families.

"When I was fourteen, I had this vision that I was going to get out. I was going to have a really interesting life, full of adventure. I was going to be really enjoying myself. I was going to be free! That kind of vision always seemed to be there. I wasn't going to stay in Tacoma, and the route out was school. I was intelligent. I had been encouraged in that direction!"

The road first opened during high school. From September through February of her junior year Dara went to France on a student exchange.

"I had my first life-transforming experience. I was an exchange student. I'd worked since I was eleven, and I saved every penny I'd earned. This person came and gave a speech about going to live in a different country and study. I was going! I said, 'Man, that sounds great. I'm going to do that.'"

Yet her mother reminded Dara, "Only rich people can do that."

"I was going to try anyway. They picked me. I spent every penny of savings and worked all summer and went. And then a whole new world opened for me."

After she came back Dara prepared for college. She wanted to go to a really good school, but she wasn't ready to go far from home. Joe and Theresa helped her prepare for the SATs. "They both helped me study for the test that would get me a scholarship, because they knew that I couldn't go to school without one. And, sure enough, I placed in the top 1 percent and from that was able to get a scholarship to the University of Washington."

When Dara finally went away to college, she was very relieved but also scared. "I was incredibly, incredibly nervous. Constantly."

"I wanted to be in a sorority because I wanted to be normal. But then

I went to those rush things and they were horrible. It wasn't really me. I just lived in a dorm."

Later Dara moved to a student co-op, where rents were cheaper and she had contact with a range of students. In her free time she wandered through the used book shops and inexpensive clothing stores in the U District. She went to art theaters and student rallies. Classes were no problem at all.

Nervous as she was, Dara reveled in being on her own. "School was a tremendous liberation. It was full of people of different backgrounds. It was hard getting to know people. We were all strangers. It had so many course offerings. It was just like being at a smorgasbord. Everything tasted good. And choosing a major was difficult."

"I changed my major about five times. First I majored in French. Then I changed to sociology and then psychology. I didn't really know what all these things were. And then I became a religion major at some point.

"I was a psych major and then I got into the honors program. It was all about doing a lot of scientific research. Rats. Then I thought that is not what I want. I started studying religion.

"I had stopped going to church, but I was really interested in religion. And then I realized that I wanted to teach comparative religion, Eastern religions. I was interested in Buddhism, although I didn't know much about it. I wanted to teach different religions in a school like the school I had gone to, because kids should learn that Catholicism isn't the only thing. Then I realized that I couldn't get a teaching credential to teach religion, because mostly you do that for public schools. So I finally ended up majoring in history, because it was my senior year, and it was the only thing I could major in and still graduate on time. I wasn't very focused."

From her first term in college Dara gradually turned away from participating in the Catholic Church or believing its doctrine. She had received a supplementary scholarship, however, and to keep it she had to participate in the Catholic student Newman Club for four years. She asserted, "I had made a commitment and I carried through on it!"

Dara associated falling from the faith with the impact of Vatican II on Catholic student life. Suddenly, Mass was said in English. The priest faced worshipers. The sacrifice of eating no meat on Fridays no longer held religious meaning. And the drumbeat of secularization drowned out the glorious religious music Dara had heard as a college freshman.

"In those days at the university there was a very good choir. It was gorgeous. They used to sing fifteenth-century Masses and it was gorgeous. Then they began to sing the new, funky folk music. They were like nursery rhymes people were singing. It was ridiculous. And one day I just didn't go to church anymore. That's not to say I wasn't looking for something that was like that first music experience—akin to religious experience which was somehow ennobling, enriching to human experience. And it's very rare. It's getting rarer, other than Rajneeshpuram and sannyasin communes.

"Apart from those sung Masses, no church I ever found had that uplifting of emotional life. It's something more than emotional life. It opens new vistas. It's like when you climb a mountain. It's totally grand because you can see for four hundred miles. Then you slide on your behind all the way down again."

In her junior year Dara represented the Newman Club on the University's Council for Student Life. It was chaired by a Quaker activist whom she came to idealize. He taught classes on peace and community through the Political Science Department, and Dara enrolled in both of them. Dara still glowed when she thought of him.

"Amazing guy. He was a Quaker who was really guided by a kind of religiousness. I guess he went to church, or meeting hall, or whatever they call it. But he just had this sort of Christian love for people. He didn't preach it, but his whole life was guided by that. I just suddenly realized the hypocrisy of people I knew who called themselves Catholic.

"I had still somehow had the idea that Catholicism was it! That ordinary Christians were somehow lazy and not really religious. So here was this guy, who was a Quaker, and I hadn't known any Quakers. But he was so much more religious and Christian or just loving his neighbor than anybody I had ever met, including all the nuns and priests I had met through my whole life."

She never told her parents that she had given up on the church.

"I recall going to church with my parents for a long, long time after that, whenever I visited them. They kept talking about the Catholic view on this is such and such. I had my own views on things.

"I started getting more political. Not that I was ever a real political leader. But I started wanting to change the world. I wanted to help poor people and disadvantaged people. I started really hating my family because they didn't care. I was telling them about starving people in Asia and black ghettoes and they would say, 'Well, you can't help everybody!'"

While taking her first class on peace and community, Dara discovered a whole new group of friends and a new set of classes about the real world and its politics. Protests against the war in Vietnam were in full swing, and Dara listened to speeches and passed out leaflets. In her final term she registered for a student-taught class about nonviolence and the university's first seminar on women's history. She felt a surge of power and responsibility. She also engaged in the process of redefining herself.

"The whole political scene was extremely sexist. All of the leaders were men. I didn't like the people for the most part. I was in protests and tear-gassed and all that sort of thing. I think I did it for the excitement as much as anything, and for the rebelliousness of it. I never got too involved in it. I was never much for party lines. I was very lost in the crowd so far as student politics.

"I had put feminism aside for a bit, because I had gotten such flack for it and very little support for it. It was my last year, and I'm taking this seminar, and it was very interesting.

"We used to have these potluck dinners and extended discussions. One woman was talking about how she had wanted to go to medical school. Instead, she put her brother through medical school. She had rare blood, and she used to sell her blood. Then her brother won't put her through medical school, even after he had gone through.

"Then she got married and put her husband through medical school, again selling her blood and working. Her brother was a doctor by then, but he wouldn't help her out. Nobody would help her out. She hadn't done what *she* wanted to do.

"I knew at this point that I didn't want to go to grad school. I didn't know what I wanted to do. And that story of the woman's sacrifices really made me think that night. And I thought about what kind of man would be interesting to me. An activist! So then I thought to myself, 'What am I talking about? What am I even thinking about? This is very vicarious. This is absurd! What do *I* want to do? Isn't that what *I* want to do?' I called up Mom and said, 'Guess what? I'm going to be a social worker.'"

Dara took exams for graduate school and earned her usual superb scores. She applied to the University of Washington and the University of California at Berkeley. Phil, the man she was seeing, also applied to

Berkeley. He could avoid the draft by staying in school, and he was interested in clinical psychology. They had met in the class on peace, and she
was truly excited about the relationship. Where sex had been scary and
secret before, another new road was opening up. Dara had hoped, but not
expected, to become so involved. But, after a decade of fear and guilt and
emotional pain, here it was. When things were difficult with Phil, Dara
remembered the long way she had come from her family and Catholic
childhood.

Sex, Gender, and Revolution

When she described her relationships with men, Dara went back to the
seventh grade. "When I was thirteen, my mother said, 'I've got to talk to
you.' She sat me down, very, very serious, and said, 'Listen, there's only
one thing that a woman has to give to a man. Save it until you're married.
Are there any questions?'"

"And I thought, 'Wait a minute!' And there wasn't a thought to ask her
a question, because I had learned not to ask questions.

"When I did figure out what she meant, from talking with a girlfriend,
I thought, 'Well, this is really strange. She must be talking about virginity.
What do you do with the rest of your life after you've given this one man
his one bit of flesh?' I couldn't figure it out."

Dara remembered that conversation with bitterness for many years.
"The total sex education that I had was when I was thirteen. This was before
I had any sexual feelings inside myself. In a way, I was very much behind
other kids. My body was developing, but my mind was very childish."

"I wasn't at ease socially, particularly with boys. I had no idea about
boys. Didn't know a thing. I had no experience.

"I had been a real tomboy. I was really athletic. The boys used to enjoy
playing with me in fifth grade. But suddenly, in seventh grade, they didn't
enjoy playing with me anymore, because they were supposed to flirt with
me, but I didn't know how to flirt. I didn't have any training in this whole
thing or models of any kind. I got really shy and felt embarrassed about
myself somehow.

"I hardly dated in high school at all. I was very insecure and very much
afraid of boys. I hadn't gotten beyond my Catholic upbringing yet!

"When I was seventeen, I had a boyfriend. My first boyfriend. He was very intellectual. We were intellectual together.

"He gave a copy of Tielhard de Chardin's *Phenomenon of Man* to me. Here was a man who was a Catholic, a monk, and who gave a whole different and equally satisfying explanation of things we had been taught to believe. Kind of mystical. Kind of neat. God is not a personal figure up there in the heavens. But there is a creative force moving toward God. This was totally mind boggling.

"But I had all the juices flowing. Anyway, there was obviously a sexual energy between us that he couldn't cope with. And he just called me up one day and he said that there are two kinds of women in the world. There are bodies and minds. 'I decided that you're body.'

"I died."

Dara made a halfhearted attempt at suicide, although she was still a practicing Roman Catholic. In retrospect it seemed to be more a call for help than a realistic desire to die. And her brother, Kevin, helped her over the immediate incident.

"I took about thirty aspirin. It wasn't that serious. I didn't tell anybody. I just fell asleep. I went to bed. I woke up at three in the morning with a terrible, terrible stomach ache. I went to my brother's room, and I told him what I had done. He got out this textbook and figured out that I should throw it up and try to drink milk. And I threw up and drank milk and threw up and drank milk and threw up and drank milk.

"And he sat up with me. I made him swear that he wouldn't tell anybody, and he didn't. Nobody ever found out. I wanted to be normal, you know!"

In college everyone in Dara's dorm discussed dates and sex. They passed around manuals on love. And in the spring of her freshman year Dara decided that it was time for her to lose her virginity. It was not a political statement or an explicit act of rebellion. It was simply a part of being a normal college girl in 1964. The earnest, clean-shaven Newman Club boys were out. She was a "good girl." They would have wanted to get married first. She started talking with one of the crew who did regular repairs on the dorm. He was a senior, seemingly sophisticated and kind too.

"In my freshman year, after my first semester, I just decided I was sick of this sexual repression in myself. I just decided to stop being a virgin. I was nineteen.

"I went out with a man I didn't really know very well. And, actually, he convinced me that I should stop being a virgin. We made love, and I just felt nothing except so much guilt.

"I went into therapy, the Counseling Center. My whole problem was around guilt about sexuality really. All my therapist ever told me was, 'Why don't you just forget about that stuff?' "

After that disastrous episode Dara went out with groups of students, but she did not date seriously until her senior year. The young man she met in her first-semester peace seminar was to become her husband.

"I spent one night with this person that I lost my virginity with, and then the next boy that I went out with was the man I married. He saved me, and I went on and got my degree, and went out to save the world.

"He was very mild mannered. He was intellectual. This was what I had learned to value in men. He was very physical too. But he wasn't into feelings."

Dara did not tell her parents that she and Phil were practically living together the summer after her senior year, when she stayed near the university to earn money for graduate school at Berkeley. Nor did she mention that the primary reason why she chose California over Washington was not the generous graduate stipend but, instead, proximity to her man. They drove down to Berkeley in Phil's Volkswagen Bug. Dara rented a room in one of the sorority houses that could not meet its quota of pledges in the radical late 1960s. She parked her clothes there and sometimes spent the night when she had to meet a deadline for a paper. Mostly, she lived with Phil in his one-bedroom apartment on College Avenue, a few blocks south of campus.

They went to demonstrations together and tried LSD. Phil spoke of brilliant images and oneness with the world. Dara fell asleep, only to wake up ten hours later with a splitting headache. They watched sunsets, studied, and sampled a huge array of restaurants from Mongolian to Portuguese. Mostly, they went to political meetings, organized and demonstrated to stop the U.S. War Machine. Dara refused to go to Mass. But she occasionally attended speeches by Catholic clergy or antiwar art exhibitions at the Graduate Theological Union.

Over Thanksgiving Phil took Dara to meet his parents in the pleasant suburb of San Mateo. His family belonged to the uppermost reaches of the middle class. Both of his parents were college educated. His father was the head of a successful West Coast advertising agency, and his mother was active on the school board and in the American Civil Liberties Union. Phil's younger sister, who went to nearby Stanford, was away at the school's program in Tours, France.

As they drove north toward Berkeley on Sunday, Phil proposed that they rent a larger apartment in his building and get married over Christmas break. His family was vaguely Methodist, but they had no objections to Dara's religious background. In fact, they were delighted that Phil had found someone who came from such an interesting, different sort of experience. Dara agreed that marriage made sense, and she called her parents as soon as she got in the door.

They would be married in San Mateo by a liberal judge who was a friend of Phil's family. Dara had no qualms about forgoing marriage in the Catholic Church. They would invite about two dozen friends and relatives and have a catered buffet dinner afterward. When Dara told her parents, Joe was resigned, and Theresa was outraged. They both attended the wedding, however, although none of Dara's siblings came, and only her older sister sent a card.

"My mother wore black to the wedding. By that time I was at the stage of just laughing." Afterward Dara and Phil spent two nights across the Bay in Sausalito at a lovely Spanish-style inn set on a hillside. Dara imagined that she was somewhere on the Riviera. Then they returned to Berkeley.

"We both kept going to school. He was going to school in social psychology, but he was what you would call an underachiever. He wanted to achieve very much, but he could never get his papers in on time. My husband and I were very much involved in politics.

"I got very much involved against the war in Vietnam. He became president of a campus antiwar group. And I did all the work. Basically, I was doing everything.

"He decided that he couldn't take any more of the doctoral program he was in. He couldn't stand it! He wanted to stop for a while and work. But we never had arguments."

Phil easily found a research job in a government-funded program on drug abuse and rehabilitation. Dara did draft counseling and finished the course work for her master's degree in social work. Her advisor urged her to go on for a doctorate, but she decided to take on a second master's program in urban planning. That came easily for her too. Four years after graduating from college, Dara only needed six months of field placement to earn a double master's degree from the University of California. Instead, Dara took time off. Phil was earning good money. She was doing good political work and might have a meaningful professional life as well. It was time to become a family.

"I thought, well, we're taking a break. We've been married four years or something. Let's just have a baby. It seemed like a good idea at the time.

"So I had his beautiful little girl. And being with her changed my politics toward women's rights. I had calmed down considerably. It was a very safe, secure environment that my husband was helping to create for me just by his being there and being so steady. It was very good for me."

For a while Dara was very worried about Tama. She had prepared for natural childbirth, but it didn't work out. "We prepared for everything, but she was single foot and breech, so I had a cesarean. I was able to stay awake during the cesarean because I just had enough adrenaline. She went immediately to my breast. She was white, but she pinked up within thirty seconds."

"But she just didn't start making baby noises." Tama had a low birthweight that caused concern. She didn't walk until she was almost two. She didn't talk until she was nearly three. But by Tama's third birthday things had come together, and she was a delight. She was active and really precocious. Those first two years were tense, however. Dara blamed herself for Tama's problems, and she rarely left her daughter.

"After my child was born, I stayed home and took care of the house. I didn't want to do anything but be with her, and that went on for the first year of her life. Then, slowly, I started to be with her almost all of the time but three-hour time slots and then come back to her. I started that twice a week—three hours on one day and three hours on another day. And then, as she grew a little older and a little older, I started to separate. She was the greatest gift I think of in my whole life."

When she became pregnant, Dara dropped out of the Berkeley antiwar movement. The peace treaty would be signed soon anyway. Student groups who wanted to organize working people like her father seemed like they were delusional. Dara had not given up trying to change the world; she just wanted to do it more gently. During Tama's first year Dara bundled her daughter up and took her to women's group meetings. Dara got together with a few other young mothers. They started talking about their personal experiences and what they meant in the context of the larger power struggle. Personal exploration became a valid expression of political concern.

"And we just blossomed. We did great. We had consciousness-raising groups and we'd read all sorts of things. And it was a very exciting time. I taught my husband to run the washing machine. You know, it was good."

Dara shied away from theoretical academic feminism or highly politi- cized books calling for separatism. She loved pithy, insightful ideas from Betty Friedan or Flo Kennedy or Germaine Greer.

"Germane Greer had a sense of humor. That was the main thing. Her writing was very lively. And she could talk about Australia and how women were treated and just make it so hilarious."

Dara enrolled three-year-old Tama in a progressive daycare facility in a brown shingled house just up the street from the duplex they now occu- pied. Her daughter needed to be with and learn from other kids. Dara sought a field placement with a feminist group in order to draw her per- sonal, political, and professional commitments together.

Less than two miles separated Dara and Phil's duplex and the battered women's center on the border between Oakland and Berkeley. Since Dara had moved into her cozy world of supportive women and sunny motherhood, the streets had become meaner. Trash littered sidewalks. Stoned teenagers begged for handouts along Telegraph Avenue. The Bay Area women's movement was as angry and politicized as the antiwar movement had been. Dara was no longer completely protected by the coziness of her new family or the warmth of her friends.

"I went from what was considered a radical in Tacoma or Seattle to what was considered a moderate or conservative in San Francisco or Oakland. And it was real active. There were a lot of separatist lesbians, and very angry, and they dominated the women's groups and the move- ment there. I was very quickly put off by it."

Some of the women in the battered women's collective criticized Dara for being male centered, for being married, for having a child and living in a nuclear family. She was "unsisterly." The biggest problem, however, seemed to be Dara's view of men. She wanted to present clients with options that included prospective relationships with supportive, nurturing men.

"The women who were controlling the center didn't want any men around at all. I mean any men of any kind. These women were straight women. A few of them might convert to lesbianism for a short period of time, but basically they weren't. This whole political idea was so uncaring. It missed the whole point. And I was a bit put out by that."

She transferred to another battered women's center, which had a reputation for providing clients with more options. Dara found the women working there to be more kindly and positive, although there were still no men at all on the staff.

"Then I went to this conference in San Francisco. That is what I remember as the breaking point: the conference on violence against women. And they had this seminar on the violence of *any* intercourse. That tells you something! It was against men, the enemy, and against the women who associate with them. And I just said, 'I'm not interested in any of this.'"

Even before the second conference Dara had completed her required hours in the field. Despite her retrograde politics, she received rave evaluations from supervisors at both placements. Dara's work with clients had been caring, committed, and effective. She wrote her joint-masters' thesis on women and urban community and graduated with honors.

To celebrate Dara's accomplishment Phil's parents took their son and his family out to a sumptuous brunch. Phil gave Dara a small gold and amethyst pendant in the shape of a woman symbol, a keepsake she still wears. The present from Phil's parents was the promise of a check for a down payment on a small house when Dara and Phil found something relatively inexpensive that they liked in the East Bay. Dara was bewildered by their generosity. Her own parents had sent a card. Although Theresa wrote regularly and both of her parents called once a month, Joe and Theresa had not visited since Dara's wedding. Nor had Catherine or any of her brothers.

Dara lined up eight job interviews with various public and private agencies. She had six offers, and she selected the job in San Francisco with a federally funded program serving urban, ethnic neighborhoods. She would be able to do everything from planning multicultural neighborhood daycare centers to counseling individual clients. Dara was pleased with herself.

The office was in a tall, yellow Victorian house. The staff advocated consensus-style decision making, where everyone had to agree on a proposal. Meetings sometimes lasted late into the night. At least once a week Dara had to stay over in one of the cheerful bedrooms on the agency's third floor. She missed Tama on those nights, but she rarely thought about Phil.

Starting Again

"I didn't start out to get a divorce. Although my husband was very, very beautiful in a lot of ways, I had never responded to him sexually at all. I was still pretty guilt ridden, so I hadn't thought anything about it. After I had Tama, I went back into therapy, and I began to realize that this was going to be a problem for me. And we tried a lot of things, but there just wasn't that click. He was my friend. I was pretty old. I had a couple of orgasms in my life. Those were not with my husband."

Dara and Phil had opened up their relationship in their first few years of married life. In the Bay Area in those times, in activist circles, sexual activity outside marriage was an accepted, strongly encouraged norm. Although Dara saw her experimentation as avant-garde, she was a conservative at heart. She had been involved with only one man besides her husband and briefly at that. And when she started staying in San Francisco, Dara found she was happier without Phil, even though there was no one else.

Phil nagged her to come home every night. He wanted to visit his parents and have all three of them stay over in San Mateo on some weekends. She refused and moved into two rooms of a collective house shared by other activists from different groups. There was a fenced garden for Tama and several friendly cats. The house was in Noe Valley, close to but far removed from the Mission District where Dara worked. One housemate lived with her ten-year-old twins, and Tama liked to stay over. Dara and Phil drifted into the process of separation.

"I didn't go back home. Tama stayed with me, and we got a divorce."

"We were very civilized, but he didn't want to separate. It broke his heart. But I was totally bored, and I knew there had to be something else."

Tama started kindergarten and adjusted to life in the big, noisy old house. Her mother picked her up from her after-school program in her old Volkswagen, and they shopped for treats at the neighborhood organic food collective or in one of the small Chinese grocery stores close to where they lived. When Dara stayed late at work, someone else from the house brought Tama home, made sure that she ate dinner, read to her, and tucked her in at night.

Six months after her divorce Dara met another social worker, one who supervised schizophrenics in an innovative halfway house run on principles developed by the radical psychiatrist R. D. Laing (1968). "I fell in love and started having lots of orgasms. I started smoking lots of pot, when I got home. Like other people have a cocktail. That wasn't good for me, but I became a vegetarian."

Dara and Greg got their own apartment close to the collective house. Tama came too, but she still had lots of contact with their old housemates. She spent weekends with her Dad, though. Phil noticed that Tama was often afraid, cried easily, and constantly sucked her thumb. She started second grade and psychotherapy at the same time.

Greg moved out in December, after Tama began sharing her problems with the play therapist, and Dara decided that she wanted to give up all drugs and alcohol and go back to the communal house. She said: "I decided to stop smoking dope. When the smoke cleared, I didn't think I wanted to live with him."

Less than a year after she left Dara went back to the Noe Valley collective house with Tama. She felt guilty about putting Greg before her daughter. "It is so terrible about my kid. The way I drug her around. She is a beautiful kid. She is very resilient. We were pretty close. In fact, we still are very, very close."

Soon after Dara moved back, she became ill, with flu and then pneumonia. She had to stay in bed for almost a month. Her housemates took care of her and Tama, but Dara decided to send Tama to live with Phil. He had a girlfriend, whom he soon married. The two of them owned a small house on Belvedere Street, down in the Berkeley flats. Tama thrived on their stable, traditional relationship. Later on, she played "little mother" to her half-brother, who arrived when she was nine. She wanted to have the same bedroom all of her life and go to the same school year after year, like Dara had done. From the end of second grade onward Tama saw her mother on occasional weekends, and stayed with her for part of the summer at most.

As soon as Dara recovered from her illness, she threw herself into her work, and everyone at the neighborhood agency endorsed her becoming head. She wrote grants that added to their staff. She still worked with individual clients, but she also sat on citywide planning boards and traveled to policy meetings in Sacramento and Washington, DC. She was building trust among Chinese, Chicanos, elderly residents who had lived in the same flats for forty years or so, and white youth gangs in the neighborhood. Dara facilitated communication between the neighborhood and City Hall and between San Francisco and the rest of the state. There was a feature article on her in the *San Francisco Chronicle*.

"My opportunities were an interaction between what I wanted to do, what I saw needed to be done, and what other people could be persuaded to try. I persuaded them to have citizen participation. A politician said to me: 'You're very politically involved, but that's not your first commitment. Your first commitment is a personal one.' He was right."

Dara sent cards and presents to Tama when she traveled on business. She collected interesting scarves and fabric remnants to hang in her bedroom. Glowing colors draped her lamps. She covered Tama's narrow old day bed with dozens of throw pillows. The room was a cocoon of warmth and light, crowned by a five-foot stained glass window that Dara had impulsively purchased at a neighborhood estate sale. The window had originally been part of a small convent that had been torn down decades earlier, and it depicted St. Christopher, the patron saint of travelers. That window became a symbol of Dara's personal quest. Although she occasionally invited men to stay over in her private space, Dara was not particularly interested in relationships or even sex. She wanted something far greater and deeper.

Her sitting room became a garden, full of many different kinds of plants. There were pots of herbs that she dried and added to the kitchen pantry. She had a fine stereo system and a music corner where she practiced her guitar. Dara's oak bookshelves were filled with materials on psychology, philosophy, and alternative religions. Phil supported Tama, and all of Dara's salary was hers alone. Rent was reasonable. She saved a lot, and she could still afford her guitar lessons, yoga classes, weekend retreats, books, records, and travel. She lived in the collective house by choice, not from necessity.

"I was most happy living communally. There were a lot of hassles with the meetings and trying to take responsibilities, but I was *living* there. We each cooked once a week, and we would have a communal, family dinner. I'd go to my room and watch television or hang out with friends. We would play music a lot, have jam sessions, and we would dance. Sometimes we would go to a movie or something. We used to have a good time."

Is This All?

"One day in March I had what you might call an existential moment. I stood up at my desk and it just flashed over me. I wondered if the rest of my life was going to be standing up and sitting down at desks. I had been at this desk for nearly four years. I was going on thirty-five. It was the sameness of it. And I really did feel that something was missing. It was spiritual in domain, but I obviously was not going to go back and be a Catholic. I had been to some Protestant churches. That wasn't it either. And so the thought occurred to me that, well, maybe a Quaker meeting would be something. There would be silence and meditativeness. Somehow that never came together.

"People said to me. 'Oh, well, you just need a relationship.' Well, I had been through a number of relationships, and that wasn't the answer. I knew that much. Richness, fullness—it just wasn't there. It wasn't like going to church was going to satisfy it. Being married wasn't going to satisfy it. Or being in a relationship, either. Because with that richness was also a certain compromise that you are making all the time to make it work. Freedom has always been a very big value to me, because obviously the first eighteen years I didn't have that much of it.

"I was just very confined somehow. My life and my vision of things were very narrow. But I knew it didn't have to be that way. I just realized that my life wasn't satisfying to me and I didn't know what I was doing."

Dara began to search in earnest. First she went to Esalen groups on Union Street in San Francisco and to other kinds of encounters for personal growth. But she desired more spirituality than the average personal growth group provided. "I had participated in some of the human growth or therapy groups and things like that. To tell you the truth, I found them a bit juvenile."

Dara tried dance expression weekends, Zen retreats, and Sufi celebrations. She read, talked with friends, and spent hours hunting through Bay Area bookstores. Then a friend recommended Rajneesh's book *Only One Sky.*

"When I first read it, I thought, 'This is really ridiculous. What is the big fuss everyone is making over this book?' Then I read it a year and a half later and I was absolutely blown away by it.

"I had a kind of spiritual frustration; I can't describe it as anything else than that. I had looked into a lot of different spiritual paths, and I tried to get into a few of them deeper. I felt in a way like a shopper who was getting a few good bargains, but I hadn't quite found the perfect outfit.

"It didn't strike me as a search. But, in retrospect, it was feeling out what the options were."

The Journey East

The summer after she read *Only One Sky* Dara decided to travel to Asia with a male friend who had recently moved out of her collective house. She had not left the United States since high school. While she longed to return to Europe, something inside tugged her toward the East. On her long weekend walks during the spring she went down to the Marina District or to one of the tourist cafes in Ghirardelli Square. She stared out to sea and wondered what lay beyond the horizon. It was the way she felt when she was ten years old.

"I had three weeks' vacation, but I asked for two additional weeks off because I was going to travel. Everyone knew that my Dad had just died. I was a frazzle. I needed some time to recharge my batteries. And so they said, 'Fine. If you go in the summer, there is nothing happening in the summer anyway.' So that is why I had most of August and September."

Dara and her platonic friend decided to go to Japan and then to India. They stayed with a family in Tokyo and then went to Kyoto. "I went to Nara and saw a huge Buddha there. I visited several Zen gardens. Americans and Zen Buddhism never seem to be really suited. Not my cup of tea."

"I wanted to see India, and I had heard all of these things about Bhag-wan—what a beautiful person he was, and the way people looked at me when they said, 'You should really go see Bhagwan.' So I went. But I was pretty straight. India itself was a bit of a shock. The ashram was just bizarre—all of these people walking around in orange clothes. And I felt alone and everything.

"We arrived in the middle of the big festival that the Indian population in Poona has. It's the biggest of the year, and everything was packed. Just trying to find a room was amazing. We were going around in the dark in one of those little golf-cart-type rickshaws, trying to find a place to stay."

The next morning Dara and her friend went to hear Bhagwan's morn-ing discourse. "A person not very tall, dressed in a white robe came in, sat down, spoke. It was eloquent. It was interesting. It wasn't earth shatter-ing by any means, but there was something intriguing about the whole experience. He was still giving sannyas and saying good-bye to people who were going back to the West. But he had begun to withdraw from verbal exchanges.

"We came out from discourse, and my friend said, 'I'm going back to the States.' I said, 'You must be kidding! For six months, you've been planning to come here and stay for three or four weeks and work on your head. And you've heard one discourse and you're leaving?'

"He stayed one more day. Then he threw his bag in the back of a taxi, drove all the way to Bombay, waited two days for the plane, got on the plane, and flew out as quickly as he could. It was a deeply emotional kind of response to a place that was totally different from what you expected.

"And I had no expectations. By the time I had been there a day and a half, I had gotten my first orange shirt. And it was so beautiful. And I didn't think I knew anybody.

"It was great. I could just bask in the sunshine and go to discourse in the morning. The ashram was a very beautiful place. It was full of very lush flowers and birds that sang sweeter than any place that I've ever been. These gardens had all been created by the people who lived there.

"The whole idea of being in an ashram was intriguing and wonderful and lovely. But the idea of taking sannyas made me very unsettled.

"I used to wear a turquoise ring. Because it was turquoise, because I was dressing up in orange to go in to the meditation hall, I put an orange thread on it. And at one point the experience of listening to Bhagwan was so intense, I snapped the thread. And he looked up to see what was going on. But it was not like it was eye contact, because I was far enough back in the shadows, so that wasn't quite possible.

"In darshan, he didn't so much relate to people as individuals or himself as a person. Think of it more as a presence, as a sense of moment that occurs when people are around him in those moments. It was something that transcended personhood. There was a sense of energy. Some would say an ocean of presence. There is some analogy to being in a lake of mild temperature and just floating."

During the second week that she visited the ashram Dara began a ten-day meditation camp, leaving her small hotel room at 5:00 A.M. in order to jog and have tea and arrive on time at the Shree Rajneesh Ashram. Participants met in a large group of several hundred, doing a series of active meditations and spiritual exercises. There was strenuous jumping and anger release during dynamic meditation at 6:00 A.M. At 8:00 participants and ashram residents heard Bhagwan speak at discourse. At 10:00 Dara usually chose a calm, breathing meditation called Vipissana, rather than arduous Sufi dancing. Lunch followed. Dara described it as "hanging out in the cafe, meeting other people."

After an audiotaped discourse from Bhagwan, which was part of the camp, there was Nadabrahma meditation. That particular meditation resonated with Dara. "In the bells meditation, you offer out whatever you have to give to the universe, and then collect back what the universe has for you. Then you are totally silent at the end of the hour." In that short daily hour Dara felt that she was discovering her current life's meaning. Kundalini was the final meditation of the day.

"Kundalini is another one of Bhagwan's meditations for Westerners. It is his feeling that Westerners have so much pent-up energy and so much repression, so much kinetic energy, that they can't sit still. So he devised other meditations. Kundalini was fifteen minutes of shaking, fifteen minutes of dancing, fifteen minutes of sitting still, and fifteen minutes of sitting totally still."

Then there would be a break for dinner and a dancing meditation called Nataraj or a music group. While Dara was with the masses in the evening, Bhagwan invited select visitors and ashramites such as Shanto to sit with him. And he would give individuals sannyas. But Dara was not among those who were selected, and she missed her opportunity to receive sannyas from the master himself.

The meditations were adaptations of Indian techniques for affluent Westerners, blending ancient practices with modern time frames. Indian names were given to exercises that owed much to body work developed in the human potential movement in the United States and Western Europe. The most important meditation, Dara was to learn later, was work. In Oregon intensely focused labor came to be defined as worship and became a means of self-actualization, much as it had been throughout Dara's life.

On the seventh day of meditation camp Dara started to weep uncontrollably. Her tears were joyful. "It was irrational, or so it seemed to me. It was so beautiful. The flowers were so beautiful. The birds were exquisite. I just felt this overwhelming sense of delight and joy and release. And I didn't understand why."

"Vipissana is the meditation where you sit for forty-five minutes and your awareness is where the breath comes. You just watch the breath, and if a thought comes into your mind, this is fine. It is not just contemplation. The thought comes in, you take note of it, and then you go back to your breathing. There was no judgment involved, which was very beautiful. For me that was a real discovery. I loved the other meditations, especially the afternoon Nadabrahama and Nataraj in the evening. But this was the first time where I was really capable of a sustained meditation like that, forty-five minutes.

"Maybe it's because of doing dynamic and being with Bhagwan and running and having a teacake and then going and sitting for forty-five minutes, maybe that's why it was possible. But to me it was quintessential meditation. The ashram made it possible to experience it, whereas in the past I had read about it in books, maybe experienced it for two or three minutes at the end of a yoga class of two hours or maybe felt a similar feeling after climbing all the way to the top of a huge hill to see spring flowers. This made it possible to actually experience it on a sustainable basis.

"I wrote a letter to Bhagwan. I said I would like to take sannyas, but I have these other commitments. And an answer came back that said see Amalia, who was a counselor in the front office.

"And she asked, 'What are the other commitments?' I said, 'Well, there's my daughter, and I also have a commitment to the neighborhood agency.' She said, 'Why don't you go and take care of those commitments, and if you still feel like taking sannyas, come back.' I was disappointed.

"That should have been the clue to me then and there. But I said, 'OK.' It seemed like if you were going to be on a spiritual path, you should follow spiritual advice, even if it did make you feel disappointed. I also asked if I could take part in some therapy sessions. And she got me into three.

"I had heard that groups in Poona really surpassed any groups in the States. I knew that I was unclear about a lot of things and was unhappy in a lot of areas in my life. I heard there were really good groups in Poona.

"One is the usual beginning point, which was called 'Enlightenment Intensive' or 'Intensive Enlightenment.' I have heard it said both ways. It's really about enlightenment and intensity. Now it's called 'A New Beginning.'"

There were sixty or so people in the group, only a handful of whom had taken sannyas. They did exercises borrowed from Gurdjieff's work and awareness warm-ups from the Esalen Institute. Then participants focused entirely on the fundamental, existential question, "Who am I?"

"It goes really deep. It's three days of isolation, except you're with the people in the group. You don't chitchat. You stay there in the room where the group is. You get your food there. It's totally focused in on yourself. You don't go out and have distractions.

"Two people would sit, and one would say, 'Who are you?' The other would speak for five minutes. Then it would reverse, and the second would say, 'Who are you?' And the first one would speak for five minutes. You sat with three people an hour, and you basically did that for eight hours a day, interspersed with some meals, some exercises, some music.

"It really brought your attention right down to the question of 'Who am I and what am I doing?' And beyond that. But that is the basic question. If you know who you are, do you know what you are doing?

"And the things I would say, 'Well, I was raised as a Catholic and I have three brothers and one sister.' Well, that's not who I am!

"Then you would try another. 'Well, I was trained in social work and urban planning, and I have a master's, and I have this job.' That's not me either, right?

"Layers and layers come off. It's just the most amazing experience. I did it again, when I came back to the States, just because it was such an amazing thing. It's a gorgeous thing. But it's very intense. That was really good.

"I can't say I came to a definition. I just was whatever I was in that moment. And that was about as far as it went. I did make some very good friends in that group, with people I later spent quite a bit of time with.

"I did centering, which was a seven-day group. It was great fun, actually. I did a bunch of others later."

After completing the groups, at the end of her visit Dara had an hour and a half session with one of the marquee therapists, who had a fantastic reputation for his instant empathy and sudden insights. They talked about her father's death at age sixty-five the previous winter. Dara had spent several long weekends in Tacoma, going back to the old house and trying to come to terms with her family.

"He [the therapist] said I was obsessing with death. I didn't disagree with the obsessing part, but nobody wanted to hear the story through to the end. I came to the conclusion that what was really happening was there had been so much love present at the time, on the day he actually died. Why did it take so long to get to that point? For that matter, why do people have trouble loving each other? Basically it seems so simple, and we screw it up all the time.

"He said all his life he was going to die young. It was just this whole self-fulfilling prophecy he had created. I can just see the whole thing. He really did make a choice in life to die young. For whatever reason, he did it. He used to work all the time. Not in a way he enjoyed."

Dara had not yet come to terms with her father's death, according to the Rajneesh therapist. Nor had she come to terms with her own life. The therapist affirmed her sense, however, that her experiences at the Shree Rajneesh Ashram had set her on a new path toward self-discovery and personal fulfillment.

"The significant part of the groups was that I got into the first one, and we were chanting, 'Why not wake up this moment?' I think that is what it was. And from understanding that the ashram was beautiful, and the people were very happy, and that wouldn't it be great to be part of this?"

When she boarded the plane in Bombay, Dara knew that she would return within the next few years. She had much work to do first, however.

"I got on the airplane and opened the newspaper. Suddenly, it occurred to me that I am on my way back to San Francisco because I have a commitment to a neighborhood agency, doing a certain, very limited thing. And here is Bhagwan! He's involved in the transformation of human consciousness on earth. And it was like a sudden flash of understanding that what I was doing was so small and insignificant compared to the life work he had set out to do.

"I was crying. I didn't want to leave. Most of the time I would drift from reading to thinking about the ashram to thinking about what I was doing. It was not like I was planning anything. It was just sort of contemplating what had happened. I had no problem with going back to work."

Coming Back, Finding Home

Back in San Francisco, Tama and Phil were waiting at the airport to take her back to the house in Noe Valley. Dara talked nonstop, describing Bhagwan's wisdom and the ashram's beauty. Tama stayed with her over the weekend and went back to Phil with relief on Sunday. On Tuesday Dara returned to the agency and to six weeks of correspondence, a shoe box full of phone messages, and a life that no longer fit her.

"I'd get up, walk to the bus stop, and take the commuter bus. I worked in a very exciting part of town, and I really enjoyed the fact that the agency was very relaxed. I could wear blue jeans and just kind of be how I wanted to be. I wanted to save the world or something, you know."

But after her month in Poona something fundamental had changed. "It was just sort of a whole series of disillusionments; I just realized I just had to save myself."

In the late 1970s federal support was drying up. Dara found that she had to let some of her staff go and that she was doing more and more casework herself. She saw tenants who were being evicted on pretexts so that landlords could raise rents or restructure their properties into condominiums. She counseled elderly homeowners who feared losing everything because of rising taxes. She worked with single mothers and newly arrived Hong Kong immigrants. One day a family of five Jewish refugees from Moscow showed up at the agency and virtually ordered Dara to find them a place to live immediately. She was overwhelmed and also angry.

"It was just the whole victim routine going on. People blamed everything in their lives on whatever it was. They were women. They were Chinese. They were old. And not wanting to take responsibility and wanting *me* to take responsibility.

"Dumping it. *You* take responsibility. Please fix it, and, if you don't, I'll dump on you! And I burned out! And now I understand why people burn out. There is a lot of resentment that builds up against your own clients because they're not taking any responsibility!

"The other thing that was notable is that when I got to work there would be competition and a power struggle going on. Definitely a constant power struggle within the agency itself. I was always in the middle of it. And there was a real male-female power struggle as well. Others might take it. I wasn't going to take it. I would get angry, which put me at a disadvantage. As long as I allowed them to upset me, then they had control. We used to sit for hours and talk about so and so and how difficult they were."

Dara had been frustrated with her job before but never so much as now. After the groups in Poona she better understood the staff's dynamics and her own responses to them. She looked critically at her colleagues, her housemates, and herself. Dara was particularly impatient with the "touchy-feely" people who tried to utilize human potential techniques without the fearlessness or sophistication of the Poona group leaders.

"The thing about the touchy-feely people that used to grate on me was that they were so dependent. They had no center. So they got their sense of identity by touching and feeling and being overweening in their kind of catering to, 'Oh, my dear, how are you?' It used to drive me crazy. And so, while it is true that sannyasins do lots of hugging as a people, there's a condition there that you don't find among the folks who are so concerned about ego need and can't get beyond that. The dependency of the touchy-feely just isn't there."

Although Dara grew edgy over her housemates' dependencies and had little time for some of her colleagues' halfhearted attempts at personal growth, she also respected the day-to-day perseverance and effectiveness of several other women in the office. She did not know them well, except at work. She was most impressed with her capable and enthusiastic assistant, who had assumed Dara's role while she was on vacation. At the end of the year Dara and Pam were working alone in the agency on a Saturday afternoon.

"Pam was just full of all the things that she had been doing in the office in the six weeks I had been away. She began to talk about an idea she had conceived and started to implement. She was all bubbling over with it, and I suddenly realized that she was capable of taking on the office. I said, 'Pam, how would you like to keep my job?' And she said, 'Oh Dara, I would love the job, but what about you?' I said, 'I'm going back to Poona!'"

Dara talked privately with everyone in the agency, and all of them liked and respected Pam. Then, at a regular staff meeting, she announced: 'I think Pam is ready to take on the office. I'm going to stay thirty days.' No one was surprised, and they greeted Dara's plan with reluctant, but supportive, assent. Her colleagues did not understand Dara's quest or her fascination with Bhagwan, but they fondly wished her well.

Dara described the process of winding down in San Francisco. It took six months instead of thirty days. "And what that turned into was making tapes about experiences we had and advice on some things, straightening up some files, transitioning some things on my desk. And telling everybody I was going."

The Saturday that she made up her mind to return to the ashram, even before talking with her colleagues, Dara also gave her housemates notice. Over the next five months she interviewed prospective replacements, working together with the other household members. They finally agreed on a pleasant gay couple. One of them was studying for a teaching certificate at San Francisco State, and the other managed a progressive bookstore. Dara sold her big brass bed, her oak desk, her plants, her stereo, and almost everything else to the two young men. She gave away the rest of the things that were unimportant to her.

"It wasn't like I was going forever. But I didn't need all these things, and this was a good way to finance myself. I had some savings bonds I had been putting aside for a trip around the world I had promised myself before I was forty. I didn't know the trip was going to begin with Berkeley. I also had some cash. I figured I could probably live a long time on that money.

"I had made a deal with my lawyer. I traded her my bicycle in return for sending me a check whenever I asked for it and doing my taxes for that year. Which she did. She was familiar with my affairs, anyway."

It was fall of 1980 before Dara finished organizing her finances, putting most of her remaining belongings in storage, saying good-bye to friends and colleagues, and enjoying a surprisingly gratifying round of good-bye lunches and dinner parties. She planned to stay with a friend from her old women's group and spend a few weeks in the East Bay hanging out with Tama, while making final arrangements. Dara's one-way plane ticket to Bombay was dated November 15, 1980. Fortunately, it was refundable.

Dara had met a number of Bay area sannyasins over the past months. She had taken some groups and attended lectures and discussions. There were surprising, troubling events at the ashram, and rumors flew. Indian revenue authorities revoked the ashram's tax-exempt status and claimed over five million dollars in back taxes. Relations between the ashram and the surrounding community were so strained that there was violence, and threats were made against Bhagwan's life. Some people whispered about a power struggle between Bhagwan's personal secretary, Ma Yoga Laxmi, and her assistant, Ma Anand Sheela (Fitz Gerald 1986, 300–308).

The most painful rumors involved Bhagwan's failing health. He had less and less contact with sannyasins because of his asthma, allergies, and back problems. Many sannyasins believed that the overcrowded ashram was no longer the best place for the master to do his work, and there might be relocation at any time. Dara said: "Word was out in the ashram that it would be a good time to take a break. If you had any family business or you wanted to visit somebody, it was a good time to go." Dara postponed her trip to India.

"I had this idea of getting some land in the country and just kind of living a rural, simple life, which I had never known. I bought a van. I sort of played hippie, because I had never done that. I fixed it up so I could sleep in the back. I bought a book on how I could buy land in the country. I had everything I needed: a little box of clothes and a little box of books and a little box of food."

Dara began to drive north. The van was too cold at night, and she was lonely. She turned around, went back to Berkeley, and sold the used van to two frat boys for a slight profit. She said, "I gave up this land business when I realized I didn't know what I was doing." Once more she stayed briefly in the spare room in her woman friend's house, and she frantically searched for a place to live. Now Dara was on the receiving end of house-mate interviews.

In less than a week, however, she found a room in a collective house on Berkeley's North Side. It was near a charming alternative shopping center with small stores selling hand-painted clothing, handmade pottery, coffee beans, and herbs and spices. Less than a month after she moved into the house, a friend of one of her housemates hired Dara to wait on tables at her gourmet grill, specializing in fresh, California nouvelle cuisine. Within three months Dara was the assistant manager.

Dara settled in. She got her textiles, books, and guitar out of storage. She celebrated her thirty-sixth birthday with champagne and a wonderful party, which included Tama. Everyone in the house was a sannyasin, and her birthday made Dara realize that it was time she made up her mind one way or another.

"I really didn't want to take sannyas. But a lot of people were asking. As you hang around and get to be a familiar face, people would say, 'Well, are you going to take sannyas?' And I would get kind of defensive and stuff.

"This one guy, who I am forever grateful to, said, 'Why aren't you going to take sannyas?' And I just blew up. I got totally upset. Something in me really turned, and I just suddenly had to look, 'Why am I so upset?'

"It is just a question. The guy is kind of pushy. So what? That's not my problem. Why don't I just say that I don't know? But I got really upset. Something about the whole experience just kind of pushed me.

"I had my reservations. I had resisted because I was afraid. I didn't actually resist; I postponed it. There was never any question about it ever. It was only a question of postponing it.

"Obviously, this man Bhagwan could see people very clearly, and that was frightening to me." She remembered her private counseling session in Poona and her own fear about surrender to a spiritual master.

The Rajneesh therapist had reminded Dara, "Being with a master saves you a lot of time." She thought about going beyond her own experience and psychological conditioning. "What was programmed into me was fear of stepping out of line. Punishment would come, never mind hell or damnation and all that shit. You would be punished right here, right now. But then you find, if you want to be successful in your own eyes or in others' eyes, you have to play at least some games the way other people play. Otherwise, they don't accept you. They've got you!

"I was reading a darshan diary, which is the evening groups with Bhagwan talking to people. I was completely blown away by the way he related to people. Bhagwan was so there. He understood people. It didn't matter where they came from or anything. He just understood. He had a great deal of humor about the whole thing. Then, in about the middle of the book, I realized I would take sannyas. That was it. There was no decision. There was no thought. There was no analysis. There was nothing.

"I didn't talk about it with anyone. It wasn't even a decision. It was a realization. This was it.

"I went to call the center in the East Bay. And I went up and got the application and filled it out and told them I was very, very fond of my name and didn't want my name changed. I was doing everything to sort of state, 'This is me and you're not really going to change me very much.'

"The mail to India took a long time. It took over a month to get there and come back. Sometimes it was over three months before they actually came back with your name.

"I got back the name Ma Prem Yashodara. It's funny the way it is, because sannyas is such a mirror of exactly who you are. I was really so willful about everything going my way. Things were operating on several different levels for me. But I got back the sannyas name and a little letter that said sannyas is a love affair."

Her sannyas name meant she could still be called "Dara," but she was also someone new. It was clear to Dara that Bhagwan had taken her wishes seriously, but he had also underscored his ultimate authority.

According to the letter from the ashram, Bhagwan had said that the name meant glorious love. Prem, a common Rajneesh appellation, was love. Yashodara was Buddha's wife's name, and it meant glorious one. In a Poona darshan Bhagwan had given the name Deva Yashodara to an older American woman who had previously followed the path set out by Gurdjieff, the Russian teacher.

Until she moved to Rajneeshpuram Dara had no idea that he had discussed the name Yashodara at a darshan recorded in the book *For Madmen Only*. He had emphasized essential goodness and discounted hard work in his excursus on the name. "The very idea of hard work is egoistic. To attain god is simple, has to be simple" (Rajneesh 1979b, 436). Four years after sannyas Dara understood what Bhagwan had meant. She doubted that she could have grasped the true meaning of Yashodara back in Berkeley.

"I would trust that any name he gave me would be appropriate. The names have something to do with the quality of the person, always. And so what I see is there's a quality and a potential in me that he sees. He's telling me that by giving me this name. That's very meaningful to me.

"I went back up to the center. I went in. There was a new person at the desk, I guess. I gave her my letter, and I didn't know how the ceremony went or anything. I said, 'I'm supposed to get a *mala*.' She reached under the desk and pulled out a box of *malas* and said, 'Pick one.' I reached in and picked out my *mala*. I walked home." That was Dara's sannyas birthday, the day she truly came to life: May 3, 1981.

"Sannyas isn't a group thing, it's a personal thing. I certainly felt Bhagwan there very strongly. More so than I ever had before."

When Dara got back to the North Side, her sannyasin housemates were waiting for her. "Everybody was looking very solemn and spiritual. And I said, 'OK, now we can all jump up and down.' And so I jumped up and down a couple of times, which lightened people up. There was a chocolate cake in the shape of a little heart."

The heart symbolized the personal, spiritual love affair each sannyasin had with Bhagwan. The man whom Dara was seeing at the time was not a housemate. He never became a sannyasin, although he later married someone else in Berkeley who was. Tony was not at all amused by the heart cake or its implications.

"It was very funny. He said to me, 'If it was a choice between me and Bhagwan, who would you choose?' And I said, 'Bhagwan!' He reacts. I said, 'Well, what did you expect me to say?' He said, 'I expected you to say that. But I didn't expect you to say it so fast.' I split up with him shortly after I took sannyas."

Suddenly, Dara could not wait to wear the sunrise colors all of the time. She bought white T-shirts and jeans and put them in a huge dye pot, along with all of the pastels she already owned. They turned the same flaming orange everyone in the Poona ashram had worn when she visited.

"I had dyed these white things. The dye was called 'brilliant orange.' It was really like things that glow in the dark. It was really funny but basically no problem.

"Once in San Francisco I ripped my *mala* off in the street. I got very angry. I went shopping with a sannyasin friend. We were going to a wedding together. I knew San Francisco, and he was visiting. I'd help him buy a suit. We went to shop after shop after shop. You can't imagine buying a red suit, a man's suit in San Francisco [in 1981].

"People kept directing us to Castro Street [the flamboyant gay district] and making horrible remarks. And he was getting more and more frustrated, and I was getting more and more frustrated. I finally said, 'Well, this is stupid. This wearing red, the *mala,* and all this. It's bizarre, if this is what we have to do to be sannyasins!' I was really angry.

"It was July, about two months after I'd taken sannyas. I grabbed my *mala* and ripped it off in a very dramatic gesture. Beads flew all over the street. I just stopped a sudden moment, and I thought, and I got down on my knees. I picked up all the beads and the *mala* and put it all back together. That was my only departure from Bhagwan."

At the same time that Dara had been carefully dying her clothes neon orange, Rajneesh dress restrictions changed dramatically. First, red, the color of her friend's ideal suit, was allowed. Then maroon was permitted. Within two years sannyasins wore every color from the sunrise. Approved shades ranged from pale shell pink to deepest purple. Bhagwan continued to dress in sharply contrasting hues of white, blue, or gray.

Styles also changed. The gauzy orange robes women and men both wore in humid Poona gave way to more conventional clothing. By 1982 fashionable Italian-cut suits and soft silk outfits were de rigueur. One sannyasin ordered pale pink button-down Brooks Brothers' shirts by the dozen. An older European woman bought several bright-red knit suits from Nancy Reagan's own designer, Adolfo.

The new dress codes reflected dramatic changes in the Rajneesh organization. Ma Anand Sheela replaced Bhagwan's longtime personal secretary, Ma Anand Laxmi. Sheela searched desperately for a large plot of land in the United States. In March 1981 Bhagwan no longer appeared in public, and in the following month, shortly before Dara received her sannyas letter, it was announced that Bhagwan had entered the ultimate stage of his work. He would remain in silence except for essential conversations with a few trusted aides.

At the end of May 1981 Bhagwan left Poona for a brief stay in Bombay before traveling to a New Jersey mansion for rest and medical treatment.

In July Sheela announced that the Rajneesh organization had purchased a 64,229-acre ranch in central Oregon. Bhagwan had plans for a utopian commune, which would serve as a model for humanity.

Little changed for Dara that summer despite the news. She continued to manage the restaurant, and people complemented her on the cheerful summer colors she always wore. No one, except sannyasins or those close to the movement, noticed her *mala*. Dara was busy learning recipes, going to the early morning vegetable market, and taking care of customers in some of the same ways she had nurtured her tenant clients a few years back. She also helped negotiate building permits for an addition to the restaurant.

At the house in the hills the telephone hummed with Rajneesh gossip. Dara heard about communal land in upstate New York, in Oregon near the college town of Eugene, and across San Francisco Bay in Marin County. That summer a steady stream of visitors leaving Poona camped briefly in their spare room or on the living room floor, before dispersing. Gitam, the northern California commune and growth center, or Utsava, the center in Laguna Beach, were their usual destinations. There were exciting personal growth groups and seminars in Berkeley, led by some of the best Poona therapists. Several of them were traveling in the United States and Europe in order to lift sannyasins' morale and to spread Bhagwan's philosophy.

She enjoyed the new Rajneesh energy in Berkeley. When word spread about the Oregon land purchase, Dara thought that she might visit someday. She had no desire to leave the restaurant, her comfortable house, or Tama. Now that her daughter was approaching adolescence, they were drawing closer. Dara and Tama talked on the phone every week, and they got together several weekends a month. She felt really good about her life, but it was changing again.

Dara possessed two areas of strength that were critical to the success of Rajneeshpuram. First, she could facilitate communication and negotiations with hostile groups in Wasco County, because of her years of experience with consensus-style staff decision making and her ability to mediate between landlords and tenants. Dara had dealt with Lefties, hippies, government bureaucrats, Chinese Americans, new Hong Kong immigrants, elderly pensioners, African Americans, and Russian dissidents. By comparison, the divisions between sannyasins and their Oregon neighbors seemed minimal to her.

Second, she had working knowledge of land-use and immigration laws. While not a lawyer herself, Dara understood federal immigration statutes. In Berkeley she became an informal immigration counselor to recent arrivals from Poona, and word of her generosity and resourcefulness spread through the Rajneesh organization. In December 1982 she received an invitation to visit Rajneeshpuram sometime soon and meet Ma Anand Sheela.

She accepted the invitation and planned to go early the next summer, after she had met several central figures in the Rajneesh legal organization, who sought her out when they passed through the Bay Area. As they got to know her better, they telephoned from Oregon with specific questions about immigration and other issues of immediate importance. Dara's enthusiasm for Rajneeshpuram grew as she became aware that her special skills would be valued. She was also influenced by contact with one of the commune's traveling attorneys, Swami Michael.

"Michael had visited. He was living at Utsava in Laguna Beach and working on a legal case down there. He had been visiting, and he stopped by. There was something about the energy he had around him. He was so excited.

"A roommate in the house, another sannyasin, said, 'You know, this morning when you left you were *here* and this evening you're in Oregon.' And it was absolutely true. That's exactly what had happened. You know, one moment I had been there and then finished."

Dara wrote a letter to Rajneeshpuram, requesting a definite invitation as soon as possible. Two weeks after she wrote Dara packed a large hanging suitcase with enough clothes for a week's visit. Several sannyasins met her at the Portland Airport. For the whole six-hour drive up into central Oregon and the commune, they chattered about Bhagwan's vision of a communal Buddhafield and potential roadblocks to utopia.

When she arrived Dara immediately responded to the sounds of building and blasting, the smell of wood at the construction sites, and the enormous vigor of the place. She felt Bhagwan's presence radiating throughout Rajneeshpuram.

"I walked in. I came for a visit. And I walked in and I said, 'This is it. That's it. There's no more question!' It was never a question of making a decision.

"I knew intuitively that it was the right thing. And there wasn't any question, once the realization was there. There's no way I can leave this place. This is home!"

Ma Anand Sheela greeted her briefly, but Dara spent a long afternoon with some of Sheela's inner circle. She was impressed with the camaraderie and sense of purpose shared by the small, lively group of attorneys and paraprofessionals who dealt with myriad issues of immigration, naturalization, and migration to Rajneeshpuram.

One day they worked to understand different legal interpretations of the Immigration Act of 1965, which had opened the United States to individuals from every country in the world. The next day she was asked to advise two New Yorkers who wanted to put their Manhattan brownstone in trust and come to live permanently at Rajneeshpuram. Everyone wanted her to stay. She didn't pretend ambivalence. Dara told them that she had decided the moment her feet had touched the ground in Rajneeshpuram. "I left to get my things, of course. But as far as the community—that was it!"

Although Dara wanted to bring Tama with her, Sheela's representatives discouraged it. Dara and Tama spent a wonderful weekend at the Timbercove Inn on the northern California coast, and she promised her daughter that a visit to Rajneeshpuram would also feel a lot like that special trip. She gave Tama the stained glass window and her guitar to keep until they were together again.

Dara's roommates offered to care for her plants and promised to come to visit her soon. They had no trouble renting Dara's room to a recent arrival from India. She worked another week at the restaurant, in order to train her replacement. Dara stuffed an enormous duffel bag with clothes, books, and some of her special textiles. Three weeks after she had returned from her visit to Rajneeshpuram, Dara was back. She loved the high desert and the way it shimmered in the hot August sun. She hoped that it would be home forever.

Rajneeshpuram

Dara felt blessed by the chill winter winds and heavy snows at Rajneeshpuram. She had few doubts about her move, although she disliked her work during the first six months. She felt pressed by life in the crowded townhouse, and Dara hated it when her roommate brought a boyfriend home and she had to sleep on the floor of another bedroom and impose on two other sannyasins. She was almost forty years old, and this was like college!

She sometimes disliked waiting for the renovated school bus to take her down to Mirdad Reception Center in cold weather. But she always appreciated the beauty around her and the glowing presence of Bhagwan, even though she only saw him briefly on his daily Drive-By. Dara felt great joy and humility in being part of the select few who were creating a utopia to guide the world into the twenty-first century.

Dara was becoming a new person once again. Everything she did, even backbreaking volunteer digging on the communal farm, was a kind of meditation. She could feel herself growing and changing. During her first two years at the ranch Dara was enthusiastic most of the time.

"The whole place is a group. Twenty-four hour meditation. People who are at a critical stage, and something is breaking through or dissolving or melting, have the option to go to dynamic meditation at six in the morning. If you really need to talk to somebody, then you go to the Meditation University and talk with a counselor, or you can book a session with a therapist. You can decide to go to rebalancing class or hiking or whatever is your best pastime.

"People who come here find they're suddenly liberated from responsibilities and cares they had in places they have lived before. There you get up and do an eight-hour day. Then maybe you have shopping, child care, house cleaning, cooking, laundry. You wind up putting in a twelve-hour day, anyway.

"So people talk about our twelve-hour workday, from seven to seven. But for the majority of time you're off work by dinner, and you don't have to cook it. Laundry is on the bed when you come home in the evening. The preschool teachers are there with the kids waiting, if you want to go and pick them up. The older ones seem to be more independent, and they see you when they get home. The whole thing is to make free space. That is speaking of the majority of time, because there are times when projects simply go around the clock.

"There is some leisure time, but a lot of people don't want it. They find they want to be totally involved with what is happening. They may volunteer to work in the restaurant or string *malas* or help with the kids. There are a lot of ways people can be involved. This is so much attuned to the kind of lifestyle I have developed over a period of time.

"There is a constant drama going on in the transformation of consciousness. At Rajneeshpuram change is constant, but there are a few things you can rely on. People who are there have chosen to be there. If they're here for any reason to do with ego, it's to understand it better. To see it more clearly. We don't believe in repressing it or turning it over and throwing it out. There is a certain kind of cooperation in helping each other see our behaviors. So you might say to somebody that you noticed that they have real impatience. That gives them the opportunity to go inside and see what it's about. Is there some pattern in their past life or some need in their present life that is giving them an urgency? The essence of Rajneeshpuram is cooperation. "I get a feeling that once before I lived in a space where things were as easy. It might have been just in dreams. The phrase Camelot comes to mind."

If this was Camelot, Dara was hardly part of the court when she arrived in 1982. She worked as a hostess, or "twinkie," for the first six months. Her job was to greet and sometimes guide curious, occasionally hostile visitors around the ranch. She rarely spoke with the important legislators, university professors, or media people who came through. Instead, Dara guided groups of high school students or collections of individual tourists who showed up at Mirdad Reception Center. Except for conversations with her hypersensitive supervisor, Ma Deva Lorinda, who was part of the inner circle, she heard nothing from Sheela or from the professionals who had invited her to help them deal with the emerging immigration and land-use cases.

"I worshiped at Mirdad. I was always getting told off because I was too compassionate to people.

"People would come in, and I could feel their nervousness, their fear of being there. I would spend enough time with them to calm them down. I was told many times that I had a bleeding heart, and that I shouldn't treat people in this way. We didn't have time to do that. We needed to be suspicious of people. Sometimes people would come in who would really act a little bit strange. I tended to spend a certain amount of time with these people to help them be comfortable.

"I was told that these aren't people we want on the ranch. I knew that these people weren't going to get very much necessarily from being there, but I didn't see why they couldn't have as nice an experience as possible. This kind of continued. Once I was asked to do something that was illegal, and I didn't do it. I just didn't do it."

Dara's life took a new turn early in February 1983. She was sent with a group from Mirdad to pick up paper and other supplies in Bend, a growing ski resort city about two hours away. The group of five stopped for lunch at a local spaghetti house. They rationalized that they were trying new recipes for Zorba the Buddha Restaurant at Rajneeshpuram. Just as they ordered, Sheela and one of her entourage descended on their table and joined the group.

Sheela was in a great mood, recounting insults she had traded with a state legislator on a local radio show. She turned to Dara and greeted her like a long-lost sister. "Where have you been? Why haven't I known that you are part of the Buddhafield? We need you."

At the end of lunch Sheela invited Dara to accompany her on a shopping expedition in Bend. They started out at a mall and then went downtown, where Sheela bought thin gold bracelets for herself. Then they hit the discount stores, where Sheela was a whirlwind of activity. She purchased supplies for her household at Jesus Grove, charming toys for Bhagwan to hand out to selected sannyasins on his Drive-By, and discount clothes to be added to communal stores. In less than three hours Sheela logged thousands on her platinum credit card, keeping up a high-spirited stream of chatter to Dara as she shopped until they dropped. Dara remembered the afternoon as something wonderful. Sheela's assistant drove them back to Rajneeshpuram as the sky darkened. By the end of the drive Sheela's charisma had mesmerized Dara.

"She's crazy about bargains. When they were first coming down, she'd disappear for two or three hours and somebody would find her with a companion at K-Mart or someplace buying bulk winter clothes or china or whatever.

"She's amazing. I can't figure her out, because she also makes some very big, important decisions without a lot of apparent background, and huge financial decisions. Somehow things seem to turn out right.

"Every time I've seen Sheela, she has been kind and gentle and caring and concerned. Funny and efficient. And I don't think I've ever heard her swear around the house."

Less than a week after her afternoon of shopping Dara received a handwritten note from Sheela requesting her to report to the Chamber of Commerce offices, which were also in the reception building. She was given her own small office cubicle. On her new desk there was a small bunch of red roses and a note from Sheela simply saying, "Welcome, Beloved Dara."

She now kept track of visitors and residents from Europe and Asia. Dara also began to work with sannyasins from other departments, traveling to the Wasco County seat in The Dalles and to Salem, the state capital. They talked with legislators to develop support for Rajneeshpuram's building plans and innovative land-use designs. Dara felt the sense of expertise and effectiveness that she had enjoyed so much during her first year at the San Francisco agency.

Later that year Dara formally resigned from the commune in order to draw a salary and receive insurance and pension benefits. Her roommate was reassigned, and she had the relative luxury of a private room. She later moved to one of the small bedrooms in Sheela's own compound. Suddenly, Dara was at the periphery of the inner circle. She did not participate in many meetings or see much of Sheela, but she still felt different and special.

Dara not only drew a salary, but she had keys to one of the communal four-wheel-drive vehicles available for use on the ranch or on business down the mountain. Sheela's assistant made her an appointment at Chiyono Hair and Beauty on Devateerth Mall. She was Cinderella. And she found a prince: a tall, rugged Australian who looked a little like the movie star Robert Redford but with a beard.

"I was married here. It was someone I actually met in California who is a sannyasin. He had been traveling around the country with his kids. He's Australian. He got into the import-export business. And he had come through Berkeley, actually stayed in our house. So I met him there, and when I came up here, and we got together.

"I think we had our celebration in spring of '83. I mean our religious ceremony, which is a form of celebrating. We weren't monogamous. It was a period of time when I was gone a lot. Work was intense. At least half of the time I was on the road with one thing or another. And it just wasn't the same for him as it was for me. For me it was my primary commitment. There just wasn't any question for me.

"For him it wasn't quite the same. He didn't have quite the same view of it in terms of a relationship. So within a year I said: 'This isn't working. We don't want the same things.'

"I don't know. I really didn't think there was anything that could be done to straighten it out. It's not like you could put energy into it and it would work out. It just didn't seem to me that was the situation. So I said that it's not working, and I filed for a divorce.

"People who are married here are not often monogamous. It is a matter of choice.

"It's fine. To me, the point is not to be in a long-term relationship or to be married and make it work. What works is to be honest and straight and clear all the time, all the way along the line. I was just reading something Bhagwan said the other day: 'Why waste time?' If it's not working and you have clarity, then you just move. Move to something else, something that is alive or something that is working.

"It's very different, and the relationships have to take on a different flavor. Here people are much more individuals in terms of relationships. People relate to each other as individuals, but they are part of a much larger unit that they are creating. People can worship with someone and not know who they are with or who they are married to. It may not come up. People are not seen as 'Mr. and Mrs. So and So.' They are seen as individuals in this whole thing. It certainly makes it easier to leave a relationship when it's not working. It's still difficult in the sense of connection with the person, but there aren't the other excuses to hang around.

"It may be that I'm not the kind of person to stay in very long-term relationships. I'm a very independent person. In our society we have an idea that everybody should be in a long-term relationship. When you grow up you're supposed to fall in love. You get married and stay in a long-term relationship to be successful. And, if you don't, you have failed somewhere. I have only very recently become aware of just how much I have been operating out of that conditioning, rather than out of my own choices. What's right for me? A lot of wanting to be in a long-term relationship has fallen away. I want to enjoy myself.

"I need about an hour of being alone every day. I just basically need it. I prefer to have a single room just for that reason."

The Fall of Rajneeshpuram

After her second divorce Dara continued to travel on ranch business. She had a room at the Rajneesh Hotel in downtown Portland and traded her little room at Jesus Grove for a spacious one at the new hotel in Rajneeshpuram. In the midst of twelve- and fourteen-hour workdays she had brief relationships with men. The volume of immigration work grew daily, as sannyasins were threatened with fines or deportation because the Immigration Services assumed their marriages were arranged for purposes of U.S. citizenship.

Dara had minimal contact with the thousands of street people bused to Rajneeshpuram during the fall of 1984. But when the short-lived "Share-a-Home" program fell apart, she worked out plans for many of the recent arrivals to leave the commune and return to their home cities. She also negotiated in disputes with the state about violations of building and electrical codes.

After the Share-a-Home program failed, Sheela grew more and more autocratic and capricious. For no apparent reason she became cold and distant to Dara. Puja, the Filipino nurse who had become Sheela's confidante, was downright nasty. Dara was moved to a small single room in a townhouse. She knew things were falling apart that summer, but Dara still labored at petitions and plans, drawing together her formidable abilities and energy. On September 14, 1985, Sheela and members of her entourage fled from Rajneeshpuram. That week Bhagwan lectured on Sheela's many crimes against his sannyasins. Dara said: "I lived with them. I loved them, yet I knew it was true."

"I just had a certain worldview or something, and suddenly it was taken away. Suddenly, you got information and realized you shouldn't have been trusting people you trusted. It's just kind of scary."

Dara tried to help hold the ranch together as more and more sannyasins left in disgust or despair. Most remained connected to Rajneesh, but they had given up on his vision of utopia. Dara sometimes worked late into the night, once again counseling refugees. But these new migrants were like brothers and sisters, fellow sannyasins whom she had known for years. They were her old friends and lovers. In spite of Rajneeshpuram's palpable disintegration, Dara still held on to the dream. She realized that she had worked too hard serving Sheela and that she needed more time for spirituality and simple, ordinary friendship. She saw those things as possible at Rajneeshpuram, now that leadership had changed and Bhagwan was speaking about freedom and diversity. This is how she described one of her days in early October, less than a month before Rajneesh himself attempted to leave the United States and travel to Bermuda.

"I slept late because I was really tired. I wanted to go to Bhagwan's discourse, so I got up. As I was leaving, a friend of mine who lives across the street called out that she was home cleaning that day. We are having a new thing. Instead of cleaning staff, we are rotating among the people in the house, so that everyone cleans one day every two weeks or something. It's kind of like a holiday. You get to house-clean, but it's like staying home and relaxing.

"So I went over and just chitchatted with her for a while. Then, as I was leaving her place, I saw some other friends. One friend was up visiting from Santa Barbara, and I went over there and chitchatted. It reminded me of a Saturday in the regular world. It felt very relaxed, even though we had a lot to do. I didn't get to discourse. It was a funny day, yesterday.

"Then I came to worship. Then I had lunch at the restaurant deck with my man friend. We don't live together, but we live kind of close by. I went back to the office to worship. We have a legal services clinic we just recently started called Rajneeshpuram Legal Assistance Fund. A lot of people have legal questions now, and we want to streamline it, so they won't have to come to the main legal office. It's just sort of a community service. If they come to the legal office, they have to charge them fees and keep file. This is just fifteen minutes where people can find out some basic stuff.

"If it's a complicated thing, we suggest people see the legal office. That was happening at the Rajneesh Hotel. I've been doing that for the last few days. It's more fun than San Francisco. Sitting in the sun with your friends. I just feel really good with people I can relate to. We're sort of in this together.

"We all say around here that worship [work] is our meditation. Recently, Bhagwan has been saying that he feels like it's a shame that we've been working so hard. We had to build the place, but at the same time it would be nice if we could have some time to meditate. We get put in all sorts of crazy situations, and you just have to find your own center.

Like working real late hours or doing things that seem kind of silly, not particularly meaningful one way or the other.

"We sit around and gossip and make each other feel better. A lot of people have left in the wake. Not that they are part of Sheela's group. But they just feel like things are changing, and it's too much for them somehow. That's also kind of hard.

"Around 7:15 I was done. I went to eat in the cafeteria, went home, and then my friend came over. I've been with him maybe eight months, nine months.

"I'm in love again. I love to be in love. The man that I'm in love with is very male. The most male man I've ever been with. Intelligent, not intellectual. With a very beautiful heart. This is strange. In a way he's a little like my first husband, but much more sensitive, but that kind of steadiness.

"Just last night I was being with my boyfriend as I was feeling very quiet in a way that I hadn't in a long time. And I was just lying next to him. I said, 'I feel very quiet lying here with you, and I feel this oneness.'

"There's a lot of harmony between us. Bhagwan had been saying, in some recent discourse that I heard about, that we're all separate. Ultimately, everybody's a separate individual. I don't really feel that right now. I just feel really close."

Dara slowly distanced herself from Rajneeshpuram during that last fall, as if she knew the commune could not last through the winter. She turned inward toward her seemingly solid, peaceful relationship, and she mused about the good things she received from being a sannyasin and being at Rajneeshpuram.

"I've found a family! I've found people who want to live in harmony. I'm very happy. A lot of people are here because they loved Bhagwan, and that's the reason they're here. And I love Bhagwan. But even if Bhagwan weren't here, this family is here, and I would be here."

At other times Dara was certain of the commune's numbered days. As part of her last formal interview, a few days after Sheela's departure, Dara responded a second time to the Thematic Apperception Test pictures, the diagnostic "tarot deck," revealing emotional pasts and sometimes foretelling their futures. She stared at the blank card in the deck, imagining a detailed picture, and Dara told this story about herself:

"There's a woman who has experienced tremendous upheaval in her life, but she has also found tremendous happiness. Certainly happiness to match the depths of despair. She certainly found heights of happiness. And she's at a turning point in her life right now. And she's looking at a man, a leader, who has tremendously inspired her and the whole group.

"She's looking at him, and she's feeling for the first time that she no longer loves him. She's not sure that she loves him. And she's thinking for the first time in years of leaving the group that she is involved with. She is sitting watching him speak. She just feels this kind of trembling inside, thinking that everything has always disintegrated around her. How much she has always been trying to keep everything together. She's wondering if maybe it's a good time. That life is creation and destruction of everything.

"It's hard to say how this story is going to turn out. She is supported tremendously by the love that is all around her. And even though she thinks many things aren't going the way she would want, there is always a way to create something of tremendous beauty. She is an infinitely optimistic person."

Dara's optimism about Rajneeshpuram was further shaken when Rajneesh tried to decamp to Bermuda and even more when he pled no contest and left the United States. On November 22, 1985, Dara heard the formal announcement that Rajneeshpuram would close and its assets would be sold. For months Dara had known this would happen. For years she had feared it would.

She stayed on at Rajneeshpuram to help sannyasins who were departing. She comforted tearful sannyasins when most of Bhagwan's ninety-six Rolls-Royces were loaded onto carriers in route to a rich Texas investor. Some people cried because they felt another part of Bhagwan was deserting them.

Dara helped organize and advertise the last "garage sale." On a sunny winter morning neighboring farmers and ranchers bought heavy equipment. The massive kitchen appliances had already been sold to local entrepreneurs. Tourists bargained over furniture or amusing "No Parking" signs. The remaining sannyasins sold or traded their meager goods. Shanto had sent money for a friend to buy her the one piece of rosewood furniture sold from Bhagwan's own compound.

Dara stood in the middle of all this, with an official-looking clipboard in one hand and a winsome stuffed goose under her other arm. The goose was a gift from one of her close friends who had left for California early that morning. Her friend had told Dara to let the goose do some of the work of organizing and caring for other people.

Dara once again lived in the Hotel Rajneesh, sharing a large room with a sitting area with her man friend. Now there were less than one hundred remaining sannyasins. Wednesday was pizza night in the spacious hotel lobby. There was live music, and sannyasins put on comedy skits about life at Rajneeshpuram. People talked about what to pack, what to leave, and what to expect from the outside world. Dara was once again positive and optimistic about her experience as a sannyasin. She said, "I feel like I've created myself."

She thought about Tama and their brief, strained visit at the ranch two years before. Her daughter was almost grown. As she made plans to leave Rajneeshpuram and move on with her lover, Dara kept reflecting about her daughter and what the future held in store for her little girl.

"Of course, I hope that she has a life full of love and joy. However, she can create that in her life, for herself.

"When she was born, I was right in the middle of the women's movement. I remember thinking that I hope that she's terribly intelligent. She can be a good businesswoman if she wants, and she can make a lot of money. I had all these ideas about success and everything. And I have none of those ideas now. None at all. I just want her to be happy. I want her to be fulfilled completely in herself.

"I hope that she is a human being who can grow up to be herself and not have other people's ideas imposed on her. That she can discover from her inner being what she is and that she can be totally it. That's *all*."

Dara was immeasurably proud of Tama. She felt another new life was beginning for herself as well. And Dara was sure that, whatever that new life was, Bhagwan would always be part of it.

Bhagwan Shree Rajneesh wore shimmering robes and woolly hats during the Oregon years. (Courtesy of the *Eugene Register Guard.*)

Ma Anand Sheela (Sheela Silverman) plotted every move. (Courtesy of the *Eugene Register Guard.*)

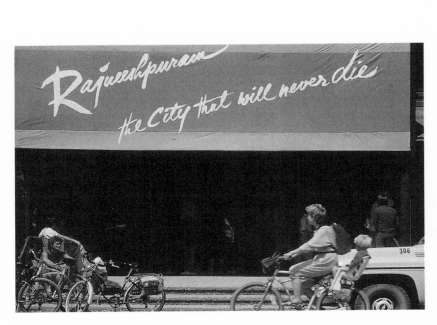

On Devateerth Mall shoppers indulged their material cravings.
(Courtesy of the *Eugene Register Guard*.)

The Rajneesh Bookstore in the mall sold hundreds of books written by or about Bhagwan along with trinkets like pens or coffee mugs that bore his image.

Workers in the fields at Rancho Rajneesh wore broad brimmed hats to protect them from the high desert sun. (Courtesy of Mike Znerold.)

An inspiring picture of Bhagwan watched over the kitchen at Magdalena Cafeteria. (Courtesy of Mike Znerold.)

Sannyasins serenely meditated in Bhagwan's presence.
(Courtesy of the *Eugene Register Guard.*)

Other Rajneesh meditations evoked exuberance.
(Courtesy of the *Eugene Register Guard.*)

Rajneesh Mandir was the community's central meditation hall.
(Courtesy of the *Eugene Register Guard.*)

Sheela sometimes served as a sentinel during Bhagwan's daily Drive-Bys.
(Courtesy of the *Eugene Register Guard.*)

Each afternoon sannyasins lined the road in order to catch a glimpse of
Bhagwan steering one of his Rolls Royces among the faithful.
(Courtesy of the *Eugene Register Guard.*)

Sannyasins bowed to Bhagwan's divinity.
(Courtesy of the *Eugene Register Guard.*)

Sannyasins said final farewells to Rajneeshpuram in winter of 1985–86. (Courtesy of the *Eugene Register Guard.*)

The towering crematorium at Rajneeshpuram was a monument to Sheela's influence. (Courtesy of the *Eugene Register Guard.*)

Chapter 5

THE SWAN

During Rajneeshpuram's last months Tanmaya poured over her tarot deck, searching for the meaning of the collapse. While the single word that might have described Shanto was *charm,* and the word for Dara was *intelligence,* Tanmaya's word was *beauty.* She stood apart because of her height of almost six feet, her grace, and her delicate, nearly perfect features. Beneath a feathery cap of black hair she had enormous, almost violet eyes; a small, straight nose; incredible cheekbones; and pouting lips. Sannyasins all over the ranch gossiped about Tanmaya and her love affairs. Less than a year before a distraught Rajneesh banker had threatened suicide because she had spurned his entreaties to live with him in Zurich. Behind her back people called Tanmaya "Our Swan." The Swan was an important person at Rajneeshpuram because of her influential lovers, her striking looks, and, somewhat less obviously, her many talents.

Tanmaya was just thirty-three—born in 1952 in the midst of the baby boom. She was part of Rajneeshpuram's "younger generation," but she had considerable prestige because of two of the powerful sannyasins she had lived with during her six years as a sannyasin. One major relationship was in Poona, the other at Rajneeshpuram. Her tarot cards sometimes foretold new developments at Rajneeshpuram or twists and turns in her love life. Tanmaya adored the cards, and she also practiced other esoteric arts like palm reading, numerology, past-lives exploration, and astrology.

In autumn of 1985 she tried all of them to get away from the pain of Sheela's departure and the possibility of Bhagwan's complicity in some of his secretary's nefarious schemes. But beyond those questions lay deeper ones about Tanmaya's own identity. She found herself staring at the number 5 card of the *Rajneesh Neo-Tarot Deck* (Rajneesh 1983). Number 5 meant the "Ultimate Accident," which was personal enlightenment. Its illustration was a scarred crone, Chyono, standing beneath the full moon. The story accompanying it was from Rajneesh's *No Water, No Moon,* but Tanmaya had made it her own, and this is how she saw Chyono's spiritual journey:

"Chyono was a beautiful young woman who wanted to be a disciple. She wanted to be on the path, wanted to be accepted. But she wasn't accepted at the monastery. She was told, 'You would disturb the monks. It's not possible for you to come in here.'

"So she went away and burnt her face and scarred her face and cut her hair and then she was accepted. She studied and meditated through the whole monastery for many years. At some point she was carrying a bucket of water. It was a bamboo bucket in a strap. She was looking at the full moon's reflection in the water in the bucket. Then the strap broke and the water came out. And Chyono said, 'The strap broke, the bamboo fell, the water came. There was no more water and no more moon.' At that moment she became enlightened."

The lesson from the story, according to Tanmaya, was that people need not hold anything back to become enlightened. She said, "You didn't have to make yourself ugly [like Chyono]. You didn't have to not be intelligent. Everything was to flower to become as beautiful as possible." This was not quite the theme in the accompanying tarot book (Rajneesh 1983, 12–13), which emphasized creating an invitation for enlightenment. But it was the meaning that Tanmaya had personally assigned to the card. Her story allowed Tanmaya to cultivate her beauty and intelligence while seeking spiritual truth. The card helped her feel her emotional center and enjoy the many benefits of her stunning looks.

Tanmaya was a flower in the high desert, whose bloom allowed her to escape some of the usual constraints of residence at Rajneeshpuram. She led a privileged life; unlike ordinary sannyasins, who were expected to be at work early in the morning, Tanmaya seldom arose before 10:00 A.M., although she guided past-lives' groups at the International Meditation University and designed spectacular, one-of-a-kind clothes for the Rajneesh Boutique. If there was a special need for her presence in a therapy group, a meeting, or a call to Bhagwan's presence, Tanmaya could force herself awake at almost any hour. Sometimes she worked late into the night counseling sannyasins or suggesting how designer clothing could be made and marketed, but Tanmaya usually stopped work by eight o'clock in order to talk with friends, dance, and be with her man of the moment. The essence of Tanmaya's contribution to the Buddhafield was neither daily labor like Dara's nor financial support like Shanto's. It was simply her physical presence.

Tanmaya's clothes were surprisingly plain. They were not strikingly fashionable or elaborately designed. But even the jeans and sweat pants she usually wore fit perfectly, outlining her endless legs and tiny, rounded hips. Tanmaya chose colors carefully, preferring soft shades of pale rose or deep burgundy that set off her white skin and natural blush. She wore relatively little jewelry except for her simple wooden *mala* and a tiny diamond stud in each ear, which she had purchased at Asprey in London with her first major paycheck for fashion show modeling. She had an ordinary Timex watch with a black ribbon band, and she only wore one ring, on the middle finger of her right hand. The ring was a knockout, an immense oval ruby surrounded by round diamonds. It had been given to Bhagwan, and later he had personally bestowed it upon the man whom Tanmaya currently lived with. Now the ring was hers.

Tanmaya had not grown up with rubies. She was born and raised middle class, with a simple middle-class name, Julie. Her father was a civil servant who moved his family to California in order to escape harsh Nebraska winters. They relocated once again, when Julie was eleven, and her family rented a huge U-Haul truck in order to cross the Sierras, settling in the Carson Valley, just outside of Nevada's capital city.

Growing Up

Tanmaya used to be Julie Elsa Morris. At home and at school she was always called Julie. Almost no one knew about Elsa. It was her mother's mother's name too. The first Elsa was a full-blooded Cherokee Indian, and Julie was always keenly interested in her own tribal roots. Although she was proud of her grandmother, Julie found the name Elsa to be just a little too close to "Elsie the Cow." She didn't want anyone outside the family to know about it.

Some of Julie's earliest memories were of strange, diffuse tensions between her parents. Although Carol and Duane Morris rarely fought openly, something was not right. "My parents were two people that always carried out an atmosphere like there was a love affair happening. So they managed. I don't know how they did it, but they managed to keep that kind of facade going for as long as I knew. Once it was out in the open, I could see things start to break down. I understood it absolutely. They were incompatible. They were wrong for each other from the beginning, but not totally."

Her mother, Carol, thought Julie was a bit unusual from the hour she was born. Julie was almost too sensitive, too alert, too insightful. Carol described her daughter as someone who was always looking and watching people. But Julie believed that her mother was a little afraid of her. Possibly afraid from the very beginning.

"I feel that childhood was kind of dark for me. Now, every year, it's getting more light and more and more free.

"I don't think there's anything weird about me, but I can see that she [Carol] thought there was something different about me.

"I felt, in a way, on the wrong planet. I never thought those words, but things felt very strange to me. Very harsh, very confusing. But I was very happy in another way. I entertained myself. I would look out the window, and I would see different things. Sometimes I still do. I would have to call my mother and I'd say, 'Is it raining?' And she would say, 'No. It's not raining.' I would just be seeing all the movements in the sky. I would see things differently, and I would ask her what it was.

"I adored her when I was a little child. I used to watch her in the bathroom. She had hair like mine. But her skin was as dark as I am fair, and I just thought she was so beautiful. I used to watch the way she talked. Her tongue. I loved her. And we were very close those first years.

"She just talked to me like an adult. She would sit me somewhere and just talk to me. Then I would just talk back to her. We had this great relationship for a few years. Then things changed.

"It was just before my brother was born. She may have been a few months pregnant with him, so I was around three. My parents had a car accident. She was knocked unconscious for ten days, or some long time.

"My father was put in jail because he had run a red light." Although Duane was out on bail almost immediately, he had his sister care for his daughter until Carol recovered. Julie recalled, "All of a sudden, there wasn't anybody there for me. An aunt who I didn't know came to take care of me. I remember, there were these basement steps. I would wake up, and I would be sitting on these steps, so I was walking in my sleep."

"And twice I even let myself fall down the stairs. I'd think, 'If I'm injured, she'll come. She would be there.'

"I don't remember this, but she said that when she came back, and she sat down, I just turned my back on her. I didn't come to her, wouldn't come to her. I was probably very hurt, and that was my revenge. 'OK, you're not going to love me, I'm going to ignore you.' I had no idea about her being hurt. I was probably very insecure. I was just left.

"We got close again. I remember us reading stories to each other. And I remember I used to draw all over everything. My walls were just crawling with images, like Sanskrit scrolls. So she got me chalk. She said, 'This is your room. You can draw on the walls with chalk.'

"I appreciate that bigness. That she let me draw on the walls. It made a mess, but it was not so bad."

What was bad was Julie's little brother, who was slightly less than three years younger than she was. "I felt she loved my brother more."

"I still wanted to be the baby. But three years seemed like a lot older than him. She still thinks of him, and not me."

Julie and her brother shared a room in Lincoln, where they were both born. But in 1960, when Julie was eight, the family moved to Sacramento. Duane had taken a better-paying job as a statistician with the California State Farm Bureau. They moved into an almost new, one-story house in a middle-class tract on the edge of town. Julie began third grade, and her brother, Tom, started kindergarten.

Julie liked her new home. The city was flat like Lincoln, but she could look up and see fluffy white clouds and the Sierras looming over the Central Valley. Sacramento had been a sleepy old California city with a Gold Rush heritage. In the early 1960s an influx of new migrants came to work in aerospace factories and the rapidly expanding state government. The true old Sacramento was disappearing, as new schools, strip malls, and housing tracts undermined the small-town values that had shaped the city's middle class a decade earlier.

On rare Saturdays Julie hiked around the foothills with her mother, searching for wildflowers. She also took solitary walks to the edge of the populated areas, treading her way through tall grass and fields. Summers were very hot, and Julie liked to go down to the community swimming pool or walk along the riverbank. At the end of summer there was a State Fair with rides and games and barns full of prize horses, cattle, and sheep.

She got excellent grades in school. Julie also had a few neighborhood friends, newly arrived daughters of middle managers who had just migrated to Sacramento to work at Aerojet. They ate lunch together at school sometimes, but Julie was so shy that she had no really close girl-friends who slept over and stayed up giggling.

"I was very sensitive. It was difficult for me to talk at all, because I was so intense. When I was in my early teens or younger, eight, I would just cry. I couldn't say what I wanted to. The communication wasn't there. The emotions were so intense. So I had to work at it to be able to come through the emotions to say what I felt. There was no possibility of me putting them aside."

"I always wanted to be more. I wanted to live an adventurous kind of life that was always changing. That was always putting me in situations where I could expand as a person, and where I could experience new things within myself."

As soon as Julie and Tom were both in school, Carol got a job as a secretary and key-punch operator with the school district. She also began working for an Associate of Arts degree at the community college, taking classes in merchandising and textiles. At home she was nervous and distracted.

"When I was in school she was always working. And there were lots of problems, but not anything in particular.

"She is very ambitious and very strong and very determined to be a success. She wants things far and above what she ever has at that moment. She wants a lot of recognition in her life."

Julie began to feel a special closeness to her father as she grew older. Although Duane was tense, distant, and often drunk, once in awhile Julie felt an emotional connection with him that was missing anywhere else in her life.

"I could see he was very intelligent, but he had almost a paranoia of not feeling good about himself. He was very spiritually beautiful when he married. But he was very hung up. When he went into the war, he was very young, too young."

Duane met Carol after he had returned from World War II and finished college, with a business degree. She was working in the offices of the same company. She had been married once before, but her first husband had died of pneumonia after a few years of marriage.

They had a civil ceremony. Carol was a spiritual seeker, attending different kinds of religious groups each month, and sometimes Julie came with her to a Unitarian meeting or a Bahai study night. Carol accepted Julie's sudden intuitions or yearnings for links to higher powers. Julie said of her mother, "A lot of people in her family were very intuitive in that way. Often she would pick up the phone and call someone across the country, because she knew something was happening. They didn't talk about it much. She is part American Indian, and they trust that psychic space."

"My mother's basic religion is Indian. She said she hated the Christian religion because she saw what it had done to her people. She said that Christianity was the cause of many, many wars. And she was raised a Christian. But she never believed it.

"She told me about Mother Nature. If you wanted to call existence 'God,' you could, but she didn't really like the name. And she said there definitely wasn't a white father sitting up in the sky with a great big long beard looking over everybody. She said there's nobody up in the sky like that.

"She believed in science. She believed in the mystery of existence. If she worshiped anything, it was Mother Nature. The wind and trees and seasons and life and the earth and the sky and the water and all that stuff. She was very Indian, basically."

Duane's father was Jewish, and his mother was Lutheran. He took his family to Christmas Eve services but to little else.

"The only memory that he had of religion at all is that he came home from kindergarten singing 'Jesus Loves Me, Yes, I Know,' and the family didn't like that. So that was the end of that. From then on, it was up to him to work out what was right and what was wrong from his own heart, rather than what religion teaches.

"The most remarkable thing about my family is that they never influenced any [of my] religion. They never taught me to believe in God or to believe in this or to believe in that. We would study religion, and they would suggest that I discover which one would be right for me.'

Duane was something of a seeker himself: "He's the one who kind of introduced me to the world of human potential kinds of things. Maybe somewhere there was a motivation for me to get more deeply into it, because that was our connection."

"With him I had a depth. All at once we would be sitting in the living room or something, feeling the sun coming in on you. We would just look at each other, and there would be a communication that went all the way in—a communication which I didn't have with my mother. Sometimes we would talk, and our talk really touched each other in a very deep space. Then it would turn, and it would go away. I think he was the first person I ever knew that was possible with.

"It's not like we went around connected day to day. But we had that possibility where he would sometimes share himself totally.

"I was also a woman, relating to my Dad as if I were a woman relating to my boyfriend, my husband, or whatever."

Those special times with her father and the closeness to her mother made up for many difficulties. Both Duane and Carol believed in physical discipline, and they occasionally spanked their kids. Sometimes Duane became angry suddenly and impulsively hit Julie once or twice, but she never considered herself to be a battered or abused child.

"It's not like he beat us or anything. At times both of them had hit me. It's the incredible tension and anger in him. Lots of incidents happened, but he's a Leo, and I'm not.

"The thing that would really bother me would be ordering. 'You do this because I said so.' A really stupid thing. Or he'd say, 'This room isn't yours, it's mine.' Stupid things to say. Or being forced to do things when I didn't think they were fair. They were not big things, but there was a tension. I was hurt by it and at times affected because I realized that kind of strain was painful to him, so I was very affected by it. He was holding himself back his whole life because of his own resentment and his own pain."

The great joy in Julie's childhood was ballet. She took lessons several times a week, beginning at age five. There was a song in the Broadway musical *A Chorus Line* called "Everything Is Beautiful at the Ballet." That was how she felt. She could lose herself in the music, and there was a reassuring sameness about the order of class and the progression of the steps. Julie knew that she wouldn't become a ballerina. She just wanted to dance.

"It was really a love, and it still is. It wasn't them telling me that I had to go. To this day, to look at dance, classic ballet or even more something like Alvin Ailey Dancers—it's just something that's very nourishing, and I love it. I begged to do it. I was doing it three times a week.

"As a kid, I was forever dancing, especially in front of my father. He loved to watch me dance. I don't know that I wasn't talented. But I had such strong feelings of inferiority that I never was able to project myself in dance. Not inferiority as a dancer, just general inferiority. But I enjoyed it, and I still love dance.

Carson City

Because she could continue with her ballet lessons, Julie hardly noticed that her family moved over the mountains to Carson City. Although it was the seat of state government, Carson was a small town of less than thirty thousand in the early 1960s. In the summertime it was as hot and flat as Sacramento, only a lot uglier, with frame houses and few trees. Reno, about thirty miles north, was where mothers took their daughters shopping and where the tiny ballet school in Carson joined its larger counterpart for dance concerts. It was where high school kids went on big dates. As Julie entered her teens, she looked north to Reno and then West, past Sacramento to San Francisco.

In high school Julie grew more and more frustrated with Carson City, describing it in retrospect as "that tiny little town and all those tiny little minds." But for the first few years things had seemed fine. Julie rarely saw her brother, who was out doing sports or hanging out with his friends. She danced, drew pictures, and took more long, solitary walks.

Julie began to imagine a life beyond what she knew. She wanted something, but she wasn't sure what. She said, "I don't see a time when I decided that I was looking for something. It seemed like, before I even knew what I was looking for, I was looking. Something a bit more. It is not like it was a totally conscious search."

The cultural shifts of the 1960s slowly crept into Nevada. Julie began to read the *San Francisco Chronicle,* and in ninth grade she helped organize a students' march for racial equality. She and her friends tried to end the quiet discrimination that kept African Americans from buying houses in desirable neighborhoods.

"A few of my friends and I went around, knocked on doors, and we said to people, 'Do you believe that America is a place for freedom, justice, and liberty for all?' 'Oh, yes,' everybody said.

" 'Well, then, why is it black people can't live in this town?' And they would say things like, 'Oh well, that's different.'

"Their basic complaints against black people were that they're more sexual. They didn't say it straight out like that, but they said, 'Well, we have to protect our girls, right?' And the next complaint was they're dirty and they make the town a mess. The next complaint was they're loud. They create disturbance, and they're violent.

"We said, 'Well, this doesn't seem right. That's making assumptions about people that may not be true.'

"So I think there were only about fifteen of us kids, and we did a little march. I was thirteen at the time, I think. We had little placards, and it was just us kids. Parents didn't join us or anything. My mother always let me make those decisions myself, but she supported me, and so did my Dad. And we marched around the town and through the city center and so forth and got our pictures taken. This was put in the paper, and people said, 'Oh, isn't this cute.'

"I think my parents raised me to really think for myself, and I did. They basically didn't want me to be a sheep."

Julie's body matured quickly and suddenly. The summer between eighth grade and high school, she grew six inches and began to develop her beautiful figure. A decade later she might have been a varsity basketball player, but that was not a reasonable option for high school girls in Carson City in 1967. Julie found it difficult to look at herself in the mirror at ballet school, although she continued to take lessons.

She remained at the periphery of the most popular crowd, invited to activities but without a best friend. Her classmates, older boys, and even some men began to notice Julie in very unpleasant ways. And at Carson High, for the first time, she had problems with her teachers.

"I made straight A's, but nobody knew I did. When I hit puberty, things took a different turn. I still made straight A's, but I got 'Unsatisfactory' in cooperation with a teacher. He was my first male teacher, and there was all that energy, and I didn't know what it was. Early in high school I wasn't interested in boys.

"I was so rebellious, I couldn't keep my mouth shut when I was in class. There was something, basically, with males that I would have this struggle with. I would provoke them, and I would make them very angry, and I kind of enjoyed it.

"Probably I did it because I got attention in class. No one else would say the things that I said. And I was kicked out of class a few times.

"I was amazed. Of course, I was a good girl in that I wasn't sleeping with men. I was in my early teens. The people I hung out with were what you would consider good people.

"The school would treat me bad. I was angry, and I didn't even know why. I would be kicked out of class for what I see now was good. I'm very glad that I said the things I did.

"Some stupid young guy who was new on the faculty came in and demanded to see something that I was writing. I said, 'No, this is a private thing, and I'm not going to show it to you!'

"He got more indignant, because it was in front of the whole study hall or something. He went on to get more and more red. And I'm very stubborn. Once I said it, there was no way out. He said, 'Go.' Actually, I think that I just packed up and went before he told me.

"I went straight to the principal, or whoever it was. It was another man. He said, 'I don't care what a teacher tells you to do. If I tell you to bang your head against the wall, I expect you to do it.'

"I said, 'I'm not going to do it.' And he said, 'So you can just leave.' And he expelled me for three days. He asked, 'Does your mother work?' And I said, 'Yes.' And he said, 'Oh, that explains it.'

"But this is what I love about my mother. I just told her what happened, and she said, 'Good.' She wouldn't have stood that either. She wouldn't have been a coward under that kind of thing."

Things got worse for Julie. Suddenly she was an outcast. The school had labeled her as incorrigible. She felt that no one was willing to give her a chance. Teachers criticized her for trivial offenses, like the short skirts she and everyone else wore.

"They measured my hems, that kind of stuff. And they treat you like some kind of whore, when you're fifteen and you've never had sex. I had a lot of anger about that. I just kind of phased out. I didn't do any work. I can seem to do things without doing anything.

"I had a horrible reputation, and I hadn't done anything." But Julie's reputation made her a moving target. In ways she felt assaulted everywhere she went.

"I would just see how people looked at each other or how men talked about it to each other, and I would be mortified. As a young girl, I just felt so terrible that they would think of anybody that way. I would be in a restaurant and just look at two men looking at me, and what they would say to each other, or the way they looked at someone else, and I would be injured. At times I would even ask my mother to change places with me, so I wouldn't have to look at it."

While Julie was sinking, her mother was stretching out and reaching higher. One day Carol let Julie skip school. They drove to Reno, where Carol managed a boutique south of downtown. It had thick carpets, soft light, and beautiful, terribly expensive clothes.

The shop had started almost twenty years before, when the city was the glamorous divorce mecca of the United States and bored rich women from all over the country had to stay six weeks in hotel suites or dude ranches in order to receive their decrees. Loosening nationwide divorce laws had slowed that traffic, but local socialites, a handful of elegant call girls, and visitors who came up from Lake Tahoe or Squaw Valley still spent large sums on their wardrobes.

Carol saw a better life for herself in the garment trade. She was hard-working and quick to learn. Already an excellent saleswoman, she was now learning merchandising and bookkeeping. She wanted Julie to share her future, and that day in Reno she enrolled her in modeling school.

"My mother took me with her, because I wanted to do modeling. I went to one of those little finishing schools [modeling schools]. It was very boring. I looked at magazine pictures when I was a kid and I thought, 'I can do that.'

"I didn't do anything they taught me, but I had that interest. I thought, 'Why not?' So I did."

The summer between her sophomore and junior years, Julie modeled for her mother's store. Although she was young, in full makeup and with her hair done in a French twist, Julie could pass for twenty. Her mother signed a release, and she posed for a few newspaper ads for a local department store while also working part time at a Dairy Queen. But she spent most of that summer lying around the house and arguing with her father, who either isolated himself after work or picked fights with anyone who was around.

In August, after a furious fight with Duane, Julie left a note, walked to the bus station, and bought a ticket to San Francisco. The famous flower children's culture of Haight-Ashbury was almost gone, obscured by dope dealers, addicts, and runaways like Julie. There were signs on telephones and lampposts begging children to come home or at least call. Julie did call her mother the day after she arrived, just to let her know she was safe. She found places to crash and tried weed (marijuana), acid (LSD), and crystal (methamphetamine). Almost twenty years later Julie still remembered those six weeks with horror. "There were drugs and men. It was a lot of confusion. I wasn't stable. I would have gotten *more* lost."

Julie came back to Carson City in mid-September, hitching a ride with a group of college students bound for Colorado. School had already started, but she didn't go back for her junior year.

"I dropped out when I was sixteen. I decided I was going to get married, and I found someone. I found someone I really liked, although I was not in love. So I told my mother and she supported me in it.

"It was like one of those moments when I looked at her and said, 'This is what I am going to do.' And she looked at me, and she could see that's what I was going to do. So she said, 'OK, I will go get you birth control pills.' So I went to a doctor, and I got married a week after I turned seventeen.

"He was older. He was nineteen. He lived in another state, but he was from Carson City. So, the same day we got married, we left and went to California. I had gone with my feelings my whole life, and this was a mature thing. This was what I was supposed to do. I knew I wasn't getting married for the rest of my life. In fact, I thought it would be one year. Not that I shared this with anybody.

"I needed to get away, and I knew this was a person that I liked. It was good. I was very emotionally upset, and I wanted to get away. I just knew that this was the right thing to do. It was very hard for me, and I cried through my wedding. I was this little soggy seventeen-year-old."

Married Life

"It was a church wedding, but not a big one. I went away with him to Davis. And I was actually with him for two and a half years. To me it was an intermediate point." Julie's new husband was a history student who would eventually go on to get a law degree. His parents now lived in San Francisco. The young couple had a neat little one-bedroom apartment in a modern complex, not far from the UC-Davis campus. At first Julie played at being a housewife, and she also took classes and tests, so she received her high school equivalency degree when she was eighteen years old.

Davis was a delightful respite for Julie. It was usually sunny, and Lake Beryessa was about a half-hour away. The community was a pleasant mixture of counterculture, students, young professionals, and old-timers with roots in farming and ranching. It was near Sacramento and the foothills of the Sierra and close enough to visit her husband Cliff's family in San Francisco. Julie did not talk about her summer in the Haight, and mostly they remained close to the Marina or strolled over to Union Street and shopped in boutiques or dined at nice restaurants. About twice a year Julie and Cliff visited Carson, staying with Cliff's aunt and uncle, instead of Julie's parents.

Julie described her first year of marriage: "I did things, but basically I kind of cooled out from the stress of my family and school. I gave myself a lot of time. I sat by the pool in the sun, got together with friends, and I screamed a lot inside."

"I wasn't ready for the world yet on my own. At times, it was almost like running away from home when I started to leave this husband. I would get to the end of the driveway, and I would look out there. I would look and think, 'This is too big, I know it's too big.' Then I would walk back.

"I kind of got a feeling of myself, in these years without parents. To me this was, is, a search.

"It turned out I eventually went to Sacramento State for awhile. I always had high hopes for school. I went in with this excitement, what it was going to give me. And I was always disappointed. I put everything into it for six weeks, and it was so boring. I tried to do this mainly for his parents, and because something in me really wanted to.

"I love books, and I've always read a lot, so I got encyclopedias. I really tried to do this university. It's not hard for me to make good grades. I think the whole time I was married I stayed in school. I can't remember dropping out.

"But during this time I went into books for classes, and I also started reading palmistry and astrology. This was the first place I started looking at myself through tarot. In some way I wasn't able to take in everything I'd see, because I needed to make my ego bigger. To build up something. To support myself. I would certainly see a lot more now, but I started then."

While she was going to school in Sacramento, Julie also started modeling again. She did luncheon fashion shows for I Magnin, a lovely women's specialty store. She also modeled for their advertisements. It was part-time work that paid a mere fifteen to twenty-five dollars an hour, but she enjoyed it. Modeling was part of the process of building her emotional strength.

"And then there came a time when it was time to leave my husband. It actually came. I met someone. I met a man, and the meeting was incredible. As soon as we walked in the room, before we saw each other, something was very different in the room. It was like what you read about. It has never happened again, and I don't think it ever will.

"It was a bit like, if there was a God, and he was playing chess up there, he would say, 'Hey dummy, don't miss this one.' There was no way we could miss each other. I was modeling at the time. I even had a wig on, and I had false eyelashes. A sophisticated nineteen-year-old.

"We just sort of met each other and oh my God! I went away, and I was shaken because I thought, 'Uh, oh, what is this?' I thought that I had really loved somebody before this, before my husband. Then I thought this will never happen again. So I married, and I hated sex and all this. And then I ran.

"I was modeling with this one girl, whom I really loved, who had a boyfriend who worked with the guy. We went back, and I drove them somewhere. I know it was *my* car, but I was sitting in the back seat talking with him [David]. Bubbles were just going, exploding in my head, and the same thing was happening for him, but I didn't know it.

"When he got out of the car and left, I lay in the back seat and started crying. I said, 'Charlie—that's my girlfriend—this is terrible. I've never felt like this before! This is awful. What am I going to do?'

"I went home, and I thought, 'Well, I will never see this guy again. That's OK. But if I can feel like this, what am I doing here?'

"And then everything became very clear in respect to my marriage. It was possible for me to love, and I didn't even know if it was love. It was just, this was happening, and it was so different from what was happening here that I left in a matter of a week or something.

"I told my husband that we were very good friends, and that was all that was ever going to go on. He wasn't interested in growth at all, and I wasn't [consciously] interested. I didn't know that word *growth,* but I was growing. And he wasn't. So we left like friends.

"I actually left and didn't even know where I was going. It was a bit the same as the time I got married. I knew I had to do that. Same thing, I knew that I had to do this. I was nineteen.

"I called a few days later. My father was actually so freaked out that he left home for three days. He was very upset. I was so scared, but it was very exciting as well.

"I just went to stay at a friend's house for a couple of days. I didn't know what I was going to do or anything. I didn't care about taking anything away from the house or about money. It was like a different world compared to what's happening now or in between.

"I really don't know how I crossed the street at times. But it was like something was taking care of me. I was being led—that's just what it feels like. And it probably won't surprise you that I did meet this man [David] again. And we lived together for seven years.

"Immediately, we slept together once, and we never separated. It was clear for both of us. He was sort of into macrobiotics¹ and things like that. I lost so much weight, because all I ate was peanut butter and bread. He thought that it was a good idea not to eat meat, so I tried it out. So, I haven't eaten meat since I was nineteen. I have been a vegetarian for a long time.

"And this all started there. There was no doctrine or anything. He was nineteen too. He was so pretty! And he was very, very talented and creative. He had a leather shop then. Beautiful. Maybe the *best.* And he was also into music. So, I was just very attracted to this person.

"It was just moment to moment. Very, very alive! And we got a place together.

"I felt more loved by him. I felt he saw me and loved me, not the image that he had of me. Most of the men I had in my life didn't know me. Most of them had a projection of who I was, that fit into their little slot of 'woman.' He was so obviously a loving person. That was a great gift for me.

"We were so close, we didn't do anything without each other. We cooked together. We shopped together. We slept together. We literally were not separated from each other for more than an hour during the first year."

Julie met her lover's brother, who lived in Modesto, another central California valley town. She also went with him to visit his grandmother near Merced. Julie's ex-husband and his family helped arrange their Nevada divorce. It was so easy that she barely noticed. She continued to model, but she also worked in David's leather store. On weekends she went to listen to him play jazz. He wrote music too, and he sat in with the Grateful Dead a few times before he met Julie.

Neither David nor Julie cooked very much. The locus of their domesticity was a big vegetable garden in back of their small, rented tract house. "We had almost every kind of vegetable that we enjoyed that could be grown in California. And we had lots of fruit trees. We had berries."

In winter of 1972 Julie looked at the drawings in *Shumway's Seed Catalog,* considering what varieties of vegetables to plant in the spring. She wanted an old-fashioned vegetable garden, with varieties that were not altered or hybrid. Julie had already ordered *Shumway's Moon Sign Book* to calculate how to plant in accordance with lunar phases. Change came as a complete surprise on a rainy Saturday in February, when David hung up from an hour-long phone call from an old friend who had moved to Europe. He came into the kitchen, put his hands on her shoulders, and asked, "Do you want to go to London?" They were gone in a month.

London Life

Julie and David found a small flat near Fulham Road, and they opened a trendy leather store in partnership with his friend. Julie designed vests knitted from leather strips. She learned to airbrush designs on velvet, and she had a neighbor sew blouses that they could sell for sixty pounds in David's store and at a popular women's boutique a few blocks away.

Julie let her hair grow long and wore Edwardian-styled lace blouses with her tight blue jeans. Soft colors like rose, gray, and mauve were the new fashion, replacing the bright pop and op patterns from a few years earlier. Their shop was decorated in those new muted colors, with stained

glass lampshades, peacock feathers, and framed reproductions of art nou-
veau posters. Within six months business boomed. Shoppers flocked to
purchase David and Julie's innovative, colorful leather designs.

"Not only were we good in America, but in London there was just
nothing like it. The possibilities were endless."

But after a few months it became clear to Julie that everything in London was expensive. Very expensive. The British economy faltered as staggering inflation set in. Affluent Asians, Arabs, and Continental Europeans
bought up real estate, forcing rental prices upward. Food costs seemed
astronomical. And Julie could not afford the imaginative one-of-a-kind
knits and patchwork dresses she longed for. Julie decided to get her hair
cut at a killingly chic salon in the recently redeveloped Covent Garden
district. She was ready to model again.

"I bought a pair of shoes and a suit, did my hair, and said, 'I'll go for it.'
I went up to the top modeling agency. I had photographs and stuff—you
have a portfolio when you're modeling—but I knew they weren't up to
the standards that this agency was. So I 'forgot' those.

"I just went into the elevator. I was going to bluff my way through this.
There were a few good-looking girls and this one woman. By the way she
was looking at me, I thought, 'She must be the agent.' So I stood there in
the elevator, and I didn't look at her. I knew she was sizing me up. We
went up, and she was the agent."

The receptionist looked Julie over, and then the agent's assistant interviewed her. They both liked what they saw, and late that afternoon the
woman she had seen in the elevator met with her.

"I said I didn't have my portfolio, but it was coming over. We shipped
all of our stuff, so it would be six weeks before the portfolio came. It was
very stupid of me not to carry it. 'However, here I am.'

"I had a lot of flair, and I knew how to come across. This was where I
was at. I had just come to inform them.

"She said, 'OK. Go over here. Someone has just come over from Italy
or something, with all this stuff. They need more people right now!'

"So it was a very big show. I told them that I could do anything, when
actually what I had been doing was small scale compared to what this was.
And then I went! First of all, the runway, the catwalk they call it there,
was about six feet high. They never did that in the States! I thought, 'Oh,

dear.' So I just bluffed my way through. They were very beautiful fashions. I went, they hired me, I did it, and then I never stopped."

About 80 percent of Julie's work was fashion show modeling, and the rest was fashion photography. In the early 1970s most advertising was low status and paid very little. A few years later, however, she did some commercial work as well. Julie's youthful good looks were much in demand by retailers who sold clothes to wealthy women who were two and even three times her age. She did luncheon fashion shows and charity evenings at some of the world's great stores—Fortnum and Mason's, Harrods, and Harvey Nichols. She also modeled for the few British designers with enough money to stage their own extravagant shows, like John Bates, Bill Gibb, Janice Wainwright, and Zandra Rhodes.

Zandra Rhodes was Julie's all-time favorite. The designer spoke with a seamstress twang and had green streaks in her hair, but her couturier originals sold exclusively at Fortnums in Knightsbridge or her own show-room. The only people who could afford those stunning, hand-painted evening dresses were movie stars, aristocrats, and the wives of Arab oil sheiks. Julie twirled around in the gowns when she modeled, but she never owned one.

After the first month of fashion shows she met David on a Wednesday afternoon. They had an elegant high tea, and then they drifted over to Asprey, the Queen's jeweler on Bond Street. Customers and clerks alike spoke in hushed voices that were muffled further by voluptuous carpets. A middle-aged man in a morning coat showed the striking young woman and her somewhat seedy consort several velvet trays of diamond earrings. Julie had always wanted something to sparkle in her ears for good luck. She was an Aries, and diamonds were her birthstone. Julie selected the next to the smallest pair of simple diamond studs and handed over several hundred pounds in cash.

"I worked the whole time, until I quit. We usually had bookings weeks in advance. I might be doing a week at Harvey Nichols or Harrod's or Saks Fifth Avenue or something like that. They didn't actually have a Saks there, but something like that. You'd have certain hours, from 10:30 to 2:30. You'd be modeling three or four shows during the lunch hour. Or you might go see the agency in the morning or schedule a photo shoot in the afternoon.

"I enjoyed it! I'm a real showoff. I love walking on the catwalk. Actually, I much preferred it to photography. Now, I think I would be very good at photography, but then I was much better at the catwalk. When I think of doing *anything* now, I think how easy it would be to do this with so little inhibition.

"I really enjoyed shows. I loved people then. I would look at particular people, and I would flirt with them. You know, proper old ladies. I would just play, and I really enjoyed that play. So it didn't matter that I was modeling or anything; I generally had a really good time doing it.

"But the people you work for were a pain. And I got bored with the girls after awhile. I pretty much took all of their problems seriously at first, and I felt sorry for them. We would have all these dressing room conversations and this and that, you know, the gossip. And I enjoyed that. But I took them seriously.

"I thought they *really* had these problems. But the amazing thing is that, four or however many years later, the same girl would have the same problems, usually with the same man or slight variations. What was amazing to me is that they wouldn't change. That was an insight for me.

"This was the thing that struck me. I would say to them, 'That's amazing, I know so many beautiful men.' Because my boyfriend was what they called a hippie. He played music, and he didn't have a lot of money. We did what we loved doing.

"And a lot of fashion girls, because they were pretty, they'd be attracted to rich men. And these men were usually a pain in the ass—not all of them but most. They owned a restaurant here and a yacht there, but these girls were not having a good time. They felt used or whatever. And so they were always complaining.

"So I said, 'Well, if you're not happy, why don't you go with someone that you would have a good time with? I know so many beautiful men.' And this one particular girl looked, and she said, 'Oh, but they're just hippies,' or something like that. And I thought, 'All right, OK, so you're choosing this, and you want it. And these are the consequences, and you don't like the consequences, and you complain about it all the time.'"

Julie started to wonder about her own future, and she began seeking answers about life. She read Western philosophy and Eastern mysticism that David recommended. For a few months she paid weekly visits to a therapist, who was similar to a social worker in the United States. She casually investigated feminist politics and also new religious movements. Despite the growing economic uncertainties and rising unemployment in England, anything still seemed possible. All Julie knew was that what she had and who she was wasn't enough for her.

"It was not like a conscious decision [to search]. How the girls were, that's the main theme. I could see that they were stuck, very stuck. I had a good time with them for an hour at lunch and when we were in the dressing rooms, but they weren't people that I really wanted to hang out with.

"I did go on yachts occasionally, and I did go to dinner, and basically I was bored. And that was that. There were people that I did meet who were beautiful, and they would still be someone who I might contact there. But basically I was bored. People would come on to me. It was just very immature."

During her third year in London Julie started reading popular books about self-improvement. She read on the tube, on buses, and in taxis going to her modeling engagements.

"I remember sitting there, reading *Gestalt Therapy Verbatim*.[2] That was one of my memories. Trying to get it into my brain, what he's trying to tell me to do and how to be. I even went and did a gestalt group.

"I didn't have any real trouble that I was even aware of, but I said, 'I just want to go, so I could expand and become more aware of who I am.'

"The gestalt therapist sat there. I just walked in, and he just sat there and stared at me and waited for me to say something, because that was the technique.

"Everyone was older and successful. They had all this relationship stuff. Hate for women and love and torture and all this. And I couldn't get in touch with anything that was very gripping. So it was kind of funny.

"I lasted a few months with that, and that was enough for me."

After that, for a year, Julie went once a week for therapy with a psychoanalytically oriented psychologist, a nice woman whose office was the den of her North London flat.

"I just sat with her basically, to untangle a lot of the confusion that was happening inside of me. And within one year I went very, very far with her. She was quite amazed with that. I was bound and determined to live happily. My whole reason for delving at all was to be a joyful, happy person and not to feel what I was feeling, which was burdened."

Julie worried about sex and sexual fulfillment in terms of personal authenticity. She was committed to David, but she felt that part of their relationship was a lie. "The whole sexual thing was a problem for me. When I was married, I hated sex. Then I met this man who I really loved, and I still hated sex. I had this feeling that I needed to do something. I didn't want to do numbers on this man. I didn't want to run my old trips. I knew that I was fucked up with this. I knew that it's not natural that I felt the way I do. So I started really looking at it. I didn't blame him. I started reading books, and I started getting a little bit into the women's movement, but I wasn't like a practicing feminist."

"I did do some meetings. When I did go, the women's lib movement, it felt very immature. It felt like they were blaming men. And to me, they were just as fucked up as we were. I *knew* that I was fucked up sexually. I knew I needed to change. And I knew how I got there. Basically, I just turned off the sexual part of me when I was fifteen. I felt sexual energy, but I didn't think it was OK for me to think of myself as being sexual."

Changes

While Julie was changing in London, her parents were also changing. She called them once a month, but she had not seen Carol or Duane since she left the States two and a half years before. One weekend her mother called to announce that she was getting a divorce. Julie was not surprised, but she was crushed nonetheless. She recalled: "It absolutely affected me. Very much so."

A month later she bought an inexpensive ten-day round-trip ticket from London to San Francisco and rented a car to drive up to Carson City. She didn't see her brother, Tom, who had moved to Chico to attend college. Her father looked wan and depressed. He was as depressing as the gloomy one-bedroom apartment he had rented near the State Library. But her mother was blooming, bursting with plans to sell their old house as soon as possible and move to Reno to open her own boutique. Julie slept in her old bed and woke up to walls covered with Janis Joplin posters and *Reno Evening Gazette* photographs of her ads and her last ballet recital. She was astonished at how different the house felt.

"I came back into the house with my mother, and I had this incredible realization. The same house, but how easy it is to be here. I can sit here, and it's OK. And I realized the tension we were living under. My father was so tense inside. There was almost like a fear in the house. So if a pen dropped you might jump."

Her father was very quiet. But he begged her to stay with him and threatened to kill himself. She said: "I snuck out that time. I didn't get it."

When Julie returned to London, she decided to change jobs. She was tired of the catwalk and wanted to try out a different side of the rag trade. She also disliked feeling cheapened by most of the men who booked fashion shows or took pictures of her. "I didn't feel on top of it," she said. "I guess I did have the feeling that there was some defeat in it."

"In England they use pet names for women a lot. They call you 'luv' or 'sweetheart,' and it's a way of men keeping on top. And I remember every time that happened, I somehow went along with it. I would be angry with myself. I must have done that hundreds of times. That didn't feel right.

"I remember some poor guy. I often have the feeling that maybe he just got up enough courage after awhile to come up to some woman and say, 'Hi, sweetheart' or something. I leveled him. I turned around in the middle of the street, and I just upbraided him from one end to the other. And he sort of turned white. I thought it would probably take him months, years, before he does that. But it was a change for me. Never again was I going to take that.

"At first it's a fight, saying: 'Don't talk to me that way. Don't say that!' But eventually it got so I could take it without saying anything but still not take it inside. I got stronger."

Julie also worried that she would soon be too old to be a top model. "I would look in the mirror. I was twenty-three, right. I would look in the mirror for signs of deterioration." It was definitely time for her to move on. She imagined that someday she would run her own business—a spectacularly artistic store or possibly her own design operation. But she needed to learn more.

In London in the mid-1970s there were dozens of spontaneous, creative designers trained in sophisticated art schools like Ravensbourne and the Royal College of Art. Many of them decamped to fashion houses in Continental Europe, and the majority who stayed behind were notorious for their collective lack of business sense. There were stories about dope in showrooms and sex on staircases. Julie wanted something better. She wanted to work for a woman.

She signed on with a small company headed by Danuta Sloan, a young woman designer with a reputation for both creativity and solid financial judgment. Julie stopped doing fashion shows entirely, although she still modeled occasionally for a few photographers she liked. She managed the showroom and modeled samples on the showroom floor. Julie learned a great deal about designing and the garment trade while working for Danuta, but the same day she started the job she wanted to move on. And Julie was terribly disconcerted by Danuta.

"She was like something out of a scandalous kind of novel of a woman who does everything to get ahead. *Everything.* She played the role out to the hilt. It was the role she made up for herself.

"The woman was something out of a cheap novel. *Scruples* would have been the one. Her face was completely covered with pancake, because she had skin abrasion, because she had very bad acne as a kid. She had perfectly platinum blond hair, beautifully bleached, and a tiny little figure and rings on every finger.

"One of the first conversations that I got to overhear her talking on the phone was to her husband. She said: 'Why did you steal my Quaaludes? You stole my Quaaludes. Don't you ever do that! I'm going to divorce you the next time you steal my Quaaludes.' It was one of those bizarre things.

"Her showroom was covered with grass mats everywhere and zebra skins. It was really beautifully done. Then there were great big black Plexiglas pillars. It was this incredible phallic feeling. Just everywhere you'd look there were these phallic symbols. [There were] mirrors, so that she could see herself everywhere, and a lot of good clothing.

"She had an incredible reputation of being the ultimate bitch. She was the most shrewd businesswoman. Everyone knew Danuta, and everyone kept away from her or else seduced her.

"I was still very young and inexperienced and had never come across anyone as—I don't even know how to describe someone like this. I knew that I had to be careful, because I was going to lose all my opportunities. What this woman was doing was trying to hook me into being with her. And I was smart enough to see that at that point. She kept on handing me clothes, very expensive clothes. And she said she'd deduct them from my salary.

"I saw that I was going to get hooked, so I didn't wear any of the clothes. I said, 'I don't want these.'

"She said: 'Why don't you want them? You take them. You need a coat. You need this. You take it!'

"I said, 'I really don't. I don't think I can afford it. Anyway, I need to use the money for something else.' So I kept myself unhooked. I lasted three months there. It was horrendous.

"I just found a tremendous amount of confusion there. I found that I also got very confused after awhile, because I started noticing that my values got really freaky.

"I was actually traumatized. Underneath this trauma, my strength was starting to emerge."

Despite all of the problems, Julie had learned a great deal from working briefly with Danuta. And, when Danuta received recognition as a major British designer in the 1980s, Julie looked back and laughed. Her next job was a complete contrast.

Julie was working at a trade show when she met a middle-aged couple who owned a well-established separates company that sold to Marks and Spencer, a large, conservative chain of stores. Julie toned down her makeup and hair, bought some nice business suits, and immersed herself in a very different workplace.

It wasn't art or even fashion, but the goods they produced were simple and of relatively high quality for reasonable prices. Many of the pieces were manufactured in Hong Kong. Julie started learning some of the international aspects of the fashion business, and for the first time at work in the London garment trade she was in a warm, collaborative situation.

"I was involved with learning importing. I was involved with learning markets. I was right there in the design room with the owners and designer of thirty years and the little nucleus of crew people, who had all been there for nine years or seventeen years.

"I had a family, and actually they had all been est graduates, all the younger people. So I had a little bit more of a rapport with those people. I had more of a feeling of involvement, where I could actually assert myself. It was nice. It was really beautiful.

"There was my career. There was everything I ever wanted there for me. If I wanted to put myself out here more, I could really have made it.

"I started seeing myself involved in another season and another season. With whether we should use this white wide or yellow wide or beige wide in this textured polyester. And to be honest, I could give a shit."

On most weekends Julie stayed home and dressed like a hippie. She went to rock concerts and jazz clubs with David, spent hours in bookstores, and attended different kinds of religious meetings, as she had with her mother in Sacramento. She felt that David and she were still seeking something together but that she was also beginning to explore on her own. She sensed that her spirit was growing.

"The whole time we were together, seven years, we were always looking at things. We were reading. I picked up a [crucial] book out of my insecurity. I went into a bookstore and picked up *The Wisdom of Insecurity* by Alan Watts. And I read two of his books before I realized they were by the same author. That's the first time I realized that people write more than one book. So I bought Alan Watts. And then I bought and I bought. I read a lot and looked at different religions.

"I checked out different religions, but something always felt wrong. I checked out Christian Science when I was married. It really had something, but that wasn't for me.

"The Children of God were very strong in London at that time, and I checked them out. There was something that was very beautiful about that. I went to a few meetings, and some guy came to me a few times and talked to me. They had a little something that they wore. I wore that for a little while. And what I realized with this one was, well, if I stayed, I'd lose my intelligence. They're very sweet and playful, but they talk the Bible. I never really did, you know.

"I would look in their eyes and feel them, and there was something lovely about it. I loved what they were doing. They were working with prostitutes and things like that. So it appealed to my altruism, but basically it wasn't for me. I would have had to go into some other person's mind or ideology rather than be myself. So I didn't go with that.

"I checked out all these different things. I never heard of Bhagwan while I was in England. I would say all this time I was looking."

While Julie was changing jobs and searching for spiritual meaning, her relationship with David frayed. They were growing apart, and a breakup seemed almost inevitable. But she still felt it was too soon.

"We were kind of splitting up at this time. We were still together, and we always knew there was a reason we were together. It was very strong. So we didn't leave each other, even though a couple of times I had other lovers and things like that.

"We were moving away a little, but we still stayed. Even today we are intimate friends, though we are thousands of miles apart, and we never see each other. We always will be tuned somehow. We stayed very close even though there was all this going on and these strong emotions.

"I thought, 'Maybe I'm wrong.' All my friends settled down. They started having babies. They were living in the country and growing their own vegetables. And I had always known, had always felt, that I wasn't going to have children. It wasn't for me. But at this point I was questioning, 'Well, maybe I'm wrong. I've looked. I can't find anything else. Maybe it's this?'

"I actually even considered having a child. I may have even gotten pregnant. I don't remember. That was a definite possibility, an early miscarriage. It was totally wrong at the time, because we were separating.

"There was no way that I could bring an [emotionally] healthy child into this world, so I was seeking. I was always looking to find a way to cleanse myself [of my badness], so that I would never hand this down to some innocent being.

"We both thought: 'Well, maybe this is it. We'll just keep on and have a child or something.' Not that we wouldn't be searching. But maybe living this life is *it*.

"It didn't feel right to me. My friends were smoking dope often, and they were getting fuzzy to me. I saw beautiful people getting a little stupid. Again, it wasn't for me.

"He was going to go back to the States to try and publish music. I didn't want to be on his trip, but at that moment I thought I needed to. There was something that needed to happen. I was going into the unknown again.

"For me it was a commitment to set myself free. I was going to be free. I was seeking. I was always looking to find a way to cleanse myself."

David sold his leather store lease and his tools and left for Los Angeles by way of Hawaii, where one of his old musician friends was farming coffee and high-octane marijuana. Julie moved in with some other friends in Hampstead in North London and tried to figure out what she wanted to do. She continued to work at the knitwear firm, but she scaled back her responsibilities and moved down to part-time. Her worried boss said things like: "What is it? What is this going to do for you?"

David was still a big part of her life, and Julie was not surprised when he called after a few weeks and urged her to meet him in Kailua Kona on the coast of the Big Island [Hawaii]. There were many other seekers who passed through Kona, including Baba Ram Dass, the former Harvard professor and spiritual leader who had written *Be Here, Now!*[3]

She agreed to join him and arranged to take an extra evening job, working at Pat Gibb's Sanctuary, an astonishing women's health club located in a former banana warehouse. Julie taught dance aerobics and wandered among jungle plants and an indoor lake. She saw tropical flowers and water lilies every day and knew that somehow they would be part of her future.

"He [David] said: 'Come! There's something! I've read a book, and there's somebody I've found who's really interesting.' I sold this and that, and I got two jobs. I *worked* just for a couple of months, and got a lot of money together. Enough money and went to Kona. This is where I heard of Bhagwan.

"So, again, I left. There are these little intervals, which I call gaps. You let go of one thing, but you have no idea of what in the world you are doing. And this was definitely one of them.

"Kona was beautiful! A sannyasin had been there and left one book and one tape. Ram Dass was on the Big Island at the same time. When I saw him in the same room, I was attracted but not attracted to go to him and talk to him. He seemed so upset with himself at this time that I didn't feel that there would be anything to communicate. But I was definitely feeling him out.

"All I knew was this man, Bhagwan, existed. Then I heard the tape. He was saying something about being God. It was one of those odd tapes, and it was a tape where you either think this man has the biggest ego in the world or he *is* [God]. I was laughing and crying inside. And everything in me was just 'Yes.'

"And Ram Dass said, 'Turn off the tape.' He said, 'If this man is enlightened I would know it, and I would go straight there. I'm not going.'

"And he [Ram Dass] was one of my heroes. Who I thought was much higher than me. I'm only beginning. And he is saying this, and my insides are saying, 'Where is Bhagwan?' And there was a book, and again I was laughing and crying. It was like all the bells were ringing."

The book was *No Water, No Moon* (Rajneesh 1975). The part that immediately resonated with Julie was Chyono's story, of course. Julie knew that she had to meet Bhagwan Shree Rajneesh.

"And so I packed my bags. I didn't go to the States with David. I went on to Poona.

"He was the gateway for me to go to Bhagwan.

"But I didn't know anything about sannyas. I didn't know that you wore red and a *mala*. I had never met a sannyasin until I walked in the gates. I took sannyas ten days after I arrived."

The Ashram

Julie's first days at the Shree Rajneesh Ashram were a blur. She remembered renting a small room in the Blue Nile Hotel, where many less-affluent sannyasins resided. A week later she moved to a small room of an old mansion near the ashram. Everyone else in the house was a sannyasin.

When Julie arrived at 17 Koregaon Park, she went to the office at Krishna House and spoke with a woman on the staff, Alana, who listened carefully to her life history and counseled her to take dancing group and an encounter group. She paid a fee, went back to the hotel to nap, and then returned early the next morning for discourse in Buddha Hall. Julie attended morning discourse every day from then on. But there was only room for about 150 people at evening darshan in Chang Tzu Auditorium, where Bhagwan counseled individuals in front of others, gave sannyas, and took leave of pilgrims who were on their way back to the West. She went four times during the next two months.

The Ashram's lush water garden reminded Julie of the Sanctuary's lake, with its water lilies and orchids. But this was real, with blue sky and clouds above masses of bougainvilleas and throngs of tropical birds. The first time she set foot in Buddha Hall for morning discourse, sitting on the floor far back in the audience of several hundred people, Julie felt that she had found her true home. A few weeks later, at discourse again, Julie recalled a dream she had during her first year in California with David, long before Poona.

"In the middle of the night, the dreams all stopped. There was nothing. It was just like a fog or a cloud. Then all at once there was this person's face. It was this older man with long white hair and a white beard and these big brown eyes and a white robe. And he was just looking at me. And it was like we were looking at each other forever. And there was nothing else. It was like I was totally awake, and I was asleep.

"Then at some point, he picked up a peach-colored sheet. You know, when you make a bed and lift up a sheet [and fan it out]. And it came down very slowly, slower than it would really. And he was still looking right in my eyes, as the sheet came down. And I woke up.

"I remember sitting on the porch later that day. I'm sitting there with David, and I told him about the dream. And I said, 'I don't know who it was, but he's the guru.' I didn't even know what that means. And that's it. I didn't actually hear Bhagwan for seven years after that, but that was the first time I met him. And, actually, I was with Bhagwan for a few weeks before it clicked. That was who it was! There's no doubt."

Four days after she arrived at the ashram Julie was completely certain that it was right to take sannyas. Her encounter group leader, however, advised her to wait just a bit longer, maybe a week. She recalled that last pre-sannyas group, "I thought it was going to be innocence, and it turned out to be a confrontative kind.

"And I did a lot of touching and a lot of meditations."

Julie remembered the day she took sannyas because she was so nervous. As she often did, she focused her anxiety on what she wore.

"The ironic part about my becoming a sannyasin was what I wore that day. I was in the fashion industry, and I was very much into the way in which I presented myself to the world. And so there I was. I went down to MG Road, which is Mahatma Gandhi Road, in Poona, and it is just a really dirty, yukky place. And I found this dress. It was not my style to begin with, not the kind of color I wear, not the fabric, nothing in the way in which it was put together. It was terrible.

"I went to iron it right before my darshan with Bhagwan, and the heated iron made the colors streak everywhere. The whole thing was completely streaked. Then, as I was going in to see Bhagwan, the girls sniffed my hair [to protect Bhagwan's many allergic sensitivities].

"And, sure enough, they smelled something, a fragrance. And they said I had to wear a scarf. So they immediately put a gauze scarf around my head. And that's the way in which I first met Bhagwan, with this streaked dress and this gauze scarf and no makeup. Just stripped is exactly how I felt."

Someone called her name, and Julie went up on the dais to sit facing Bhagwan. He sighed, pressed his finger on her invisible third eye and told her that her new name was Ma Anand Tanmaya. *Anand* meant "love," and *Tanmaya* meant "to be absolutely absorbed." "Your path," he said, "is going to be that of being lost." He admonished Julie to become completely lost in each moment, each activity. Then she could stop watching herself and others. She would become free once she forgot about herself totally.

"So here, doing meditations, keep this continuously in mind, that you are to lose yourself. If you are dancing, then dance so totally that only dance remains and you are not there. If you are humming, hum so totally that humming is there but you are not there."

Bhagwan continued, "You have to practice losing yourself, getting lost—that is the meaning of Tanmaya."

Tanmaya was crazy about her sannyas name from the very first. "When I told people afterward about my name, and I was so pleased, they said, 'My God, that's so heavy.' Most people are named sweet-smelling flower or something. But I always related to it."

Like many other Western sannyasins, especially those with complicated Sanskrit names, Tanmaya had a number of nicknames. Some people called her Maya, others Tanyi. But the nickname that stuck was TM. This always brought smiles to sannyasins from the San Francisco Bay area, many of whom had participated in Mahareesh Mahesh Yoga's transcendental meditation, which was termed *TM*. Tanmaya was not yet known as "the Swan," because she was a new sannyasin, with no distinct place in any ashram network or its organizational hierarchy.

Tanmaya did a number of groups, and after two months she had the honor of being invited to live at the ashram, in one of the warrens of small sleeping cubicles. She began to design simple clothes, supervise sewing, and take a few more groups.

She had been in touch by letter and telephone with both her father and mother. Her father's letters dwelt more and more on the dark side of things, and her mother was clearly worried about him. Tanmaya shared her worries with other sannyasins, and one day she was summoned to the office and offered a round-trip, first-class ticket to San Francisco, if she would deliver a small suitcase to another sannyasin in the Bay area. She was told nothing about the contents, although at the time ashram funds were being transferred through travelers' checks sent abroad (Franklin 1992, 142–48). She readily agreed, and her trip was pleasant and uneventful until she reached Carson City. It was clear to her that her father had always been seriously emotionally disturbed.

"He wasn't having overt problems before. What I didn't know was that he was always threatening suicide to my mother, so my mother was always in a panic.

"There was a lot of tension. And I actually got his passport. I did everything so he could come to Poona, and he didn't come. So it was a very good lesson for me, because I did everything I could. But you can't put their feet one in front of the other.

"He wanted a guarantee. You can't tell him that! I could say that I know it's going to be beautiful for you. That I know that you're going to get through these things, and it's going to be fine. But you can't guarantee it.

"I've made it in my life. I've stepped off into the unknown many times, not knowing if it was going to be OK or not. I left husbands and money, not knowing anything certain but just knowing this is the way I'm moving. He wasn't willing to do that.

"He actually threatened me [with suicide] when I was leaving. And he was so angry that I wasn't going to stay with him. But what can you do?"

Tanmaya went back to the ashram with relief, but she traveled again to Carson City within a few months of her return. This time her father was physically ill. He was dying of cancer. He asked her to come, and so did her mother.

"I knew when I left he would die. And within a year he got cancer and died. To me that was his choice. It was suicide in a way. Suicide with cancer, to me. He made his choice, and I had to feel that was his choice. I don't know if there was anything else I could have done. I shortened the dynamic for him so he could do it and then read to him from Bhagwan. He loved it. He was very touched. My mother would also be there, doing Kundalini and reading the books, and she loved it too. But he died."

Her father wasted away in front of Tanmaya. A visiting nurse came for about an hour, and her mother arrived after work and stayed through the evening, when she returned to her new husband. After Duane died, Tanmaya's brother came for the funeral, and they both stayed for a week in

Reno, with her mother and new stepfather. He was a successful stock-broker and investor, who looked far younger and healthier than Duane ever had. They had a big house on Skyline Boulevard, where Tanmaya could step out on the deck and watch the twinkling city lights. But late at night it was still country, and Tanmaya could take comfort in the smell of the sagebrush from the nearby high desert and the coyotes' muffled wails.

Carol had converted the family room downstairs into a spacious home office, where she did bookkeeping for her boutique and also amused her-self designing textiles and clothes with a Native American flair. She wanted her beautiful daughter to stay and become her business partner someday soon, but Tanmaya was eager to return to the ashram and to Bhagwan. She viewed her mother as trapped by her new, affluent life.

"What I saw in her was a sort of prison. Always a feeling of never get-ting there. Never, ever having enough. Although she has all the material things that any woman would want, I viewed it as a prison.

"When I came back from my father, I went to work in the *mala* shop. I worked there for three years. I made the beads and the *mala*. I had a lot of love for it. I used to take them into the house where Bhagwan lived. Not to his room but into his house, which was like being in an esoteric school. This was like a priestess coming into the Temple and walking down these long corridors, which I loved very much. I'm an inner person in that way.

"I loved going into this house and taking the beautiful *malas* for people who took sannyas that night. I love this in the Meditation University—the corridors and then you come into a room where all these inner things happen."

Tanmaya also designed and made the wooden boxes that Bhagwan per-sonally bestowed on sannyasins who would soon journey away from the ashram. Some people considered them "magic boxes" because they were thought to sustain contact with Bhagwan. Tanmaya said that when you were away but needed Bhagwan's advice, you could place the box close to your body and somehow experience his help.

After her return Tanmaya received invitations to a number of evening darshans, where she was seated in the first four rows. Her new status reflected her recent involvement with one of Bhagwan's longtime sann-yasins, a tall, handsome Scandinavian who had the honor of living in Lao Tzu House, the master's compound. Swami Joshua did different kinds of troubleshooting around the ashram, and he ran important errands in

Bombay for Laxmi, Bhagwan's personal secretary. His position and influence came from the fact that he was among Bhagwan's earliest West-ern devotees. Tanmaya still sustained a warm friendship with Joshua at Rajneeshpuram, although they had long since ceased to be lovers. After she introduced us, she said: "He looked so gorgeous. He has been with Bhagwan for so long, and he knows all the little things. He's doing odd jobs. He's just come to accept himself as lazy and feels much more happy now, now that he has accepted himself. One of those lazy men who don't chase women. He's just one of those guys who can move around and not do a lot. And he'll admit to that."

While she was still sexually involved with Joshua in Poona, Tanmaya became attracted to Rakesh, a man who was closer to her own age. Tan-maya felt that the sexual chemistry between her and Rakesh was different than anything she had ever experienced. And she admitted that the ten-sion between Joshua and Rakesh heightened her pleasure with each of them.

"Being in triangles has been an incredibly growing situation over the years. For me it's always been a matter of finding out, of being as alive as I am. If we allow our total energies, we're going to get into trouble, and I get in trouble occasionally.

"I'm not always walking around feeling sexual, but I'm almost always walking around in my energy, and sometimes that is definitely sexual. I let myself get caught up with somebody, and at first I can rationalize it like this or that.

"Someone is paying attention to me, and I need attention because my boyfriend is always away or he's always working. In terms of awareness I realize that there is a point where I decide that I'm going to go a little bit unconscious here. 'Please, just a little bit unconscious,' so that I can get turned on, because I want to feel that. I have to actually make a decision to let that happen. You could pinpoint those times where I decided just to tune out for awhile, just so I could feel good.

"We sort of played for a long time before we had anything sexual hap-pening. I love secrets. In some ways I will talk about everything and be very clear and straight and honest, and in other ways I'm very female. The thing that felt best to me is that it was very secret. Now, my secret tended not to be very secret. To me it was a secret. It's the part of me that loves the dark rooms and the hiding. To me that's the exciting part.

"Once I've talked about it, I'm not nearly so exited about it. Now it's just normal. And I know that's part of the unconscious as well. The intrigue.

"What was very interesting about this one was that I could watch it step by step. 'OK, now I'm doing this, great.' It was hard to believe it, but I was still caught up enough to go ahead and do it. And I ended up loving this guy. He's a very beautiful man."

Tanmaya spent fewer and fewer nights with Joshua in Lao Tzu House. She now shared a bed with Rakesh, who had been a humanities professor at SUNY–Stony Brook and now worked as a leading Rajneesh therapist. She learned a lot from Rakesh, sitting in on the groups he led and providing him with her emotional support. While continuing to make *malas,* Tanmaya cultivated her esoteric abilities. She earned extra money by doing detailed, insightful tarot readings, and her new boyfriend offered to teach her how to lead groups. "All this energy I had. I realized how much I can see people. When I was young, I didn't have that facility of communicating it. So this time I gave it endless space. I had to sit there, hear how he was talking and working with people. I wasn't put on the spot."

Gradually, Tanmaya began to assist Rakesh actively in his groups. He trained her, and she even supervised a two-day past-lives' workshop by herself. Tanmaya had found her calling. "I don't know if I should have been doing it all along, because I had to go through all these things that I went through. But it certainly is a love of mine now. I didn't realize what a close link I had with the subconscious or with that inner world. Now I am realizing more and more that I'm developing that or have developed it in the past without knowing it. To help people fall into the subconscious or walk around in there."

In 1980 Tanmaya often felt lonely, because Rakesh traveled to lead groups at Rajneesh centers in Western Europe and the United States. Tanmaya had several brief affairs, and at the beginning of the new year, 1981, she fell in love once more, with Tarik, a visiting sannyasin who was a partner in a large San Diego law firm. Bhagwan gave Tarik special dispensation to wear ordinary colors at work and place his *mala* inside the shirt, but his firm's managing partner still wanted to get rid of him.

When Tarik encountered Tanmaya in Poona, he was negotiating the sale of his share of the partnership and starting to work full-time for the

Rajneesh legal organization. Tarik asked Tanmaya to come with him to southern California, where she could lead groups at the Laguna center.

Rakesh agreed that a trip with Tarik might be good for Tanmaya because the ashram would soon be moving to a new site, either in India or the United States. Tanmaya left for California in April 1981, just before Bhagwan went into silence. Tarik, now a full-time Rajneesh attorney, met her at Los Angeles International Airport, and drove her down to Laguna in a rented convertible. Her mother was delighted that Tanmaya had returned to the United States, and they visited each other three or four times over the next year.

Tanmaya luxuriated in Laguna for a year and a half before she moved to Rajneeshpuram. While Tanmaya did some counseling of sannyasins, she accomplished many other tasks there. Utsava, the Laguna Rajneesh Center, was involved in litigation with the former owners of the property. She was a supportive companion to Tarik, who was working fourteen-hour days and commuting to Oregon. Tanmaya did not mind doing all sorts of chores around the center. She spearheaded a giant communal vegetable garden, like her old one in Sacramento. Tanmaya described her niche as doing "anything and everything. It was a communal lifestyle. Make dinner, go shopping, clean, paint the house, whatever was needed."

"I didn't know what was going to happen to me. It was like 'Who knows?' I knew that I wanted to be at the ranch." She accompanied Tarik on some visits, and one day late in 1982 he surprised her with an invitation to come to live with him at Rancho Rajneesh. She readily accepted.

Rajneeshpuram

At Rajneeshpuram Tarik and Tanmaya were a couple, sharing a spacious, airy room. Tanmaya tried to telephone her mother at least once a week and arranged to visit Reno with Tarik. She was pleased with her mother and stepfather's friendliness and their obvious affinity for Tarik. "My mother adores him, actually," she said.

Carol sent her daughter spending money and wonderful care packages with things like makeup, a natural bristle hair brush from England, or Swiss eyebrow tweezers. Carol also visited Rajneeshpuram and praised the beautiful setting and warm people. But it wasn't enough for Tanmaya.

"The first day she [Carol] was here, someone came to sit down at the table. He had been doing groups with me, so he had respect for me, but he had energy. I said, 'This is my Mother,' and introduced them. She said she had been visiting her children—there are just two—and discovering them again. And he said, 'Well, your children must really have changed over the years.' Of course, he was tuned in to me and thinking about how she must feel about how I've changed.

"She said something like, 'Yes, I still talk to my son like he's nineteen, but he's really a grown-up person.' And he [the sannyasin] looked at me, and I looked at him, and we were both surprised that she'd totally forgotten me in that way. But I wasn't hurt. It was just interesting because when she thinks of children like that, she thinks of him. And then she turned to me, and she said, 'She was always old.'

"I saw that she had no flexibility in her life. To me what she considers security I consider a burden. And I see that it satisfies her in a certain way. It keeps her from feeling her own existential insecurity—that life is fragile and is going 'poof.' Here today, gone tomorrow."

Despite the continuing tension with her mother and the political turmoil at the ranch, Tanmaya loved living at Rajneeshpuram. She rationalized Sheela's abrasive behavior and imperious demands the way many other sannyasins did. Sheela was like an alarm clock; you might want to throw her against the wall to get her to be quiet, but she woke you up.

Tanmaya was also troubled because she saw so little of Tarik, who often traveled on legal business. Nevertheless, Tanmaya found herself developing, truly blossoming, because of the therapy groups she led and the individual counseling sessions she facilitated. She was particularly fascinated with the possibilities and meanings of past lives. As she described the sessions she facilitated, Tanmaya merged the esoteric and mundane.

"I take things Bhagwan has said, and then I try to figure out how we can create a situation in which these things can be applied in a practical way. And then we do exercises in groups to discover if what he is saying is true or it isn't true.

"I have never asked anyone to believe what I say to them. In fact, I tell them at the beginning, 'Don't believe what I say to you! I'm going to present some things, and I'm going to make some suggestions. Then if, through your own experiences, you discover that it is also true for you— great. If you discover that it isn't, believe yourself. Not anyone else!'

"I ask people in a session to imagine they are floating backward in time. And they float back to a time when they possibly had a past life. And because we use this technique of imagining floating backward in time, sometimes the whole session feels like you're imagining things.

"And I ask people if that feeling, 'I'm just imagining things,' is there. Try not to force the feeling to go away. In fact, it might be the truth. Why should it go away? Let it be there. If something is coming up for you, it has value, even if it's just your imagination. It helps you look at yourself. It helps you see what is inside you.

"If, in fact, past lives exist, I think that death is probably the most important part of the lifetime. If they were a Japanese samurai in a past life and now they're an American-born woman, then something about that person didn't die when the samurai died. And I would like to find out what that is. If you can remember a death and find out that you go on— the body falls away, but something that is you continues.

"That would help people no longer be afraid of death. That's my purpose. Because the less afraid we are, the more willing we are to be courageous and to tell the truth. One of the reasons that people can be manipulated and controlled is because of their fear of death. If a person wasn't afraid of death, he could be authentic.

"When a person goes back and remembers a past life, they can see that they're repeating a pattern in this lifetime. If they can experience that activity consciously, then that brings an awareness of it. Once something is conscious, it no longer has a control over you that you're unaware of."

Tanmaya's description of past-lives work affirmed devotees' basic shared assumptions that each and every one of them possessed a true, core self that should be uncovered and explored. Her words about awareness and authenticity also revealed some of Tanmaya's own inner struggles with Sheela's growing autocracy and capriciousness.

After the Share-a-Home program failed in late 1984, Sheela grew desperate to retain her power as Bhagwan's personal secretary, and she worried that Tanmaya and other therapists might organize resistance or even overthrow her. Sheela vehemently criticized Tanmaya and the other therapists at a public meeting. She tried to shut down the International Meditation University, but it had too much support from Bhagwan and from sannyasins at Rajneeshpuram and other Rajneesh centers. Tanmaya felt lonely and confused, and once again she found herself falling in love with another man.

"A few days a month, I'm very sexual. I think it's like that because sex is very natural to me now. When I was more hung up with it, meaning I wasn't clear with myself, I would have been thinking about it more.

"Sometimes, the sexual just isn't relevant for me at all anymore. It's not that I will never have sex, although I did go for a whole year before this triangle. I was celibate for almost a year.

"This was after the AIDS announcement [March 1984], and all those things. The way we understood the message was that if you can be celibate, do. I said, 'Well, let's try.' It was just a mutual agreement. If you can, do!

"We try and listen to the messages as finely as possible. You know, read between the lines. 'What is He [Bhagwan] saying?' And in a way it was possible, because the relationship I was in [with Tarik] was very loving and very warm.

"I guess the energy changed between me and [Tarik], the man that I was living with. He could definitely tell something was going on. At first it was very beautiful for him, because I was giving him a lot more energy. And after awhile it was like, 'OK What's going on?' I said: 'I do have energy for someone. And I didn't expect it to happen like this.'

"We knew from our past experience, I had more sexual energy than he [Tarik] does. 'Well,' he said, 'Why don't you move out? Do it that way, because it's too hard for me to do this [triangle].'

"I didn't want to do that [move out]. But something was going on this time. This is the growing part of it. This time I wasn't going to be manipulated by anything.

"This can also be manipulation. [Tarik should say,] 'Why don't you move out?' And then I should say, 'Never mind. It doesn't need to be this way. Everything is very beautiful.'

"So I said, 'OK, I will.' And I was upset about it the next day, and I wrote to Bhagwan. I did all these things. But I went ahead and did it. I moved out, and I went with this guy, and it was really nice. It's very confusing in a way."

Tanmaya wrote to Bhagwan and told him that Tarik had suggested she move out. She received a letter that appeared to be signed by Bhagwan. He urged her to go ahead and try a new relationship.

"Even back in Poona, the game from Bhagwan to me was to listen to what's right for you. It was the big message to me. 'Don't move around. Be clear.'

"I feel that he would never tell me anything that wasn't possible for me. He's not trying to hurt us. And I know that he's right."

Tanmaya's passion subsided after about three months. In early summer of 1985 she moved back to Tarik's quarters. "Even though we didn't know if we would ever get back together again, we came through this last one quite beautifully, with very little blame. Blame occasionally, but basically it was good. And I was very pleased with myself in that I let myself go through it again: Step right out of the known. And maybe nothing comes together. Maybe I get out here, and there's no possibility of ever going back. This unknown is everything I love."

"I have sexual energy, and I don't have to go with it. Or maybe I can take it back to my boyfriend. I can share it with him. He is very open about that kind of thing, very open. If I've been with somebody else, he wants to feel it and experience it. 'Tell me everything. Tell me anything.' Not that he didn't go through things, but over the years there was much and much less."

After they reunited, Tanmaya and Tarik were included in some of the small, select audiences privileged to hear Bhagwan lecture once more. She and her lover discussed Bhagwan's exciting new discourses and cautiously whispered about Sheela's waning power. Secrets about political intrigue rekindled Tanmaya's interest in her old lover. Tanmaya's intuition, as well as her many sources of information about Rajneeshpuram's internal politics, told her that Sheela's arbitrary rule would soon end.

Sheela and a number of her confederates resigned their positions and left Rajneeshpuram on September 14, 1985. Tanmaya was relieved because it was now clear to most sannyasins that the verbal attacks on her and the other therapists had been part of Sheela's twisted attempts to grab more and more power. "It's very tumultuous. And I see that I've gone through different phases. Some people were hurt and upset at first. I was a little bit smug, a little pleased about these people leaving. Not about people being hurt. I didn't even know about that yet. But when I heard Sheela left and all that, I was shocked. There's a part of me that loved Sheela and most of those people. But we were so repressed here at the university. We [therapists] happened to be one of her pet hates."

Tanmaya and the other therapists strived to address the personal dimensions of Sheela's departure, encouraging other sannyasins to learn lessons from their experience with autocracy and move on to new levels of personal growth. "These whole recent events that have happened with Sheela. If there's a mistake, the mistake is she isn't looking inside. The fact that she was intoxicated by power and misused it is, I think, normal. I feel very sorry that she got involved in illegal, criminal acts, but I don't condemn her. I'm sorry because I've seen how much it hurt her and some other people. I'm very, very sorry. But I don't condemn her."

In the aftermath of Sheela and her lieutenants' departures, national media broadcast tales of crime and conspiracy at Rajneeshpuram. FBI, state, and local law enforcement agents searched buildings for weapons and biological warfare laboratories. They also questioned former spouses and parents of sannyasins all over the country. Hundreds of sannyasins feared they might be arrested or subpoenaed, even if they had done nothing illegal. Tanmaya called her mother.

"I called her the other day, and I said I just wanted to let her know that I might be arrested in the next couple of days. I'll call you in a few days to let you know how it is, but, if you see something on television, you don't need to worry. And she said, 'Oh God.' And she laughed. And her laughter was so beautiful. What I love about my mother is that she respects who I am and what I do with my life."

Tanmaya was surprised that legal authorities displayed relatively little interest in her, despite the fact that she was now a longtime sannyasin herself, who had some personal contact with Bhagwan. They talked with her mother and asked Tanmaya some questions but to her knowledge did little else. She dreamed about the investigations and the FBI. They weren't scary dreams, just problem solving.

She stayed on at Rajneeshpuram, determined to help heal other sannyasins and remain close to Bhagwan. She said, "There's so much happening in the commune that needs dealing with and that needs our help and support."

Tanmaya tried to think of the many difficulties at Rajneeshpuram as a series of life lessons. The hardships were opportunities for growth. And the aftermath presented possibilities of becoming spiritually and physically closer to Bhagwan.

"The mystery of this place is so magnificent that it's wondrous. It's just wondrous. I can't talk about it without having tears come into my eyes. It's nothing that you can just write home and tell your friends about, because it's words. We have all used all these kinds of adjectives to describe more ordinary kinds of things. And, as Bhagwan says, it's totally ordinary. And that's the extraordinary part of it.

"Everything has just been a wonderful flow. It's like I've forgotten myself, and the meditation is happening more. You're doing something where you're totally involved, and you're no longer thinking of something that is burdening you. Somewhere you've left. You're no longer your personality. You're now totally part of whatever you're involved in. You're absorbed in it. That's what has been happening for me more and more.

"There was a period [soon after Sheela left]. I don't know what exactly triggered it, but I felt I lost my center, and I fell back. I closed off. It felt like a trauma, because I felt in the dark, so the feeling is like walking in the dark and not knowing where you're going and not knowing exactly how you're going to function. Not really knowing how to fake it anymore, like I used to. But knowing that I have to continue, and it's going to pass. Reminding myself not to be too hard on myself, to accept myself and not to pass judgment. Because that's all part of living with Bhagwan.

"There was a period when I just wasn't dancing. Not being able to dance and not being able to connect with him [Bhagwan], as I had been no more than a few days before, put me into quite a trauma. Again, I felt myself burdened. It was a panic a little bit inside me that I was going to go back to one point in my life where I wasn't flying, where I wasn't dancing, where I wasn't being spontaneous, where it was more of a charade instead of an authentic way of existing."

Tanmaya's personal dark period ended in October, as sannyasins picked up the pieces that Sheela had left behind. Bhagwan was once again in regular contact with all of his devotees, lecturing to large groups and appearing in public. In the evening, after media interviews and darshan for a small, intimate group, he danced with bemused reporters or with sannyasins lining the path between his Rolls-Royce and Sanai Grove, where he had just lectured. Tanmaya described her rediscovered joy through contact with Bhagwan. She waited for his party to come back out after his lecture and actually danced with him. "I went out, and I thought, 'I really want to dance with him.' And he came straight for me, and he just danced with me. It was so beautiful. It was exactly what I needed. Something was so calm about this. I'd let go and come back, and I'd look, and I'd just start dancing again. It was so sweet, very sweet."

As the fall lengthened, Tanmaya wondered whether Rajneeshpuram could survive. She meditated more and cast astrological charts for herself and Tarik. Again and again, she laid out her tarot deck. She told herself: "If everything finished today, if Bhagwan left or whatever, I would be fine. I'm here! As long as I can still not see the end of something, that's all there is."

But within a few short months, like the water and moon in Chyono's bucket, Rajneeshpuram disappeared. After Bhagwan departed from the United States, in November, so did Tanmaya. She was so physically and emotionally exhausted that she wanted to sleep for a month, possibly two. She flew to Stockholm with some other Rajneesh therapists, however, staying at Rajneesh centers and offering free groups to help European sannyasins understand the collapse of Rajneeshpuram and sustain their faith in Bhagwan. She awaited news of Bhagwan's plans and lived in the moment. During the time following the end of Rajneeshpuram she thought about Chyono's story and meditated on her favorite message from her spiritual master: "You are here to disappear."

Chapter 6

LESSONS?

Tanmaya did not disappear, although Bhagwan left and the ranch crumbled. In the immediate aftermath of Rajneeshpuram she neither attained enlightenment like Chyono nor abandoned her identity as a sannyasin. Instead, Tanmaya, Shanto, and Dara all carried on, making the best of difficult situations as they had so many times in the past. Despite their community's collapse and the staggering revelations about crime and abuse, all eleven women who formed the composites staunchly affirmed their commitment to Bhagwan. They believed that they had emerged from Rajneeshpuram exhausted but much wiser.

Their rationalizations transformed Sheela's exploitation and vindictiveness into meaningful life lessons. The women, like so many other sannyasins, were convinced that Bhagwan had not interceded and salvaged his communal vision because he wanted them to be responsible for their own lives. They spoke of his nurturing intentions, likening their spiritual master to a mother bird who had forced them out of the warm nest of his protection and into the air. Sannyasins might fall at first, but they could eventually fly. Amid the disintegration, the women still believed that their time at Rajneeshpuram had been well spent and that their pain allowed them to grow, as it had so many times in the past.

The sannyasins' elaborate justifications stunned me. How could these productive, perceptive women absolve Bhagwan of any responsibility for the disastrous utopian experiment? How could each of them set aside their years of emotional and physical stress in central Oregon? The fact that the sannyasins moved ahead, however, was an essential lesson for them and also for me. The women had learned to trust themselves during their sojourns in the high desert. They had grown emotionally, although not necessarily in the directions that they initially believed.

This chapter interprets some of their discoveries and describes some of mine. It is about the broader meanings of the sannyasins' life histories. As I have mentioned throughout, this book is about the women of Rajneeshpuram, but it isn't about them alone. I hope that readers who have come to know Shanto, Dara, and Tanmaya have also reflected on what their lives have in common and what the three sannyasins can tell us about ourselves and our friends. The sannyasins' personal accounts hold theoretical and practical implications for millions of other American women. The interactions of the sannyasins' lived experience with the academic frameworks presented in this chapter create new understandings or grounded theories (Glaser and Strauss 1967).

Theories from the sociology of gender, psychoanalytic sociology, and the sociology of religion frame this chapter. I hope, however, that readers can consider them without becoming entrapped by abstruse analysis and debates. Academic theory and research are essential for developing important questions and evaluating their empirical answers, but they tend to be very slow reading. The sannyasins' voices and personal histories remain the crucial elements in this book, and the theories simply permit us to consider their wider implications.

Because Shanto, Dara, and Tanmaya embodied all of the women sannyasins I interviewed, I will continue to refer back to their three life stories. Yet I will also break down some of the information about the eleven individuals who formed the composites and introduce some material from the life histories of the eleven women in the comparison group I described in chapter 2. The comparisons allow me to examine how specific kinds of personal attributes and life experiences predispose some women to search for their identities within cults or in some other defining relationships.

Each sannyasin and each matched comparator illuminate the ways in which people are affected by their times, their parents, and their own choices. All of the women came of age as dramatic economic and political shifts reshaped America in the decades after World War II. The decisions they made in the midst of massive social changes reflected both their social locations and also their emotional development. Deeper understandings of the sannyasins' lives broaden our view of how other women develop firm senses of self separate from their mothers, come to terms with feminizing fathers, deal with problems of spiritual meaning, and establish lasting, loving bonds.

My perspective on the women of Rajneeshpuram reflects two seemingly incompatible areas of sociology: rational choice theory and psychoanalytic sociology. Throughout their lives the sannyasins made decisions rationally, calculating how to maximize their material and psychological well-being with a minimum of sacrifice (Iannaccone 1995). Their emotions, however, somewhat limited the possibilities that they weighed, because their childhood experiences defined their preferences and constrained their decisions. They searched for fulfillment in self-actualization markets because their childhood religiosity and their early experiences had influenced their adult goals. Once the women had defined specific realms of choice, much was available within each one. They could select among dozens of different goods, services, and affiliations, blending the therapeutic and the sacred.

The Road to Rajneeshpuram

When Shanto, Dara, and Tanmaya were sixteen or twenty-one years old, no one could have anticipated that they would become sannyasins. In retrospect, however, it is possible to identify signposts that mark their conversion and commitment as almost inevitable. If Bhagwan had not been there, some other defining relationship with a charismatic individual probably would have changed their lives.

Before looking more closely at selected directions, I would like to consider all eight of them. These directions do not constitute inevitable routes to conversion, nor are they a set of orderly, narrowing sequences that screen out the less committed with each additional step. Instead, they are like twisting, entwined paths in a garden, and the more paths a woman pursues, the more likely she will discover the shelter of a defining spiritual relationship.

Eileen Barker (1984), a British sociologist of new religions, emphasizes the unpredictability of conversion and commitment. Joining a new religion like the Rajneeshees is not all or nothing. Conversion, for anyone, is neither a certainty nor an impossibility. Most people share some of the longings that compel searches for ultimate truth. But it is necessary for a blend of personal predispositions and social serendipity to combine at just the right moment in order for someone to join and remain part of a new faith for a year or more.

None of the women took a direct route to Bhagwan. All of them tried out psychotherapy and movements for social change, and most of them also sampled other spiritual disciplines or religious groups. They encountered the Rajneesh movement at turning points in their lives, when each of them was already seeking some higher meaning and purpose. If they had not found Rajneesh, some of the women might have gone on searching, while others could have connected with a different spiritual leader.

Even after they dip into the spiritual or therapeutic marketplaces, few individuals turn their backs on their old lives and jump into a cult, as the sannyasins did. Most people who enter those markets are simply consumers of spiritual goods and services who rarely affiliate with a spiritual movement. Moreover, only a small number of those who do affiliate stay for more than a year and become active, committed members like the sannyasins in this book (Barker 1984).

Most individuals, whether they are seekers or not, take less extreme steps than the sannyasins. They assuage their yearnings for connection and validation in other kinds of relationships. Those relationships, whether they are spiritual, therapeutic, or personal, are not so totally demanding, nor are they as rewarding as being a sannyasin was for the women of Rajneeshpuram. Few connections provide people with the same possibilities for the synthesis of love and work and the blending of materialism and spirituality. Most people, moreover, seldom feel that they are always close to someone with supernatural power, as the sannyasins did. The sannyasin women had extraordinary needs for love and confirmation. Heart-to-heart connection with Bhagwan fulfilled them.

Choices between success and emotional or spiritual fulfillment are complicated. The women of Rajneeshpuram seemed extreme when they relocated to central Oregon, but their decisions were not so different from the mundane choices other women make in prioritizing their own needs, the needs of people whom they love, and the demands of their work. Many women, possibly most, make idiosyncratic career decisions based on love, families, therapy, politics, or religion, although different choices could facilitate their occupational goals.

Questions of personal identity and interpersonal connections routinely eclipse careers, especially for women who are caregivers. The
women of Rajneeshpuram were enmeshed in mid-century American culture, differentiated by the intensity, not the nature, of their experiences,
so their lives very much resemble those of other women of the same age,
social class, and ethnicity.

What we see in the women's decisions to follow Bhagwan is the intersection of biography and history. The relatively brief affluence of mid-
century America, the second wave of American feminism, and the dramatic shifts in the structure of American religion comprised the social
contexts for the sannyasins' great hopes and expectations. Their emotional vulnerability and their childhood relationships with their parents
shaped their personal predispositions for connection with a charismatic
figure. I will briefly discuss the eight social and personal experiences that
the sannyasins in this book all shared.

*The first path to Rajneeshpuram was social transformation that generated new
possibilities but offered no clear, guiding collective values to ground individuals'
crucial decisions.*

Shanto, Dara, and Tanmaya had different class backgrounds, but they
all shared in postwar America's material blessings. The three women
browsed for exotic goods, ideas, and experiences in the international
marketplaces open to Americans who came of age after World War II.
Even Shanto, who was submerged in the feminine mystique of the 1950s,
weighed different possibilities for self-actualization well before movements for social change shook the foundations of her middle-class life.

The second wave of American feminism brought the sannyasins
increased awareness, educational opportunities, occupational rewards,
and possibilities for intimacy and self-knowledge. Changes that began at
the end of the 1960s promised each woman opportunities for fulfillment
and freedom from the obligations of middle-class marriage. The many
social changes the women experienced paradoxically created a pervasive
sense of frustration, which sociologists have labeled "anomie." The
women had almost too many interesting choices, without definite guidelines for their decisions.

Varied choices do not necessarily create anomie, but, when people cannot define their important decisions in terms of clear values or anchors for personal identity, they often feel rootless and confused. The women experienced particular frustration and confusion around sudden, fundamental changes in gender roles. The changes and varied opportunities became deeply problematic for them because they had few, if any, fixed values to guide them.

All of the sannyasins had grown up with religious meanings, but each woman had turned away from them. By their mid-twenties every one had discarded traditional organized religion and explicit religious values. Later in this chapter I will look closely at each sannyasin's religion, because all of them were deeply influenced by the secularization and decline of liberal Protestant faiths, the Roman Catholic Church, and American Judaism.

The experience of prior rewards from religiosity created the second path to Rajneeshpuram.

The women defined their searches for self-identity as quests for meaning and value. All of them had considered some versions of spirituality in their earlier searches. They were familiar with the language of faith, and they had occasionally tasted the sweet rewards of emotional connection with some sort of higher power.

Because they knew and appreciated spirituality, the women were open to Bhagwan's philosophy. In fact, as Shanto observed, they may have been seeking spiritual answers all the time. At earlier points the sannyasins had merely turned to the wrong sources with their questions about existence and its purpose.

The Rajneesh movement reconnected them with the spirituality that their families had discussed but seldom lived. People who had grown up with few religious messages would probably resist spiritual groups, seeking political or scientific answers to their fundamental questions and fears about life (Hoge, Johnson, and Luidens 1994). The women of Rajneeshpuram had all been exposed to some of the rewards of spirituality, and they were able to hear and appreciate the ephemeral music of the sacred.

Each sannyasin had become discouraged with her childhood religion, and each one sought fulfillment in many other spheres before turning to spirituality once again. The women asked much of themselves and of their surrounding social milieu. When they approached religion, education, achievement, or intimacy, their perceptions of great prospects almost guaranteed them disappointment. The sannyasins' needs for affirmation and love were intensified by the surrounding social conditions of affluence and choice. Nothing seemed certain, and the women's apparently limitless possibilities created endless difficulties for them. The more they achieved, the more empty they felt.

The third path to conversion involved a huge chasm between real life and the desired life.

All of the women had experienced an enormous separation between their daily routines and the lives they had wanted to lead. Often, they had no idea of what had caused their dissatisfaction. Before finding Bhagwan, Shanto, Dara, and Tanmaya were deeply, consistently discontented. The women could and often did perform superbly, but their investments in relationships, education, and work never brought any of them the satisfaction that they had anticipated. Until they risked everything with Bhagwan, the sannyasins placed emotional side bets that allowed them to leave their previous love and work commitments and repeatedly seek other sources of rewards.

Great distances between the mundane and the ideal are familiar to many people, but the sannyasins inevitably defined that contradiction as one that they could remedy if they achieved yet one other specific goal. The women began their varied searches with single-minded certainty that they would finally discover the key to their true characters. Shanto looked to education, Dara turned toward identity politics, and Tanmaya considered an unconventional combination of glamour and counterculture. None, however, found what they were seeking. Their constant discontentment reflected the fragility of the women's self-identities as well as the possibilities available to them in a rapidly changing society.

Fragility reflecting childhood and family relationships denoted the fourth path.

Throughout most of their lives none of the women could adequately answer the question, "Who am I?" Their many gifts often made them uncomfortable and vaguely ashamed. The women looked to others to provide mirrors that would confirm their self-worth. Their precarious senses of self intensified both their confusion about choices and their dissatisfaction with conventional religion and other aspects of daily life. The displeasure with their lives also reflected the fact that the women's important adult decisions were frequently based on what they did *not* want, rather than what they wanted. They were often uncertain of their own needs and desires, but the women knew beyond any doubt that they could not allow themselves to become like their mothers.

The fifth path was dread of resembling their mothers.

The sannyasins viewed their mothers as both powerful adversaries and pathetic victims. Each sought symbolic differentiation from her mother through varying levels of education or occupational attainment. No matter how their mothers had behaved, the sannyasins could not forgive them for failing to provide enough nurturing to them as they were growing up. On the other hand, no matter how complicated their relationships with their fathers had been, all of the women saw them as interesting, exciting, and sympathetic. The sannyasins sought to be entirely differentiated from their mothers and still remain feminine enough to hold the attention of men who met their idealized memories of their fathers.

The sixth path was idealization of their fathers and their daughter-father relationships.

Throughout their searches the women looked for situations that would allow them to define and maintain the boundaries between themselves and others while still establishing meaningful connections. Their desires for connection involved the many rewards of having been Daddy's girls. The sannyasins' real or imagined bonds to their fathers had allowed them to feel special and treasured. Their fathers' reinforcement of their femininity had confirmed their feelings of personal goodness and worth, while, in contrast, their mothers made them feel embarrassed and angry.

In different ways the sannyasins' fathers validated their daughters' emerging womanhood, but their fathers had not encouraged them to discover autonomy through achievement. The women had looked to careers, intimate relationships, psychotherapy, politics, and, almost inadvertently, spirituality in order to recapture their paternal connections that could allow them to define their own identities.

Each woman came to believe that she had always belonged in Bhagwan's protective shadow, because each needed a defining relationship to feel whole and complete. No sannyasin had embarked on an explicit quest for religious attachment, but, once they rediscovered their spirituality in Pune or at a Rajneesh center in the United States, each and every one of the women felt that she had returned home. Part of being home was acquiring a new family made up of other sannyasins.

The seventh path involved comradeship and collectivity in spiritual exploration.

Interpersonal networks were important to the process of conversion and commitment (Stark 1996a, 73–94). All of the sannyasins joined friends or lovers when they explored the marketplace of personal growth therapies and spiritualities. Longtime intimates who took sannyas well before they did introduced two of the women to Bhagwan's philosophies and encouraged them to become sannyasins themselves.

The other nine women traveled side by side with other unaffiliated seekers and sampled varied philosophies and religious groups. Only two of these women, however, actually took sannyas at the same time as their companions. The rest became acquainted with the sannyasins' way of life in the company of others, but they made their leaps of faith on their own.

The social networks supporting the women's commitments developed and consolidated through collective meditations and Rajneesh therapy groups. Profound friendships and absorbing love affairs unfolded through the intense, absorbing group experiences that encouraged instant intimacies. At the Pune ashram and Rajneeshpuram emotional bonds also strengthened when sannyasins drew together to support one another in the face of external threats to their community.

Love for Bhagwan, however, was the central, shared bond that cemented their friendships and romances with one another. Sannyasins talked with one another endlessly about the meanings of his words, the power of his insights, and the mysterious ways in which he facilitated their personal growth.

Surrender to Bhagwan himself, a powerful personal divinity, was the eighth path, marking the end of the road to spiritual fulfillment.

Every one of the women experienced Bhagwan as a vital, intimate spiritual master. Intense, close connection to their divine teacher was the essential element in their faith. Although Rajneesh therapists might do some of his work, each woman felt that she and her spiritual master communicated directly and personally. Moreover, his essential spirit guided their every activity.

There were two levels of communication between master and sannyasin. The women all shared highly personal imagined dialogues with Bhagwan, and they also experienced more generalized self-searching that they believed their divine master guided.

Bhagwan's spiritually direct relationship to each of his sannyasins motivated their sacrifices and enhanced the other rewards of being devotees. Although most of the women had little, if any, physical access to him, each believed that she could communicate directly through meditation, dreams, and interpretations of esoteric signs from Bhagwan. He symbolically mediated every difficulty they encountered. Their charismatic connections with Bhagwan compensated for the sannyasins' emotional fragility and allowed them to feel protected by great powers.

Many other religions also center around gods who live in their devotees' hearts. Members of fundamentalist Christian faiths turn to equally personal relationships with Jesus when they are troubled. Others, like liberal Christians or wiccans, look inward to find some generalized, transcendent spirit.

The women of Rajneeshpuram, like so many other women, needed a powerful rescuer to watch over them. They also needed ways to look into themselves, tools to contemplate and consider who they were. Charismatic connections with Bhagwan strengthened each sannyasin at the same time that it bound and limited her, in many of the same ways that falling in love creates layers of intricate emotional bonds.

The sannyasins' times, their relationships with parents, their needs for self-definition through external validation, their friendships, and their desires to do something great with their lives eventually led them to Bhagwan. He attracted these talented, frustrated women because he framed the world in spiritual terms and promised intimacy and protection. Their spiritual master made it possible for them to focus inward and, at the same time, continue to cultivate and apply their many talents.

Accidental Achievers

None of the women I interviewed, neither the sannyasins nor the comparison group, could foresee the many career options that would open to them from the 1970s onward. The youngest groups of comparators and sannyasins, who were all born after 1950, were the only ones who always expected to work outside the home. Yet even members of that last cohort had few explicit educational or career goals until they left school or graduated from college.

It is disconcerting to remember the curious ideas about women's work that most middle-class Americans shared in 1960. In recent memory there was widespread consensus that women were biologically programmed to be men's helpmates and housekeepers (Skolnick 1991). At that time the tradeoffs for middle-class white women appeared to be clear and obvious: Achievement in a male-dominated world required women to sacrifice their femininity. The womanly alternatives to such denial were ill-paid jobs in pink-collar service work, school teaching, social work, or, instead, marriage and child rearing.

The sannyasins' lives all changed because the second wave of American feminism allowed women to reconsider gender ideologies, assert their rights, and transform their aspirations. The women experienced feminism in many ways, depending on their ages, but it offered each of them new personal entitlements. For the successful women who became sannyasins, feminism represented a mandate to become the most actualized and satisfied person possible. Each one took that mandate completely to heart, because none of them had ever developed a stable, autonomous sense of self.

The feminist movement and the seismic shifts in opportunities bowled over *all* of the women. Both sets, sannyasins and comparators alike, had to consider and adapt to sudden, vast changes in the educational and occupational landscapes. Reconciling what they had learned as girls with the changing times was both a welcome task and a confusing challenge for all of them.

None of the women in either group had planned to become recognized achievers in business or male-dominated professions, and all of them had been somewhat surprised at their success. Almost every woman was an accidental careerist, moving ahead on the crest of the successive waves that destroyed a great deal of formal, overt gender discrimination in the American labor force (Whittier 1995).

The sannyasins' concentration on achievement was intense and almost desperate in contrast to the eleven women in the comparison group. The nonsannyasins felt pleased and lucky to have rewarding work, but they viewed their careers as only one part of lives that included friends, parents, partners, and many other interests. One of the comparators, for example, was amazed at her own achievements, although she had displayed considerable interest and ability since childhood. "I was just in the right place in the right time when they were looking for a token. I always wanted to do something, but I was still a product of the sixties, where I thought I would not necessarily work full-time."

On the other hand, the women sannyasins had defined educational or work commitments as all-or-nothing struggles. They believed that they had to succeed at their chosen goals in order to differentiate themselves from their mothers and find their identities through achievement.

Shanto and the other women her age had looked toward education and professionalism for liberation from their personal battles. Their generation had been galvanized by Betty Friedan's *Feminine Mystique* (1963). She defined the housewife's problem with no name and suggested that women needed higher education and work outside the home in order to be fulfilled.

Dara's cohort had reconsidered their marital destinies while they were still in college, and the *Feminine Mystique* seemed rather tame and dated compared to Germaine Greer's (1971) caustic humor or Shulamith Firestone's radical manifesto *The Dialectic of Sex*. Dara valued professional success as both a means to escape her mother's fate and also as a way to become an actor on the stage of history that developed through the social movements of the Vietnam era.

Only Tanmaya's generation took work outside the home for granted. Like Shanto and Dara, she threw herself into the labor force, but, unlike the other two women, she had always assumed that she would do so. Work provided respites from her family when she was a teenager, and later it was an escape from her first marriage and then from her long-term liaison. Tanmaya also found the garment trade intrinsically fulfilling, and she discovered possibilities for transforming herself into someone new with each successive career change.

The women who took sannyas asked for more rewards from work than the stimulation, social status, and solid paychecks that motivated the women in the comparison group. They hoped that their professional situations would be second-chance families, providing emotional support and complete personal validation that they had never had before. Shanto's abilities as a financial deal maker flowered within her second marriage. Dara sought solidarity and empathy in the neighborhood organizations. When Tanmaya joined the conservative sportswear company, she viewed her coworkers as a family offering her a warm, safe haven.

All of the woman of Rajneeshpuram wanted fellowship and community in the workplace. Each one of them implicitly asked, "Will you love me for my talent and dedication?" And *only* Bhagwan and his other sannyasins finally answered, "Yes!"

They also asked a second burning question of their colleagues and employers. It was the one that had haunted them throughout their lives. They wondered, "Who am I?" Once again Bhagwan offered them an answer, or at least ways to discover the answer themselves.

Shanto summed up how all of the sannyasins felt about their professional triumphs. "And once I had achieved doing it, I could drop it."

The sannyasins had all experienced the socially constructed tensions between womanliness and accomplishment. Each of them described the painful pulls between her parents' expectations and her own goals. Moreover, each had been torn between the demands of loving relationships and her desires for personal fulfillment through education, work, or other relationships.

The women were able to come to terms with those contradictions only when they encountered Bhagwan Shree Rajneesh and his sannyasins, who lived in spaces where work had been transformed into worship. The community and the spiritual meanings associated with work at the ranch were what they had desired all along. The women had achieved in order to discover the sacred within themselves. They had asked religious questions of the material world. Once they began to inquire within the spiritual marketplace, they could at last come close to the positive identities that they had sought all along.

Religious Travelers

The sannyasins' spiritual voyages began at the particular historical moment when many denominations declined, and Americans by the millions sought meaningful spiritual experiences. Each woman lived out the tremendous shifts in religious organization and involvement that reshaped American religion. Their searches for spiritual meaning and religious structure illustrate the widespread processes of shifting religious identification and affiliation within the religious marketplace.

Bhagwan was at once his sannyasins' teacher, their therapist, and their divine inspiration. He tacitly approved of Sheela's labeling a series of his 1985 discourses as *The Rajneesh Bible* (P.ajneesh 1985b). After Sheela's departure he denounced her establishing the religion of Rajneeshism and claimed that every codified, Western-style religion contradicted his philosophy (Carter 1990, 227–30). Despite these disclaimers, the movement around Rajneesh remained profoundly spiritual. The sannyasins shared in the key elements found among all religions: belief in some higher power, collective organization, an overarching doctrine, and regularized attempts to come to terms with higher powers (Stark and Bainbridge 1985, 5–6).

Coherent, albeit vague, spiritual principles lay beneath Bhagwan's capricious leadership. The Rajneesh movement stood out and seemed bizarre to Oregonians because it changed so fast and because it so blatantly incorporated the politics, sexual experimentation, and materialism associated with the late 1960s. Bhagwan's personal unpredictability and pluralistic spirituality infuriated outsiders, who claimed that the sannyasins were making things up as they went along. The sannyasins were indeed inventing their religion, but similar processes of innovation and elaboration occur in all vital faiths, as leaders and believers encounter new external circumstances and varied internal demands.

The central elements in sannyasins' faith involved affirmation of Bhagwan's divinity and power in the intimate, highly individualized master-devotee dyad. Personal gods ranging from Haitian *vodou* deities to Roman Catholic saints to Jesus all function as advocates and advisors in devotees' daily routines, just as Bhagwan did for the women of Rajneeshpuram (Brown 1991).

The second important aspect in the sannyasins' spirituality was the diffuse religiosity that allowed the women to look into themselves and commune with some higher, collective goodness. This was a transcendent spirituality connecting them to something ineffable that lay far beyond Bhagwan himself. From the time they became sannyasins every woman had individually cobbled together her own spiritual development, combining therapy, meditation, and thoughtful reading and discussion. While living at Rajneeshpuram, however, each of them emphasized only one of Bhagwan's three central orientations: the emotional, the political, or the mystical.

Shanto took the emotional path, plunging into the spectrum of Rajneesh therapies and meditations that led her to come to terms with her past and affirm her present ardent emotional connection to Bhagwan. Dara shared Shanto's emotional intensity and belief in Bhagwan's historic importance, but she responded most to his fusion of the personal and the political through the communal vision that appealed to her intellect. And Tanmaya passionately embraced the movement's mystical elements, like past-lives' explorations, crystals, palmistry, energy rebalancing, auras, and tarot cards.

Each one emphasized different parts of Bhagwan's philosophy, but all of the women grounded their daily practices in profound commitment to him. Celebrations brought together the sannyasins' diverse approaches to spirituality. Many of the women worked double shifts during the summer festival, tending to paperwork and food preparation for thousands of visitors, with no time to experience the power of mass celebration. But more mundane communal events, such as Drive-Bys, meetings, showings of videotapes, or Bhagwan's discourses during the final months, bestowed the profound rewards of collective emotion and expression.

Protestants, Catholics, and Jews

The women embraced Bhagwan because of, not despite, their childhood religious environments. All of them grew up in families who spoke of and affirmed realms of faith and spirituality (Lofland 1981, 50–62). Although they were highly critical of their parents' religious practices, the women had absorbed spiritually oriented frameworks. While Shanto discounted her family's Jewish solidarity, Dara condemned Roman Catholic secularization, and Tanmaya longed for more sustained exposure to her mother's Native American spirituality, each woman was familiar with and attentive to spiritual significance. Bhagwan's message resonated with the women because he touched on their earliest memories of meaning.

Each sannyasin exemplified different ways people relate to religion and spirituality. Tanmaya grew up in a household where her mother cultivated spiritual development that was detached from formal religious affiliation. Shanto's experience was the reverse, in that Judaism defined her family's history and cultural identity. Yet her religion never provided a sense of the supernatural or a personal, caring God. As a young girl, Dara found both spiritual experience and formal, religious structure in the Roman Catholic Church, but the ephemeral spirituality seemed to disappear with the enactment of the dictates of Vatican II.

Bhagwan fueled devotees' dissatisfaction with their earlier religious orientations, cementing their bonds to him with jokes and jibes aimed at every major Western religious tradition. He focused specifically on Jews and Catholics while taking on Protestant faiths generically, through broadsides against Christianity and its distortion of Jesus' role as a spiritual master. His special scorn for Catholics and Jews reflected the demography of Rajneeshpuram.

In the 1983 survey of 635 sannyasins, almost all of whom were American, about 30 percent reported Protestant backgrounds, 27 percent Roman Catholic, and 20 percent Jewish (Latkin, Hagan, Littman, and Sundberg 1987). Among those three major faiths, only Protestants were significantly underrepresented, with about two-thirds of the U.S. population affiliated with those religions, compared to the 30 percent of sannyasins.

Despite the underrepresentation of Protestants among American sannyasins, in his Pune discourses and in his later talks at Rajneeshpuram, Bhagwan attacked Jesus and the New Testament with the same vicious humor that he critiqued Roman Catholics and Jews. Bhagwan called Jesus a neurotic victim of his own ambitions and hallucinations who wanted to become the Jewish messiah at any cost. The Crucifixion was fabricated, and so was the resurrection. According to Bhagwan, Jesus faked his death on the Cross. He later slipped out of Jerusalem and settled in Kashmir, where he lived to the venerable age of 112 (Rajneesh 1985b, 141–63).

Some sannyasins laughed uproariously at the scenario of Jesus being alive and well for many years in India. It was a joke, an outrageous device to alert everyone to Christianity's fundamental falseness. A handful of devotees thought the information might possibly be accurate, once again demonstrating Bhagwan's superior wisdom. Tanmaya did not care one way or the other. By the time she came to Rajneeshpuram her fragile identification with her father's Lutheran roots had simply disappeared.

Tanmaya voiced the same apathetic disengagement characteristic of other nominal mainline Protestants who diminished, changed, or dropped their affiliations during the decades after World War II (Hoge, Johnson, and Luidens 1994, 95–162). The real spirituality of Tanmaya's childhood involved sharing her mother's sporadic religious quest and her personal Native American mysticism.

It was somewhat surprising that Tanmaya and hundreds of other Protestants came to Bhagwan at all, because they could easily select other, less deviant options through strict Christian groups, providing faith, intensity, and community. That so many Protestants chose to follow Bhagwan indicates the weakness of their former ties and also testifies to the power of the master's charisma, the importance of communalism, and the allure of the movement's many rewards.

The awesome sense of supernatural presence, which Tanmaya occasionally experienced at home in connection with her mother, permeated the Roman Catholic Church, which Dara attended as a little girl. She never forgot the particular smell of that incense, the beautiful, incomprehensible Latin Masses, the mysteries of confession, and the pictures of saints. Even before she was in kindergarten Dara had shared an indescribable sense of the sacred during some Masses.

Her religion was embedded in every corner of Dara's early childhood. It was in her name, selected from the approved Catholic names enumerated in Smith's *Baptismal and Confirmation Names.* It was in the fusion of ethnicity and religion on her street. It was in the school she attended in the early grades. Roman Catholicism was a central support of the Kelly family's unity.

The Catholic world began to recede when Dara's parents pulled her out of parochial school in the middle of third grade to enroll her and her brother in public school. She started to question the ultimate authority of the church because of her father and mother's conversations regarding the transfers. Dara still participated in catechism class, tried to emulate the saints, and took philosophy and ethics very seriously while attending Catholic high school. By the time she entered college, however, Dara had serious doubts.

Catholic values had not prepared her for the challenges of adolescence or her own sexuality. The church no longer put her in touch with the transcendent, nor did it deal adequately with earthly dilemmas of racism, war, and poverty. Although Dara had to belong to the Newman Club in order to keep her university scholarship, she stopped going to Mass and put her energy into movements for social change. Throughout her twenties and early thirties Dara sought reconnection with her earlier sense of the ineffable, seeking collective experience that took her beyond herself. She tried political activism, socially meaningful work, relationships, and personal growth groups. Nothing worked, until she journeyed to India and recaptured spirituality in Pune.

While Dara's religious decisions reflected highly personal concerns, they were deeply embedded in structural changes that transformed the Catholic Church in the mid-twentieth century. The turning point in her religious life and the lives of other American Catholics came in the early 1960s, when Pope John XXIII convened the Second Vatican Council (Finke and Stark 1992, 255–75). The Pope initiated a four-year *aggiornamento,* an updating and reassessment of contemporary Catholic practice, which confused many faithful members.

Over the four years changes came one or two at a time, but, when Dara entered college in 1963, her priest had already begun to face his parishioners instead of the altar, and he said Mass in English. Somehow Mass was no longer so unique and uplifting when Dara could understand every word. She had additional regrets when the church abolished the restriction against eating meat on Fridays. There were no more midnight countdowns, special occasions when she and high school friends would head down to the local Bob's for the burgers that marked the end of their day of sacrifice, which had affirmed their group's distinct religious identity (Finke and Stark 1992, 262).

When Rajneesh attacked the Roman Catholic faith, he leveled general criticisms against the Vatican, priests, and saints, but he reserved his harshest words for two living luminaries, the Pope and Mother Teresa. He castigated the Pope for destroying the earth's fragile ecology by restricting birth control. According to Bhagwan, Pope John Paul II, or "Pope the

Polack," supported poverty and starvation, because he greedily encouraged his followers to breed and swell the ranks of his church (Rajneesh 1985b, 152–53; Gordon 1987, 163).

Mother Theresa fared even worse. Bhagwan asserted that she was a criminal whose false humility cloaked her ruthless ambition to win the Nobel Prize. Mother Teresa was a Roman Catholic because she needed hungry Indian orphans to demonstrate her limitless charity. She could only receive the prize if orphans were available for her to aid (Rajneesh 1985b, 152–54).

Dara laughed at her master's rash condemnations of the Catholic Church, but she also enjoyed them. Although she doubted that his outrageous stories were completely accurate, Dara believed that his exaggerations woke people up to the hypocrisy of traditional religions. True justice and equality lay in each person's discovering the truth of their own beings. Dara had redefined herself and her spirituality by means of her personal covenant with Bhagwan. By focusing on herself, Dara could once again become part of a transcendent collective vision.

Jews were stunningly overrepresented among sannyasins at 20 percent, in relation to the small national proportion, which hovered at about 2 percent. Any reader skimming over publications by and about devotees could not help but notice American Jews, a number of whom were highly visible and relatively powerful within the Rajneesh organization (Franklin 1992; Rockland 1989). Shanto's story illuminates the three central, related reasons why so many middle- and upper-class American Jews joined Rajneesh and other cults in the 1960s and 1970s. First, pressures for assimilation forced them to compartmentalize their lives and deny parts of their own identities. Second, anti-Semites, both in the American present and in their families' recent European pasts, dramatically affected their self-conceptions. Third, Hitler's Holocaust had an overwhelming impact on American Jews growing up in the 1940s and 1950s.

Shanto felt demands for assimilation everywhere. The ideal American behaved according to the Protestant ethic of individual achievement and looked and sounded as if she or he traced roots back to England, Scotland, or possibly Germany (Aguirre and Turner 1998). Her parents resisted complete Americanization, and they never decorated a Christmas tree, Anglicized their last name, called their children Christi or Noel, or remotely considered dropping their synagogue affiliation, as did some more assimilated Jews. The Bernsteins migrated to the suburbs, however, voluntarily separating themselves from their ethnic roots, as did so many other immigrants' children. Shanto grew up in a neighborhood where American, not Jewish, customs prevailed.

Anti-Semitic Americans often protested that they did not hate all Jews. They said that they only discriminated against Jews with certain problematic attributes, and they selected the attributes to justify whatever arguments they wanted to put forth. Jews could be too orthodox or not religious enough. They could be too wealthy or too impoverished, too uneducated or too cultured, too pushy in business or too passive in the face of Hitler's persecution. Jews, trying to assimilate or simply avoid discrimination themselves, internalized similar invidious differentiations (Fanon 1963).

Shanto felt estranged from herself and her roots, never knowing how far to broaden her horizons. Her childhood reflected the dilemmas of assimilation and anti-Semitism, which plagued Jewish American life. These problems took on greater weight and meaning for Shanto's generation and for younger Jews because of the Holocaust in Europe. The Holocaust was a shameful secret shared by several generations of American Jews, who did not want to consider the ways in which a century of assimilation in Europe had ultimately worked against Jews in almost every European nation. Nor did they want to confront the myriad implications of the basic fact that anti-Semitism had not been vanquished along with Hitler. So, Shanto grew up with silence and secrecy about the Holocaust (Lipstadt 1993).

Bhagwan often told anti-Semitic jokes or commented about the Holocaust as part of his commitment to heal through uncovering pain. The dozen or so Jewish American sannyasins who had survived the European atrocities were often publicized, with the implication that the survivors' presence at Rajneeshpuram affirmed Bhagwan's work as a healer and peacemaker (*Rajneesh Times,* March 9 and April 6, 1984). The meanings of being Jewish devotees, however, remained open questions and sometimes open wounds.

In the published discourses from Pune, Rajneesh sometimes offered beautiful descriptions of Jewish contributions to humanity, while at other times he held Jews responsible for the Holocaust or joked about their avariciousness, poor hygiene, disgusting habits, or complicity in the concentration camps (McCormack 1985, 14–15, 109–11). Yet, despite the constant confrontations with anti-Semitism, Jews found special benefits at Rajneeshpuram.

Shanto and other Jewish sannyasins came together in religious and cultural community, similar to the shtetls and ghettos their grandparents and parents had forsaken. There were small reminders of Jewish traditions everywhere at the ranch, from Hassid Cafeteria to the klezmer music Rajneesh musicians played during the July festivals to the naming of the "Chosen Few," who first heard Bhagwan break his silence. By embracing Bhagwan, the sannyasins were finally assimilated without the pain of being too Jewish for America and without the loss of their collective history.

The three sannyasins' religious histories superficially appeared to be as different from one another as their personal histories. But, in fact, each of the women played out the historic decline of established denominations and the concomitant rise of other competing faiths. Because religion never lost its importance to them, each sannyasin had to deal with spiritual meanings in order to create a centered self and find out who she really was. Spirituality, however, was only part of the selves that the sannyasins sought.

Fragile Selves

The women's charismatic attachments to Bhagwan and their personal spirituality reflected their own emotional contradictions. Each of them was an assertive, accomplished adult, yet each felt vague and vulnerable much of the time. Bhagwan's protection diminished their troubling doubts, but those doubts never vanished entirely. Throughout their lives the women possessed fragile selves, rather than integrated, mature ego identities (Goldman 1997; Miller 1981). When they experienced marked emotional pressures at work or in their relationships, their centers did not hold, and they lacked trust in their ability to function as complete, distinct individuals. Again and again, they asked the question presented in the Rajneesh Enlightenment Intensives: "Who am I?"

They sought some essential identity that was theirs alone, differentiating them from other people. Shanto desired a meaningful life, as she attempted to find "the truth of how I was." Dara believed that "something was missing," while Tanmaya wanted "a feeling of myself." Each one strived to create an autonomous, integrated self during her adult years, with the same fervor and intensity characteristic of an adolescent girl's pursuit of adulthood (Pipher 1994). The sannyasins turned away from their past and tried to recreate themselves over and over, ostensibly ignoring their many previous experiences.

The women believed that they could discover a *single* key that would somehow unlock their true selves. They had looked for the key in many different places. Yet all but one of the women sought psychotherapy before coming to Bhagwan, and they tried out a bewildering range of therapies, from classic psychoanalysis to pharmacology to the far reaches of New Age. During their searches every one of the eleven women had the intuition that she possessed a true core identity, hidden and distorted by layers of frustrating experiences and relationships. The sannyasins pursued their identities in many contexts, but in every situation they looked in the mirrors of others' faces in order to affirm the positive aspects of their own selves. They searched for validation of their worthiness, confirmation of the fact that they were good enough people.

When she did not receive abundant emotional support or affirmation, each woman became in turn frustrated, depressed, and enraged. Each one personalized and felt pained by mild interpersonal difficulties or simple miscommunication. Shanto's two husbands and three children sorely disappointed her when they did not validate her enough. Her circle of affluent housewife friends also let her down. Dara ran through the same emotions in her marriage and then in her demanding work as an administrator and advocate at the neighborhood agency. And Tanmaya became frustrated, depressed, and then angry when she failed to find her true self in her relationships with men or in the admiring eyes of fashion show audiences and garment trade colleagues.

At their most despondent Shanto, Dara, and Tanmaya questioned the meaning of their whole lives and wondered if they even had a right to exist. Yet, when things went well for them, they were optimistic about their unique qualities and their capacities for shaping a better world. Their inordinate sensitivity to social life around them and to others' opinions and feelings made the women perceptive, often beguiling companions. That same sensitivity, unfortunately, also made them unrealistically vulnerable to the routine setbacks of daily life.

The sannyasins were by no means disoriented or interpersonally disorganized, even under the grinding work schedules and ominous surveillance at the ranch. They maintained cohesive, relatively realistic self schemas most of the time, but the women exhibited vulnerabilities of character and brittle, easily wounded feelings. Until finding Rajneesh, none had a sense of emotional center or integrated self that could sustain them through the interpersonal and material thickets that seemed particularly dangerous in the 1960s and 1970s.

The fragility I describe lends itself to clinical characterizations. Narcissistic vulnerability seems particularly apt because it describes individuals with fragile selves who search unceasingly for confirmation in others' eyes (Goldman 1997). I would not label the sannyasins as clinically narcissistic, however, because that differential diagnosis is not applicable in the context of my research. Narcissistic personality disorders involve highly specific sets of interdependent symptoms that are relatively rare (Horwitz 1991). It is important to visualize a spectrum of emotional fragility, and the sannyasins' represent part of a wide normative range, shading into clinical narcissism.

Like the word *cult,* the term *narcissism* has been transformed into a general cultural broadside with negative connotations. Social critics such as Christopher Lasch (1979) and Tom Wolfe (1976) remade a technical diagnostic concept into an inclusive condemnation of millions of Americans who participated in movements for personal and social change in the 1960s and 1970s.

All of the women shared a common set of traits marking the fragile self, described by Alice Miller in *The Drama of the Gifted Child.* Miller, a writer and former psychoanalyst, discussed talented, emotionally vulnerable adults remarkably similar to the women before they came to Rajneeshpuram:

> In everything they undertake, they do well and often excellently; they are admired and envied; they are successful whenever they care to be—but all to no avail. Behind all this lurks depression, the feeling of emptiness and self-alienation and a sense that their life has no meaning. These dark feelings will come to the fore as soon as the drug of grandiosity fails, as soon as they are not "on top," not definitely the "superstar," or whenever they suddenly get the feeling they failed to live up to some ideal image and measure they feel they

must adhere to. Then they are plagued by anxiety or deep feelings of guilt and shame. (1981, 6)

The sannyasins were sensitive, perfectionistic, and frequently envious of others. In spite of their many gifts and their abilities to function superbly in varieties of social settings, they seemed to lack self-esteem. While the women sustained long-term interpersonal ties with friends, mates, and their own children, they never seemed to empathize completely or achieve full, mutual interdependence with their loved ones. When those closest to them could not meet their emotional needs, the women abandoned them, in part motivated by fears of their own capacities for anger.

Shanto was willing to leave her first and second husbands and her teenaged children, although she had pangs of regret. Dara did the same with her spouse and young daughter, similarly motivated by the urgent desire to find herself. And Tanmaya went from one long-term lover to the next, using those relationships to get away from her family and then to move on to successively more rewarding lifestyles.

Although their choices differed, each woman needed to build distractions into her life in order to avoid the feelings of inner confusion and emptiness. Shanto insightfully described the distraction she sought in her endless rounds of country club activities. Dara distanced herself from complete interpersonal commitments by means of routine political struggles and personality clashes. Tanmaya made her life more interesting through dramatic subsidiary liaisons that limited her risks in her most significant relationships. Even when they invested great amounts of their time and emotions, all three women needed side bets in order to avoid full interdependence with another human being, for that person would inevitably disappoint them by not fulfilling their needs to be emotionally confirmed and fully protected from the vicissitudes of daily life.

Mothers' Antagonists, Daddies' Girls

The women first felt vulnerability within their families. Each wanted to rise above those early experiences by reinventing herself. Although I began to talk with sannyasins hoping to discover why they left their hard-won credentials and their successful careers, I discovered that their answers to my questions were unexpectedly less about work than they were about love. The women achieved in order to find the love and validation that they had never experienced as very young children.

They believed they could affirm themselves only if they escaped their mothers' fates. Yet their mothers were always with them symbolically, and they compared their own successes and failures with those of their mothers (Chernin 1985). Even the sannyasins who were almost fifty years old, and who had adult children of their own, continued to reflect almost daily about their mothers and their relationships to them. They constantly measured themselves against their mothers, comparing themselves with the same emotional vehemence as emotionally embattled thirteen-year-olds (Pipher 1994, 101–14). In their comparison and contemplation the sannyasins also worried that they had been difficult daughters, somehow contributing to their mothers' confusion.

All of the sannyasins' mothers, even those three who worked outside the home, had put their families first and primarily invested themselves in support of their husbands and children during their daughters' childhoods. The sannyasins chose to labor at education and careers in order to differentiate themselves from their mothers, because they were still bound to them and had never attained full emotional autonomy.

The eleven sannyasins described their mothers as preoccupied women who, because of their own difficulties, were often incapable of offering their daughters sustained emotional confirmation and predictable support. Their mothers' personal problems ranged from family financial failure to emotional isolation to addictions to severe depression to frustration with their husbands' emotional instability. For many different reasons the sannyasins' mothers never rose above their own emotional circumstances. They neither offered their daughters validation nor encouraged their eventual autonomy.

Throughout our conversations all of the women described their desires to be as different as possible from their mothers and, in most cases, to be almost opposite in every way. Their insistence on being unlike their mothers was so intense and so pervasive that it almost sounded as if they were saying, "I will not *be* my mother." Every one of the eleven sannyasins voiced profound discomfort with her mother and their emotional ties to one another. Shanto said, "I didn't respect or admire most of the way she was." Dara not only criticized her mother but also sensed that they were so different from one another that "she was an alien creature to me." And Tanmaya, who sustained a more positive relationship with her mother, still felt "there were lots of problems" and wanted to lead a very different kind of life. None of the women's mothers represented role models for them.

While the small numbers of individuals in this research made it possible that this common thread was really a matter of chance, the marked similarities in the ways the sannyasins viewed their mothers was striking. Four of the eleven comparison women who were not sannyasins, however, also resented their mothers. One of them sounded remarkably like her matched sannyasin comparator when she said, "I fought constantly not to be like her [mother]!" These four dissatisfied daughters' accounts suggested that mothers alone were not responsible for the sannyasins' passionate searches to discover keys to their identities.

Nevertheless, unlike *any* of the sannyasins, most (seven) comparators discussed predominantly supportive feelings and attitudes toward their mothers. Six of their mothers had strongly encouraged their daughters' educational successes and subsequent careers, while only one of the sannyasins' had. Moreover, a number of women in the comparison group emphatically appreciated and admired their mothers, describing them as "mature, caring, deep women."

Even the most positive comparators' relationships with their mothers were not consistently easy. Some of their mothers were too ambitious for them, wanting their daughters to succeed in ways that they had not. Other mothers were overprotective and intrusive, unwilling to allow their daughters to aspire and then fail. All of these ambivalent comparators worried about their mothers' traditionalism and their overinvestment in housewifely roles. Yet, even though they articulated varied concerns about their mothers, ten of the eleven comparison women still preferred their mothers to their fathers, and they viewed their mothers as generally competent individuals. In contrast, *every one* of the eleven sannyasins, no matter what her familial difficulties, vastly preferred her father.

Their emotional recollections of childhood and adolescence suggested that sannyasins' fragile senses of self developed from their relationships to their mothers and also their encounters with their fathers. They described complicated interactions with their mothers, their fathers, and with and between their fathers and mothers. All of these interactional patterns contributed to each sannyasin's emotional vulnerability. In contrast to their sustained ambivalence or antipathy toward their mothers, however, all eleven sannyasins had connected emotionally with their fathers, who encouraged their daughters' flowering femininity and sexuality.

All but two sannyasins had grown up with both of their parents living in their household. The two sannyasins whose fathers died while they were still children nevertheless idealized them, fantasizing about what their fathers were like and what they would have wanted them to become. Moreover, both of these women seemed to hold their mothers partially responsible for the deaths. Similar idealization of their fathers combined with ambivalence toward their mothers to define sannyasins' feelings toward their parents.

The sannyasin women were truly Daddy's girls. Dara spoke for all of them when she described her father: "He could bring a liveliness. . . . Maybe that's why I related to him more." Whatever the men's real situations were, the sannyasins' fathers symbolized a vast, exciting world of possibilities and power (Chodorow 1978). All of the women's mothers had bowed to prevailing gender ideologies of their times, stressing their husbands' leadership within their households. The sannyasins described their fathers as distant men who were often preoccupied with work, while their mothers were their daily companions. That distance also made fathers special in their daughters' eyes.

The two daughters whose fathers had died imagined that their lives would have been much better if they were still alive. One recalled her father remarking that she would be a beautiful bride, and her stepfather reinforced that theme, often telling her that the most successful women were dedicated wives and mothers.

None of the sannyasins' fathers wholeheartedly encouraged their daughters' academic aspirations or helped them plan careers, but they consistently reinforced traditional femininity (Johnson 1975; 1991). Shanto, who grew up in the early 1950s, received clear messages from her father: "Women are just totally women. You don't ever think of making A's in school." Dara received similar advice as the 1960s approached: "My parents said I couldn't be a doctor because I was a girl." And later, in the 1960s, Tanmaya's father ignored her high grades but appreciated her charm and comeliness.

Each sannyasin described different kinds of intense, uplifting emotional bonds to her father. Their emotional ties involved unspoken understandings and connections, which the women had trouble describing with much specific detail. Fathers of women in the two younger cohorts, Dara and Tanmaya, confided in their daughters about problems they had with their wives, while the fathers of the women in the Shanto cohort had delivered harsh evaluations of their spouses to their family as a whole, while their wives were present.

One sannyasin described the essence of the intense emotional bonds between fathers and their daughters in this way: "As every little girl loved their dad, I loved my dad also. I can't say that he spent a lot of time [with me], but I think that we had a lot of quality times together. And I think it was as much me contributing to those quality times, because some were in me being that child. I was also [symbolically] a woman relating to my dad as if I were a woman relating to my boyfriend, my lover, my husband, or whatever."

The sannyasins experienced different kinds of boundaries with their fathers, but all eleven of them described uniquely rewarding bonds in fact or fantasy. Those bonds with their fathers were of central and continuing significance to all of them. Because of their unique closeness, the women forgave their fathers' shortcomings in ways that they could not forgive their mothers.

The fathers of the women in the comparison group appeared to be almost as removed and distant in daily life as the sannyasins' fathers were. Several of them traveled on business for months at a time. Except for one woman whose mother was clinically psychotic, however, none of the comparators' fathers engaged in the long critiques of their wives or had chummy discussions with their daughters regarding their mothers' shortcomings. And, with that one exception, the comparators all felt closer to their mothers than they did to their fathers.

All of the comparators' fathers, even the most traditional of them, supported their daughters' accomplishments and career aspirations. One man complained, for example, that his girl rather than her brother had won a high school sports prize, but he accompanied her to the lettermen's banquets, loudly applauded her award, and encouraged her continued athletic achievements in college.

The sannyasins never mentioned this kind of support from either their fathers or their mothers. Their mothers were distracted, usually ineffectual role models unable to confirm their daughters' senses of personal value or validate their autonomy. Their fathers reinforced traditional femininity, not independence or achievement. This family configuration was almost guaranteed to generate problems when the girls became adults. Its impact can be best understood in terms of the object relations approach to psychoanalytic theory (Chodorow 1978; Gardiner 1987; Mahler 1968; Winnicott 1964).

The general object relations perspective provides the compass for charting the direction of the personal dynamics that compelled the women to become high achievers and then take sannyas. All of the varied approaches within object relations emphasize the importance of relationships with parental figures in shaping strong or fragile selves.

The women of Rajneeshpuram described troubled childhoods and adolescences in detail, but they spoke relatively little about their earliest years. Tanmaya alone remembered what it was like to be a three-year-old, but the other women had difficulty remembering much about their families until they were older. While many object relations theorists underscore the importance of infancy and early childhood, later childhood and youth may reflect patterns set in the earliest, often forgotten years. Moreover, nurturing and validation throughout childhood and early adolescence are more important to emotional development than many people believe (Kohut 1984; Miller 1981).

I first explored mother-daughter relationships because most object relations theorists underscore mothers' significance. Winnicott, for example, wrote that the foundation of healthy self-regard was built on "good enough mothering," which involved sensitivity, responsiveness, and empathy (as cited in Chodorow 1978, 77–91). Recent feminist theorists such as Nancy Chodorow (1978) and Miriam Johnson (1991), however, have refocused attention toward the interdependent relationships with both mother and father. Family configurations and also the social conditions influencing families are the sources of lasting emotional vulnerability.

The sannyasins grew up in a culture that emphasized and valued women's work as wives, mothers, and caregivers just like the traditional object relations theorists did (Gilligan 1982; Gilligan, Lyons, and Hammer 1990). After World War II their parents' generations had seized on

the words of Benjamin Spock, who was himself much influenced by
object relations approaches. At that time cultural dictates stressed the
importance of mothering devoted to self-sacrifice, empathy, and affirmation of others. All of the sannyasins saw their mothers as falling far
beneath that high mark. Their mothers had never been ideal parents, nor
had they even met their daughters' needs. The women never absolved
them of real or imagined transgressions.

As young girls, they seldom fantasized about becoming wives or parents resembling their own mothers. Most of them, however, wanted to
nurture in the abstract, longing to care for humanity and receive love and
recognition from the world at large. They imagined themselves becoming
doctors, missionaries, psychologists, scientists, or even saints. The sannyasins connected love with achievement. It was a generalized love that
would allow them to leave their mothers forever, be validated by powerful individuals like their fathers, and find their own identities at last.

Someone to Watch over Me

In order to avoid resembling their mothers in almost any way, the sannyasins searched endlessly for some real or symbolic rescue by a career, a
social movement, or an individual who would stand between them and
their mothers' fates (Benjamin 1988). Bhagwan embodied this kind of
liberator, representing both a lover and a father to the women of Rajneeshpuram. Because he was so much larger than life in his role as a
charismatic leader, Bhagwan elicited devotion from them, which no previous relationships had inspired. Even when they threw themselves into
new quests or relationships, sannyasins had always held something of
themselves back, until Bhagwan persuaded them that they could only find
their true identities by surrender through sannyas.

Bhagwan was a vital, personal spiritual teacher and divinity. Shanto,
Dara, and Tanmaya believed that he invariably watched over them. Like
members of many other strict, intense religions, the sannyasins symbolically communicated with their deity almost every day. Almost every sannyasin had written him letters at one time or another, certain that Bhagwan personally dictated each response. Tanmaya sought guidance about
her intimate relationships, and Dara wrote to him about her confusion

and waning devotion. No matter what the state of Bhagwan's health, the intricacies of communal politics, or the external legal pressures, every woman was sure that her master would guide her with candor and compassion. And, when they searched their souls to discover answers on their own, they still believed that Bhagwan's spirit directed the solutions that they discovered.

Different sannyasins infused various details and occurrences with spiritual meanings that connected them to Bhagwan. The 108 stitches on a regulation major league baseball corresponded, for example, to the 108 beads on the sannyasins' *malas,* a similarity that several of the men sannyasins considered to have profound metaphysical significance. None of the women mentioned it. Every sannyasin, however, endorsed Bhagwan's interpretation of the beads' symbolizing the many different ways in which each devotee could find a personal spiritual road. There was always space for individuals to create highly individualistic spirituality in terms of Bhagwan's higher power and philosophy.

Sannyasins owned caches of objects representing their intimate emotional connections with their master. Along with the ubiquitous *mala* and locket with his picture, the women also wore gold rings or necklaces decorated with facsimiles of Bhagwan's signature or the communal emblem of one bird flying in the shadow of another. Wooden boxes, like the one Shanto received when she took leave of Bhagwan in Pune, often lay under their pillows at night.

Those who never visited Pune found comparable powerful charms to connect them with Bhagwan as they slumbered. For example, one woman pressed the withered roses that had once decorated his car during a Drive-By, and another slept with the luminous tail feather she had swiped from Bhagwan's personal peacock. Two of the women had received hats or robes that Bhagwan had once worn, and they valued those above everything else they owned.

None of the objects associated with Bhagwan had specific symbolic significance, but each sannyasin created private, personal ceremonies with some of her artifacts combined with the small, framed commercial photos of Bhagwan that every one of them owned. Some of them placed improvised offerings like a polished river rock from the Rada (John Day River) or a cookie beside a picture of him. One had calligraphed and mounted one of Bhagwan's phrases that had touched her deeply. Several of the women had great affection for a framed picture of Bhagwan drinking a cup of tea, and each one of them chatted privately with his image while unwinding over her own tea or coffee.

Nowhere was the singular relationship that Bhagwan emphasized more evident than in sannyas' names. Each woman, like every other sannyasin, believed that her new or revised name was a direct, carefully considered gift from her master. Shanto, Dara, and Tanmaya all interpreted their names to be both affirmations of who they were and visions about who they could become. New names signified dropping the past, finding one's essential self, and being fundamentally reborn through Bhagwan (Rajneesh 1979a; 1979b). When they received them, and after that throughout their careers as sannyasins, the women interpreted varieties of meanings and constructed innumerable reasons why Bhagwan had selected that particular unique appellation to help her along the path to self-actualization.

Reading through scores of published *Darshan Diaries,* I learned that many sannyasins were given the same name, an issue that sometimes drove Sheela's assistants wild as they tried to keep records about each devotee. On a more philosophical note, did the five Yuddhistras or seven Satya Bhartis share the same essential personal attributes? This was unclear to everyone I asked.

While each sannyasin believed that her assigned name drew on her unique innermost qualities, it seemed to me that Bhagwan bestowed new names almost randomly, altering the nuances of their meanings with facility and ease. Nevertheless, each woman valued her name, because she was sure that she was treasured and unique to her spiritual master.

Since Bhagwan represented an idealized rescuer, fantasies of protection and proximity to greatness colored the women's interpretations of his every word and act. They read meanings into everything their master did and rationalized his flaws, just as many women do in their mundane intimate relationships. Like the sannyasins, millions of women desire men who are interesting and exciting like their fathers, but most of all they fantasize about men who can master the social world and protect them from emotional harm and material difficulty. Bhagwan embodied the ultimate liberator. He was the sannyasins' fairy-tale prince, rescuing maidens who were imprisoned by their own emotional fragility.

Many other kinds of religious women relate to a rescuer who is a supernatural being. He may be a spirit, a deity, or perhaps an enlightened leader. He is a personalized higher power who will understand and protect them. Romantic love permeates their religiosity. This idealized figure resembles a romantic partner, because he is someone to whom they can confide their cherished hopes and deepest fears. The spiritual patriarch is seldom part of the contemporary earthly world, unless he is a living spiritual master. Bhagwan was the ultimate idealized leader, and he fulfilled the women's most grandiose fantasies. His remarkable insight, intelligence, and self-presentation were empirical attributes that sannyasins dramatically amplified because of their own emotional requirements and hopes.

Shanto's, Dara's, and Tanmaya's lives were all fundamentally changed when they became participants in the charismatic process—the ongoing interaction of their immoderate personal needs with the presence of a spectacularly gifted leader and spiritual guide (Camic 1987; Johnson 1992). Because of their relationships to Bhagwan, the women at last developed sustained senses of self-identity and personal worth.

Bhagwan loved, guided, disciplined, and imparted knowledge to his sannyasins, just as an ideal father would. Much like the transference process in psychotherapy, the charismatic dynamic allowed the sannyasins to recreate their intense, half-remembered feelings of childhood and redirect them in the present (Coles 1977, 192–210). Some Rajneesh therapists explicitly discussed the ultimate transference on to their master, but the transference I describe is less a clinical phenomenon than an everyday process that is, to some extent, part of everyone's life.

Bhagwan himself, however, assumed a classic psychoanalytic stance in describing his symbolic role as a therapist for all of his sannyasins. Yet he was not the usual therapist who urged his patients to examine and leave behind their extreme loyalty to him. Merger with Bhagwan's spirit, not termination, was both his and his sannyasins' ultimate goal. Surrender and recovery were endless processes, just as they are in twelve-step addiction programs.

Sannyasins idealized Bhagwan as an omnipotent, powerful, and historically important figure. Through association with him they were able to feel strong and whole. The sannyasins felt their own personal value grow because they were connected with someone so extraordinary. Being a sannyasin made each woman expand in her own eyes, as connection with

Bhagwan's greatness affirmed her goodness and merit (Kohut 1984, 204–7). The women could become emotionally centered because taking sannyas allowed them to escape any remaining possibilities of being like their mothers. Bhagwan protected them from the parental criticisms they had internalized and from the routine sacrifices associated with femininity in our culture. Affiliation with him, like connection with their fathers, confirmed their lifelong differentiation from their mothers and affiliation also allowed them to distance themselves from, but still remain supportive of, their fathers.

Similar processes of differentiation through idealization can occur in other strict religions, in therapeutic settings, in marriage, and in romance. In all of these contexts idealization of an adored, powerful figure allows women to feel better about themselves. Their relationship defines their identities. Endless love of someone special permits women to feel emotionally whole (Norwood 1988). When an idealized patriarchal figure becomes central to their own emotional well-being, women deny or excuse their beloveds' shortcomings. Thus, they can remain secure in the face of difficulties encountered within the relationship itself. The sannyasins ignored, rationalized, and reinterpreted their fathers' emotional difficulties, their lovers' and husbands' problems, and Bhagwan's role in the collapse of Rajneeshpuram. They forgave and idealized their master, because they could not afford to jeopardize their new identities and feelings of autonomy and efficacy. Although Rajneeshpuram disintegrated, during the immediate aftermath of its collapse all of the women emerged with their commitment intact. As sannyasins, they had finally defined and understood their own needs for sustained validation within spiritual contexts.

Most of the eleven remained connected to Bhagwan for many years afterward, and those who dropped sannyas discovered other masters and spiritual disciplines offering comparable support and fellowship. Their master had made his sannyasins a promise: "I will become part of your healing process." So long as they sustained a defining relationship with a powerful figure and communicated with a higher power, the women could remain whole and free. Bhagwan never healed his sannyasins' emotional wounds completely, but he made it possible for them to accept and cope with their own fragility.

Some Implications

The women of Rajneeshpuram journeyed through the outback of spirituality, far from the denominational mainstream, but the religious and emotional paths they pursued were simply narrower and rockier versions of
those that many women travel. The difficulties they encountered, their
separation from the outside, and the stigma they sometimes endured as
sannyasins were overshadowed by the exultation and delight of their spiritual connection to Bhagwan. For the sannyasins religion became joyous
emotional experience, satisfying their long-felt hunger for faith, intensity, and community.

The sannyasins treasured their connection to their powerful, protective spiritual master. Through Bhagwan they also discovered other people
to whom they could become close, because they all shared in idealizing
him. The bonds sannyasins formed with one another affirmed their commitments to Bhagwan while providing them with solidarity and emotional support. As the women became involved and committed devotees,
they inevitably distanced themselves from their families and old friends
and interacted with other sannyasins to the exclusion of almost everyone
else (Lofland 1981, 50–62; Beckford 1975). For all of them fellowship
was simply an added benefit of their attraction and charismatic connection to their master (Kohut 1984, 193–99).

Like the movement surrounding Bhagwan, every successful religion in
the United States provides powerful rewards of interpersonal fellowship.
Moreover, like the Rajneesh movement, all of these other faiths have also
changed courses in order to hold members and attract new converts
(Finke and Stark 1992). Rajneesh began his work as a spiritual teacher in
the Indian tradition and then changed to embrace Western followers and
personal growth psychotherapies. Within the boundaries of each religion,
ranging from evangelical fundamentalism to wicca, active members also
develop their own rituals and impart personal meanings to their doctrine, much as the women did.

Bhagwan's assertions of representing the future of religion may have
been more accurate than anyone suspected at the time. Recent, rapidly
growing independent Christian churches, such as Calvary Chapel and
Vineyard Fellowship, provide members with opportunities for personal

growth, although they do not necessarily offer them new selves. Like the communal city of Rajneeshpuram, they offer diverse programs, meeting every imaginable human need from child care to crisis counseling (Shibley 1996). The new churches respond to devotees' emotional needs, left unsatisfied within other cultural contexts. Like the sannyasins, members of these and many other current faiths in the United States share therapeutic sensibilities, and they are similarly concerned with emotional development, individual identity, and interpersonal authenticity. Fellowship and mutual support are linked to personal growth through spirituality, just as they were at Rajneeshpuram.

Bhagwan's creative interpretations encouraged each sannyasin to construct her own religious meanings and embellish the master-devotee connection. The sannyasins' general, unabashed pride in their improvised spirituality drew public attention to the movement's many excesses, first in India and then in the United States. The hilarious and tragic paradoxes of Americans' naive seekership can affirm the theme in the Upanishads: Sacred knowledge can destroy fools (Mehta 1979, 28). All seekers are foolish in their own ways, however, trying to comprehend and come to terms with higher powers. Change and improvisation are embedded in vital religions, and sannyasins' spontaneous, highly personal spirituality reflected the wider, postmodern world.

The three women fell in love with Bhagwan, just as other women might fall in love with a different personal divinity or an idealized partner. The sannyasins' accounts indicate that in most ways they were not so different from many, possibly most, of us. They illuminate some of the choices considered, but often not taken, by other women who came of age with the second wave of American feminism. The women of Rajneeshpuram lived on the edge, burning with a passion to find themselves. Their intricate quests offer greater understanding of both the short-lived communal city and the seemingly timeless contradictions of femininity in our time.

Epilogue

DOWN FROM THE MOUNTAIN

Sheela's precipitous departure on November 14, 1985, marked the beginning of the communal city's end. After that, Rajneeshpuram disintegrated with remarkable speed.

Bhagwan denounced his former secretary and her inner circle two days after she decamped. He informed his devotees, the media, and law enforcement officials that Sheela had instigated and implemented dozens of wicked criminal plots. Sannyasins opened all of Rajneeshpuram to state and federal investigators, who swarmed onto the ranch, accompanied by roving packs of news-hungry reporters.

The upheaval and intense scrutiny proved to be far more extreme and lasting than anyone living at Rajneeshpuram had anticipated. A few influential sannyasins heard warnings that a Federal Grand Jury had indicted Bhagwan himself and an arrest warrant was imminent. On October 28 federal agents apprehended Bhagwan in Charlotte, North Carolina, when two chartered Lear jets carrying him and members of his new inner circle stopped to refuel while en route to Bermuda.

According to his companions, Bhagwan had merely embarked on a Bermuda vacation to restore his physical well-being. Authorities believed that he engaged in unlawful flight in response to the forthcoming warrant, and a federal judge refused to grant bail (McCormack 1985, 115–16). Somewhat ironically, that same day Sheela and two of her collaborators were arrested in West Germany, charged with attempting to murder Bhagwan's personal physician during the last Summer Festival at Rajneeshpuram (Carter 1990, 234).[1]

National news media flashed pictures of Bhagwan in chains, surrounded by grim-looking marshals. Sannyasins at the ranch saw images of their shackled master and wept for him and also for themselves.

After spending eleven days in prisons in South Carolina and Oklahoma, Bhagwan was returned to Oregon, where he posted bail of a half-
million dollars and pled not guilty to multiple charges of immigration
fraud. His loyal followers worried that the ordeal had ruined his fragile
health. Tales spread about his exposure to contagious diseases, violent
inmates, and biological hazards in prison. The week after his return to
Oregon, however, Bhagwan was ready to travel once more. He pled no
contest to two charges of immigration fraud, paid fines of $400,000, and
agreed to suspended sentences and probation outside the United States.
After telling the judge, "I never want to return to the United States,"
Bhagwan immediately returned to his communal city and boarded a private plane at the Rajneesh Airstrip (McCormack 1985, 116). Hundreds
of remaining ranch residents sang and danced to show him their elation
at his freedom. On November 22, 1985, sannyasins heard the formal
announcement they had long dreaded: Rajneeshpuram would soon close
forever.

During the following months Bhagwan traveled from India to Nepal to
Europe and South America in search of a permanent home in a nation that
would permit him to gather his devotees together once more. Sannyasins
publicly termed Bhagwan's wandering "The World Tour," again putting
the best face on a problematic situation. Bhagwan and his close associates
shuttled desperately through more than a dozen different countries, all of
which rejected his applications for temporary or permanent residence
(Gordon 1987, 210–32). Risk and uncertainty hung over the tour.

Bhagwan's first destination was the Himalayan village of Manali, but
the Indian government refused extended visas to key members of his
entourage, and they began their desperate wandering. After lengthy
negotiations to work out an understanding that foreigners could not form
a huge permanent commune around their master, the Indian government
finally notified his representatives that Bhagwan could return to the old
Shree Rajneesh Ashram in late 1986. Within a few months he once again
spoke in Buddha Auditorium.

The ashram, which has become known informally as Pune 2, flourished once more as a destination for sannyasins and seekers. New meditations, spiritual exercises, and growth groups rejuvenated the movement.
Some of the faithful changed their sannyasin names to mark the transition, while others held fast to the original name that Bhagwan had

bestowed. Bhagwan changed his own name in 1989. First he was Osho Rajneesh and then simply Osho. The ashram became the Osho Commune International. It is a place for experience, personal development, and merger with the whole of existence. Although Osho "left his body" on January 19, 1990, the movement continues through his undiminished spiritual presence.

His image, words, and philosophy are everywhere in the commune and in his worldwide centers. Most of his American sannyasins are baby boomers, now well into middle age. But there are lively contingents of younger devotees from Japan, Germany, Italy, and countries that had been part of the old Soviet bloc. Affluent, Westernized young adults still seek self-actualization.

Former residents of Rancho Rajneesh have gravitated to places with good weather, active alternative cultures, and spiritual diversity, usually on the West Coast or in the Southwest. In the United States concentrations of old ranch hands and newer recruits live on the Hawaiian Islands of Oahu and Maui, in Seattle, the San Francisco Bay area, the Los Angeles region, Boulder, Sedona, Santa Barbara, and Santa Fe. There are smaller enclaves near Boston, Madison, New York City, and Nashville. Following Osho's emphasis on synthesizing material comfort and spirituality, few devotees stay for long in cities like Detroit, Amarillo, Mobile, or Fargo. They seek out tolerant and beautiful places, where their professional skills and countercultural experiences are appreciated.

Because of long memories and lingering hostility from outsiders, sannyasins in Oregon and Washington maintain low collective profiles, although they rarely hide their individual affiliations. Residents of Rajneeshpuram are now teachers in Portland, therapists in Eugene, innkeepers near Ashland, law enforcement personnel in Deschutes County, engineers in Olympia, and computer programmers in Seattle. A gourmet sandwich shop in Seattle's bustling Pike Street Market features a Zorba focaccia honoring Osho, and sannyasins make a point of stopping by for a snack when they are in the neighborhood. While no longer a force in the region, sannyasins are still very much part of it.

The largest concentrations of sannyasins live near the Osho Academy in Sedona, Arizona, and the Viha Meditation Center in Marin County, California, and devotees from other places in the United States often visit or correspond with them. Wherever they are, devotees often gather together to visit and meditate. Some travel to Pune when they have the time and money, although their trips are less frequent than they were a few years ago.

Most of the women who comprised Shanto, Dara, and Tanmaya conform to these general patterns, living in the western United States and remaining loyal to Osho. They have usually kept some form of sannyasin first name and added it to their last name. Ma Anand Tanmaya, for example, might now be Tanmaya Morgan.

All but three of the eleven women visited the Osho Commune International in Pune for lengthy sojourns. Those three who had not spent time in Pune 2 left the movement, as did one other woman, who drifted away almost a decade after Rajneeshpuram disintegrated. The seven others are still faithful Friends of Osho, living together with other devotees and hoping to spread his word into the next century.

The Aftermath

Soon after Bhagwan's plane circled the central Oregon hills one last time, all of the women made plans to leave Rancho Rajneesh. Like other sannyasins with independent financial resources or negotiable professional skills, each woman weighed several different options. Shanto joined three friends from the ranch and rented a California mansion, but she was ready to move when Bhagwan called upon her. Industrious Dara stayed on at Rajneeshpuram, once again aiding people in pain. She arranged other sannyasins' departures and helped organize the distribution of ranch assets. The foundering Rajneesh organization dispatched Tanmaya to European centers, in order to bring messages and support to beleaguered and bewildered sannyasins abroad.

Both Shanto and Tanmaya were driven to the Portland Airport in large, comfortable cars, which were not sold until most of Rajneeshpuram's other assets had been distributed. Dara left later, with a sannyasin couple who offered her temporary lodging in the guest quarters of their sprawling colonial-style house in a Portland suburb. Like the three women, other sannyasins from every stratum of Rancho Rajneesh clung together in small groups or couples, resting and trying to make sense of the past four or five years of their lives.

During the diaspora none of the women had immediate financial worries. Shanto received regular earnings from her substantial portfolio, and the Rajneesh establishment continued to support Dara and Tanmaya. These three sannyasins left the ranch in style, and they made the best of being out in the world, buoyed by friends and their still unwavering faith that their master would guide their futures.

Other sannyasins who remained faithful left under less fortunate circumstances. One group of four women and a man, who were friends of sannyasins I had known fairly well, camped out for an evening in our Eugene, Oregon, living room in late December 1985. Dara and other overseers had decided that another fifty people had to leave Rajneeshpuram as soon as possible, and these five were among the remaining residents who were encouraged to venture out.

One of the overseers drove them down through the canyon past Antelope and Madras to Redmond, the Deschutes County Seat, where they took a Greyhound Bus to Eugene and arrived late at night. They were exhausted but gracious when they introduced themselves, peering out from the rosy hoods of their damp, down-filled parkas. Each visitor had crammed a sleeping bag and every other possession into three relatively small suitcases or duffle bags. They were loaded down with their clothing, small gifts from friends, favorite stuffed animals, tarot cards, crystals, photographs, tapes of Bhagwan, and various personal mementos from their years in the communal city.

All five relished visiting a cozy home, with a fireplace, wall-to-wall carpets, two small children, and a friendly Old English sheepdog. Little heat, no dogs, and few kids remained at Rajneeshpuram. The visitors were wistful and dispirited. Nevertheless, they had decided to follow Bhagwan on part of his European tour before all of their money gave out and they had to return to the States to find new homes and jobs.

The guests were gone before dawn, bound for early flights to Brussels and then to Crete, where they hoped to be near Bhagwan and listen to his lectures twice each day. They left me charming thank-you notes, and, to further lighten their burdens, they left flashlights, a down-filled comforter, and tapes.

Their greatest burden was being on the outside, in a world they had left years before. It had little structure compared with the ranch, and whatever work they chose was unlikely to offer the interpersonal rewards that they had found in their communal city. Sannyasins like these five, without professional credentials or specific skills, had to fill huge four- and five-year holes in their resumes (Gordon 1987, 211–12). But devotees with businesses or academic jobs often helped out less fortunate sannyasins, offering them references or sometimes employment. One Northwest millionaire recommended dozens of sannyasins on the basis of excellent work in his household or businesses. Most of their work was indeed excellent, but they had carried it out at Rancho Rajneesh.

Looking back over more than a decade, many sannyasins have found that their years at Rajneeshpuram provided them with unexpected occupational possibilities. Their experience in central Oregon could sometimes supply extra cachet to their resumes.

Several sannyasins received graduate school fellowships, because curious admissions committees found that their communal sojourns added weight to their high test scores and excellent grades from years past. Psychotherapists, landscape designers, health care workers, public relations consultants, entrepreneurs, importers, computer designers, and engineers in creative fields also fared surprisingly well in reestablishing their careers or embarking on new ones. Even now they seldom share their Rajneeshpuram histories with their business acquaintances, but these sannyasins have built solid professional reputations on skills they honed at the communal city. Their creative problem-solving approaches and their concerns with process as well as outcomes enhance their abilities to function in business or the professions. Their recent occupational successes are embedded in the focus, skills, and intense work ethic that they had developed at the ranch. None of these individuals has grown rich, but they survive comfortably within the middle class.

Many sannyasins made the most of the twists and turns of their lives, redefining their parents' and sometimes their own ideas of occupational success. For example, an attorney had supervised one of the ranch's large communal kitchens because he lacked credentials to practice law in Oregon. When he left the ranch, he had no career direction at all, except the desire never to practice law again. After housecleaning, waiting on tables, and wandering, he started a restaurant, employing other sannyasins and outsiders as well. Explaining his current entrepreneurial success, he said: "Need makes you smart. We had to come up with an answer to life."

Coming up with an answer to life after the ranch meant deciding about work and resettlement. Spiritual issues had already been resolved. Most

Rajneeshpuram residents continued to believe that they had found the answer to their fundamental questions about life when they took sannyas. They believe that continued connection to Bhagwan nurtures their personal authenticity. From the time they became sannyasins to the day Bhagwan fled from America to his announcement that he had become Osho and on past his death, the majority of sannyasins affirmed their spiritual surrender. Even those who renounced Bhagwan usually continued to see him as an essential and meaningful part of their histories, somewhat like a former spouse.

By sustaining their faith, sannyasins resembled others who are active members of communal new religions for at least two years. Those years fundamentally alter devotees' goals and ways of looking at the world. Long-term members seldom renounce the spiritual priorities acquired as part of an intense collective religion. Even if they disengage or if their groups collapse, they usually remain faithful to the alternative spiritual stances they have adopted (Goldman 1995a; Jacobs 1989; Wright 1987). They may move closer to the mainstream, but they retain the overall frameworks that they have acquired through their earlier commitment.

In many cases the more outside rewards individuals give up, the less willingly they abandon their alternative spiritual stances (Iannaccone 1995; Stark 1996a, 163–89). Individuals who sacrificed much want to affirm their decisions. Even when they adopt new affiliations, believers continue to build on the ways of looking at the world and the practices they acquired during their years of intense commitment. The eleven women abandoned a great deal when they journeyed to central Oregon, but when they left Rajneeshpuram they took their reconstructed selves with them.

Leaving and Believing

In 1986 I mailed surveys to all of the women I had interviewed at length and a number of other sannyasins as well. In 1997 I interviewed nine of the eleven women who formed the composites and an additional eleven women who were both high achievers and are or had been sannyasins. Their priorities remain unchanged. I found that their experiences in central Oregon cemented all of their identities as seekers of spiritual truths.

Liquidation of Rajneeshpuram had already begun before any of the

eleven women in the composites disengaged. Two women dropped sannyas within a year after they scattered, and two others loosened their ties
later on. Now, eleven years later, at least one sannyasin in every composite no longer considers herself to be committed to Osho. Because of these
changes and the addition of eleven more respondents to continue to preserve anonymity, I will discuss issues, rather than Shanto, Dara, and Tanmaya, in the rest of this epilogue.

After the initial pain and bewilderment attending Sheela's departure,
all of the twenty women struggled to redefine the Rajneeshpuram experience as a positive one of learning to let go of their egos and expectations. The nine sannyasins in the composites who still felt positive about
Rajneeshpuram two years after leaving continue to consider the ranch as
a kind of mystery school that had deepened their self-knowledge. One of
the early baby boomers spoke of "No regrets. Some understanding of the
human condition." A younger sannyasin observed, "My love of Bhagwan
grows ever deeper, richer, stronger."

In contrast, the first woman who disaffected could never overcome the
failure of her dreams. She wondered whether Bhagwan had lied, and she
obsessively dissected the meanings of the communal collapse. When she
left Rajneeshpuram with her lover, and the two of them returned to his
hometown, they still thought of themselves as sannyasins. Three months
later, in February 1986, they were free agents in the spiritual marketplace. She wrote to me: "We have no intention of following B. anywhere.
. . . Life is still very good."

This early baby boomer, who was one of the women who became
Dara, shed her affiliation over a brief time, in the company of a supportive partner. It took the couple several months, as they both settled into new lives, entirely isolated from regular contact with other
devotees.

The other early defector, part of the composite Tanmaya, dropped
sannyas impulsively and angrily. She had embarked on a mission to the
European centers when she discovered that Sheela and possibly Bhagwan
had secretly terrorized her. Her partner and several close friends also
dropped sannyas suddenly and publicly at the same time.

She asserted: "This time, when I tuned into the place that had for nine
years registered a clear 'yes,' I got an equally clear 'no.' There was a wob-

bly time. You can imagine. But I never really looked back. For me, there is no going back. I don't feel there is anything left for me to learn there." Shortly after writing this, she joined another spiritual group, led by a recent Rajneesh apostate.

The other two women in the composites who no longer think of themselves as sannyasins gradually disengaged over several years. They barely knew each other and lived thousands of miles apart, but their stories were remarkably similar. Both of them were hardly aware that they were in the process of dropping sannyas. Almost without their volition, each one's ties to Bhagwan slowly stretched and finally snapped. They still move among sannyasin networks, although they have other friends as well. One of the women who drifted away described her sustained bonds: "When I am in a room with sannyasins there is an openness and authenticity that is not so easy to find!" And old friends who knew these two from the ranch refer to them as "closet sannyasins." Each retains space in her heart for Bhagwan.

Some individuals close to the current inner circles in Pune separate those who remain loyal to Bhagwan from defectors. For the most part, however, sannyasins draw few distinctions between devotees who dropped out and those who are still formally part of the movement. Although they condemn the apostates who published lurid exposés about Bhagwan and Rajneeshpuram, they usually speak with warmth and concern about old comrades.[2] This was a common theme among all of the sannyasins who talked with me recently: "No matter what, you never really drop sannyas."

Another former sannyasin noted that she would always have a community of the five hundred or so former and current sannyasins living in the San Francisco Bay area. "It's like living in your own hometown. They are my tribe," she said. She elaborated and described being a sannyasin as similar to being an American Jew. Both were cultural identities embedded in her core self.

Most current and former sannyasins share similar interpretations. They believe that devotion to Bhagwan is embedded in a broad approach to life and that spiritual surrender transcends religion. Even when someone casts aside their sannyasin name or tries to denounce or erase past experiences as a devotee, the connection remains.

A Dozen Years Later

The two women in the composites who left Bhagwan within the first year had disappeared from sannyasin networks over the past decade. When I last heard from each of them in the early 1990s, they were still focused on their personal growth through intense spiritual commitments. The other nine were surprisingly easy to find because they kept in touch with old friends and acquaintances from Rajneeshpuram in the same ways that people who had been active in movements for social change in the 1960s and 1970s keep in touch with their old comrades (Goldman and Whalen 1990).

When I began to contact nine women from the composites and the additional eleven, I was disconcerted that some whom I scarcely knew remembered me vividly. One recalled helping push my muddy station wagon out of a deep rut in the rain-soaked county road near Mirdad, the visitors' center, and another described the professional blue blazer I wore on my first few visits. On the other hand, other women whom I knew far better had no idea who I was when we first began to talk on the phone.

Just as they recalled different things about me and my research, the women recalled Rajneeshpuram with different levels of detail. Those who are deeply involved with the current Pune commune, Viha in Marin County, or the Sedona, Arizona mystery school had vaguer memories of the ranch than the women who live at a distance from the movement's current spiritual centers.

Sannyasins active in current projects concerning Osho said, "Living in the present is a full-time deal!" In contrast, individuals who had disengaged or established residence far from any Osho centers remembered Rajneeshpuram with striking clarity. Some remain in a kind of bubble, and their experiences at the ranch seem more real to them than recent events. Everyone I talked with, however, still thinks of the ranch as both the worst and the best of times.

During the summer of 1995 about five hundred former ranch residents met in the San Francisco Bay area for a ten-year reunion. Two of the eleven women in the composites attended. Several others sent love and long messages, which were read aloud. The four women in the composites who had disengaged by that time did not go, but the two disaffiliates who spoke with me mentioned the reunion and had enjoyed talking about it with friends who had attended.

The "Meeting of the Tribes" affirmed the centrality of Rajneeshpuram to the life histories of almost everyone involved. An issue of *Viha Connection,* the magazine published by the center in Marin County, was dedicated to the tenth-anniversary celebration, and sannyasins described the lasting impact of the Oregon experience.

Newer sannyasins often treat old ranch hands with the same deference and awe that the previous generation reserved for individuals who had been with Bhagwan when he still occupied his tiny apartment in Bombay in the early 1970s. Their years at Rajneeshpuram have taken on mythic significance to many of those who were at the ranch as well, although Osho Commune International increasingly minimizes the importance of the Oregon experiment.

Official descriptions of Osho's dream for a new kind of humanity and references to his timeless spiritual presence overshadow the old memories of Bombay, the earlier Ashram, and, most of all, the ranch. Unofficially, however, Rancho Rajneesh still symbolizes timelessness for many sannyasins. It was a moment of youth, no matter how old they were. Veterans of the 1960s, in midlife, could recapture the exhilarating collective optimism that had filled them earlier, when their lives seemed to hold endless possibilities.

Even now, when some of them are eligible for senior citizens' discounts, the women rarely mention their own aging or death. In some ways they remain forever young, still affirming their own endless potential for personal growth and spiritual development. All of their voices are buoyant, and their lively inflections and enthusiastic conversational styles sound amazingly youthful.

Most of the women insist that they feel as young as they had at the ranch, although most of them have encountered the recent deaths of parents and dear friends, as well as Osho's. The idea that their master will live on in each of them makes his demise less final and lends an urgency to their own future deeds, so that their own spirits might also continue.

Four of the women in the composites recently passed through serious health crises of their own. All of them believe that meditation and spiritual joy allowed them to overcome cancer. The women have confronted recent personal adversity with the same emotional resources they drew on when Rajneeshpuram collapsed, asserting that dire circumstances teach them to live in the present moment. They minimize their physical decline and instead concentrate on ripe, meaningful maturity.

Almost all of the twenty women I spoke with look as young as they feel, according to their own account, confirming photographs, and descriptions from friends. Some have had cosmetic surgery. None has gone gray, and many have tried a range of hair colors in order to bring their outer selves in line with their inner youthfulness. All of them exercise regularly, and they meditate to become more peaceful and aware.

One woman had put on weight, but the rest were as slim as before. All but one still buys her clothes in sizes ten and below. They laughingly refer to "Dorian Gray" or "pacts with the Devil" to explain decades of comeliness and their apparent defiance of the laws of aging.

They wear every hue, in keeping with Osho's wishes. Most, however, still maintain a soft spot for sunrise colors. Some are fashion forward, wearing new designs and scouting the latest trends, while others favor comfortable natural-fiber clothing or buy vintage silks at flea markets.

During our recent conversations we chatted about the experts who help the women feel so young: an innovative manicurist, a fabulous massage therapist, an outstanding herbalist, an insightful chiropractor, or a talented acupuncturist. They described the power of botanicals, henna hair treatments, the Zone diet, Pilates exercise, Niha, and Tai Chi. These exchanges highlight the women of Rajneeshpuram's sustained concern with body and soul together. Integration of material and spiritual life is a continuing element in the sannyasins' worldviews.

Relationships

Only three of the eleven women from the composites are still with their partners from the ranch. Within two years of the collapse the other relationships disintegrated. All of the composites who had married sannyasins who were foreign nationals split up. Two of them explicitly discussed their immigration arrangements with me, but all of these women believed as one sannyasin stated: "We were never really together."

None of the composite women live in an intentional community, although three reside with small groups of other sannyasins. Most live with or near their current husbands or long-term partners, but the women continue to prize private space and time alone. Three described their strong needs for extra personal space as reflective of their old loss of so much privacy at Rajneeshpuram. In every case sannyasin or ex-, the women value their personal growth more than intimacy. The "I" remains more important to them than "thou" or "we."

Their partners resemble the women intellectually and emotionally. Playfulness and enthusiasm are traits that the women look for in a mate, but the most important element in their soulmates is spiritual commitment. The women bond with individuals who also focus on themselves and their personal paths. The men—or, in one case, the woman—in their romantic lives are also seekers who share in the pursuit of self-actualization.

Every woman also sought understanding and support from her children, if she had them. Some children were close to their mothers, while others disappointed them, and within the same families children had different kinds of relationships to the sannyasin women. The happiest connections were between mothers and the children who had remained with them, lived at the ranch, and had been raised as sannyasins. The other relationships that worked reasonably well involved women with children who were already grown before their mothers became seekers.

One sannyasin woman, for example, looks to her sannyasin son as a spiritual guide. Another lives with her adult daughter and considers her to be a close friend. I talked briefly with the daughter, a charming and articulate devotee whom I remembered as a little girl on a Rajneesh school bus. She clearly reciprocated her mother's feelings of closeness and interdependence, with shared faith in Osho sustaining the intimate bond between them.

Other maternal connections were more ambivalent, especially for those women who had left one or more children behind with their husbands. Some of these children have become closer to their mothers, but most of the women's children still struggle with anger and emotional wounds from their earlier abandonment. As the women recounted these difficulties, they sounded hurt and perplexed. While their own children might be voicing some of the same kinds of pain that the women had articulated about their own mothers, none empathized or perceived any similarities to their own earlier emotion.

One sannyasin, whose son's "religion" is financial success, has sent monthly care packages of Bhagwan's books for more than a decade, hoping that he will someday understand her quest. I heard about a dozen adult children's marriages that were incomprehensible to the women. Daughters or sons had married Mormons, evangelical Christians, orthodox Jews, or members of some other group that the sannyasins classified as inflexible and irrational. They wondered why their children sought answers in such strict, rigid organizations. "How could he choose to live this way?" one asked. They completely failed to identify their discomfort with what their own parents might have felt decades earlier, when they themselves had left the mainstream to journey to Pune or central Oregon.

The women from the composites who had no offspring seldom regretted their childlessness. They believed that they were not meant to mother, and some of them talked about problems they had with their current stepchildren, nieces, or nephews. Bhagwan's many warnings about how bearing children made self-actualization difficult compelled two of them to have abortions during their twenties and thirties, and another had scars and endometriosis, which she attributed to negligence or possibly malevolence on the part of Rajneesh clinics. Although their accounts held some sadness, none of these three believed that motherhood would have been good for her.

Some of the other eleven noncomposite women I talked with described their childlessness as one of life's great tragedies and believed that Bhagwan, for whatever reason, had deprived them of a basic experience. They put off children until age made it difficult to conceive. One of these women said that infertility was "the most significant sacrifice to be with Bhagwan."

Work and Worship

While some women missed having or being with children, none regretted leaving either her marriage or changing her career aspirations in order to become a sannyasin. Even those who were no longer sannyasins felt relieved to have redirected their earlier commitments. One of the women, who had adolescent dreams of an affluent life that combined marriage and a vague but prestigious career, summed up all of these descriptions when she spoke of her gratitude to Bhagwan: "That period at Rajneeshpuram was like I was shot to the moon to deflect the life I was moving toward."

After the ranch she and others who reentered the labor force spoke of bringing Osho into the marketplace. Even if they dropped sannyas, the women saw their work as having some reverent, meditative dimensions. For these spiritual reasons and perhaps from post-ranch burnout as well, none of the women who had been attorneys now practices law.

A number of sannyasin women tried real estate sales in the 1980s because they were convinced that their intuitions could bring the perfect people to the perfect property in booming markets. Only one, however, remains in the field today, specializing in luxury properties for well-heeled buyers who are less concerned with mortgage rates than realizing their personal fantasies.

Another successful professional provides "a good spiritual environment" for consumers of upscale clothing, and another owns a gallery where she makes buying chillingly expensive art a "fun experience." One sannyasin is a successful public administrator, bringing Osho into her professional world because of her willingness to listen to others, to consider group process, and to work almost ceaselessly. The other sixteen do not do such lucrative work. They are teachers, counselors, herbalists, and physical therapists.

Although the majority of the twenty women opted for diminished careers in order to actualize themselves, they have few immediate financial worries. Some receive regular incomes from inheritances or personal investments, ranging from adequate supplements to exceptional entitlements. Even the most entitled women still work, set in their beliefs that spiritually informed, creative labor is an essential part of self-actualization. The core of all of their self-actualization, however, is some form of meditation.

All but two of the twenty still keep pictures and other mementos of Rajneesh with them. Most, including those who dropped sannyas, refer to him as Osho rather than Bhagwan, and they maintain continuing imagined dialogues with their spiritual master. Even a woman who is an out-spoken critic of Rajneeshpuram sustains these ethereal conversations, splitting the good Bhagwan of the old Shree Rajneesh Ashram from the bad Bhagwan/Osho of Oregon and Pune 2. She continues to meditate and listen to old tapes, believing that if some vision of Bhagwan ever took off the wool hat he wore in his later days, "he'd be *my* Bhagwan again." One of her treasures is the small picture of her and her master together in India.

The other women who display or carry Rajneesh's pictures all continue to imbue these images with unique meanings. One described the special twinkle he had during her darshans with him. Another tells of "a gift giving back," because her favorite photograph depicts him in robes made of material that she was allowed to purchase and give to his seamstress.

A lapsed sannyasin describes Osho's tapes as "so nourishing and so tasty" she can usually forget about his insensitivity and egoism. Most of the others, whether they were active sannyasins or not, also depicted their spiritual relationships with Osho through images of nurture and sustenance. They spoke of themselves as "starving" for connection after his death and "gorging" on his tapes, books, and pictures.

Osho continues to be the enduring center of practicing sannyasins' lives. Said one: "Osho is always with me. I constantly try to integrate meditations and Osho's teachings, as I understand them, into my life. Sometimes it's easy, and sometimes it isn't." Another woman stated, "I am daring to live the wisdom and learn the art of living."

In fact, every one of the women I spoke with recently was absorbed in "tending the flowers within themselves" and living Rajneesh's philosophy. The primary difference between practicing and lapsed sannyasins was whether Osho and his teachings remained *the* foundation of their lives or whether Oslo's wisdom was one of several foundations. Active sannyasins were monotheistic in their commitment to Rajneesh, and lapsed ones tended to find the wisdom of the ages in a number of places.

Three of the twenty women sought more answers through psychotherapy, working with secular therapists who could help them make sense of their inner conflicts after the ranch collapsed. They spent as little as three months in therapy and as long as four years. Said the four-year veteran of post-ranch therapy: "I dropped the past with open arms. When He let me down, the only place to go was inside."

She still meditates informally and, like the other women who turned to psychotherapy, once again browses in the spiritual marketplace. Although they search with intensity, these three seekers vow that they would never again surrender so completely as they had to Bhagwan. Nevertheless, they and other lapsed sannyasins look to masters whose styles, teachings, and affluent, educated followers resemble Bhagwan's. Among those they mention are John Roger, whose Movement of Spiritual Inner Awareness has attracted rich Californians like conservative media personality Arianna Huffington, and Andrew Cohen, who advocates a synthesis of Eastern and Western wisdom and cultivates somewhat younger followers.

These men are less influential with former sannyasins than a recently established woman spiritual teacher. The teacher, Gangaji, has influenced all of the lapsed sannyasins who talked with me recently. She is an attractive baby boomer who looks like the sannyasins themselves. When she traveled to India in 1990, searching for her core self, Antoinette Varner met her master Poonjaji, who is also known as Papaji. He renamed Antoinette as Ganjaji and instructed her to carry his wisdom to the West, where she now has headquarters in Boulder, Colorado, not far from the Osho Meditation Center.

Although one former sannyasin came to Boulder to visit, the others first heard her lecturing in other places in the United States. Her message is almost indistinguishable from Rajneesh's: "Explore your Self" (Gangaji 1996, back cover). She asks seekers, "Are you willing to surrender all conditioning?" (40). If the answer is yes, Gangaji provides individuals with ways to discover their inner cores.

Reading Gangaji, I observed eerie similarities between their new teacher and the women themselves. A gentler version of Bhagwan, Gangaji had been elevated by her own Indian master in a way that some of the women had fantasized Bhagwan might choose them. They, too, recognized a mirror of their ideal selves in their new teacher.

One lapsed sannyasin said that she sits in satsang with Gangaji because "she is not a guru, but she is a sister and a friend. We could not have a disciple/master relationship, because we are too much alike." Another remarked, "I feel peaceful with Gangaji, and I like her because she is an American woman like me!"

Criticizing those who now look to Gangaji, a deeply committed sann-yasin asked: "Why are these sannyasins hopping from *satsang* to *satsang?* Osho has everything!"

Jessica, who influenced me to look more closely at the women of Rajneeshpuram, was another seeker who did not find everything in Osho. She eventually chose to define herself through a high-powered career, rather than spiritual commitment. When she feels unusually stressed, however, Jessica restores herself through Rajneesh meditations she learned twenty years ago in Berkeley.

Like so many of the sannyasins from Rajneeshpuram, she remains attractive and enthusiastic, even after a decade that included a bitter divorce and other disappointments. Jessica romanticizes herself as the modern equivalent of a nineteenth-century *femme des lettres* who has fash-ioned her personal and professional identities in the face of societal con-straints. She cobbles together her spirituality from different sources: Rajneesh, Afro-Caribbean traditions, and her own Lutheran roots. Occa-sionally, remembering the meditations in Berkeley, she "dances 'til she trances."

I asked Jessica if she knew that Rajneesh had died, and she said that kind of finality was terrifying. She believes that his molecules and his spirit are still out there. So do the other women whom he touched in one way or another.

Final Images

Throughout the Pune commune, Rajneesh centers, and every corner of their private lives, the women who built Rajneeshpuram encounter ever-present reminders that Osho is always and forever with them. The theme is: "Never born. Never died. Only visited this Planet Earth between December 11, 1931, and January 19, 1990" (Osho 1996, 282).

Yet, in spite of Osho's timelessness and their own yearnings for endur-ing youth, sannyasins cannot completely suspend the rules of aging. Throughout their adult lives the sannyasins questioned and sometimes defied social norms, but some things cannot be changed. They have had to consider their own mortality, however fleetingly. The women are no longer quite so energetic as they once were. Most of them now live more quietly and cautiously than they anticipated, moving closer to the American mainstream than they believed possible when they tried to construct utopia in Oregon.

The Osho movement in America is graying, and they have not recruited large numbers of young adults. Nor have sannyasins replaced themselves, because of their own low birthrate. There is no new generation born within the movement. But, although the residents of Rajneeshpuram dipped well below zero population growth, a surprising number of younger sannyasins are their children, nieces, and nephews. The movement's new blood now comes predominantly from Europe and Asia, where youth movements are just beginning to embrace the spiritual and psychological gentrification that defined the baby boomers' quests for self-actualization.

Longtime devotees are bemused that their generation no longer occupies center stage in the world nor possibly among the Friends of Osho either. At a recent private gathering honoring Osho, sannyasins remembered life at the ranch and wondered, "Where have all the discos gone?" They recalled the days when they could party all night and work all day. And they still imagine recreating those times.

Paul Simon's sentimental song "Still Crazy after All These Years" ran through my mind throughout that evening. And I once again considered how the sannyasins seem to represent the essence of the generations that came of age in the wake of World War II. They tried to become their best selves and experiment with new ways of living, bringing enthusiasm and innovation to our culture, while often ignoring history and collective obligation. The sannyasins remain certain that they can continue to grow and recreate themselves at any age, and they think of retirement as just another stage in the long, long life of Zorba the Buddha.

The Friends of Osho go on because they recruit and hold affluent, talented devotees from a number of different nations. Since they are privileged individuals, sannyasins are influential in their societies. They are taken seriously without suffering extreme political repression, and they can remain engaged on an international scale (Stark 1996a, 29–47). While there are now probably fewer than twenty thousand active sannyasins worldwide, they continue to have more influence than their num-

bers suggest, because they are linked by sophisticated computer networks, they provide spiritual goods to a wide market of esoteric
consumers, they come together regularly in small groups, and they have
contact with national centers and the Osho Commune International in
Pune.[3]

Wherever they are a decade after the ranch collapsed, and whatever
they feel about Rajneeshpuram or Osho now, the women still believe in
taking personal risks. All of them say that stepping out of the mainstream
was worth it to them. One sannyasin voiced the ardor of their commitments when she urged me: "Tell people that we are loved! Osho loves us
and we sannyasins love each other." That search for love is what brought
the women to Bhagwan and to Rajneeshpuram, and the love they experienced is why all of them still value their passionate journeys.

Appendix A

Interview Questions and Follow-Up Questionnaire

Interview Guide for Women and Men at Rajneeshpuram

General Notation to Interviewer

These questions are designed to chart a direction of a conversation. They are to encourage individual's comments and insure that certain information is covered. It is not necessary to read each question or to phrase it exactly the same way every time.

Feel free to use probes and follow individual's own comments, if they seem to open fruitful areas for understanding.

Before the second interview, check tapes/transcripts to make sure that all of the information was covered and to suggest directions for the second interview. At the end of the second interview, check demographics: age, marital status, educational and occupational histories.

Introduction

The purpose of the study is to discover why people who had achieved occupationally or academically found that those rewards were incomplete and made a decision to take sannyas. We may talk twice or possibly over many meetings; it's a matter of choice. Each of our discussions will probably take one and a half to two hours.

During the interview I will show you six cards from the Thematic Apperception Test (TAT), which was originally developed in the 1940s. These cards have been shown to thousands of people, who have made up stories about them, as I will ask you to. I am interested in comparing sannyasins to the larger population and to a matched group of nonsannyasins.

The TAT is also a nice way of warming up and loosening memories. The cards are sort of an academic tarot deck. We will look at the cards in the middle of this first interview or at the end, whichever seems to be most comfortable, and then again, the next time we meet.

Questions for First Interview

1. Tell me about the day you took sannyas.
2. What led up to it?
3. Was religion always important to you?
4. Can you describe a typical day shortly before you found Bhagwan?
5. What about a typical day now? How about describing yesterday.
6. Where did you grow up?
7. What were your parents like?
8. What was your family like?
9. What was high school like? Were you a "good" girl or a "bad" girl in high school?

10. What about college/graduate school (if applicable)?
11. Did you ever have any experience with psychotherapy?
12. Did you do Rajneesh therapy in Poona or in the United States? Do you do it now?

Questions for Second Interview

1. Have you meditated regularly? Do you meditate now? If so, which meditations?
2. Do you have any current intimate relationships? What are they like?
3. What about past relationships?
4. Any marriages?
5. Any kids? (If yes, where are they?)
6. What do you think of the AIDS precautions and policies at Rajneeshpuram?
7. Can you describe a particularly satisfying or "peak" experience that has occurred during the past year?
8. Any frustrating or low experiences? Can you describe one?
9. What work do you do/have you done at Rajneeshpuram?
10. How is your health?
11. In high school, college, or after were there any ideas or books that were important to you?
12. Any meaningful quote you can think of from Bhagwan?
13. Anything else?

After each interview, describe the person, their mood, appearance, etc. Also describe where the interview took place.

Follow-Up Letter Sent in December 1985

Dear [sannyasin's name],

Since your last interview, the changes have been extraordinary. I am sure that this is both a time for sorrow and joy for you. If you would like to discuss your experiences, your feelings, plans with me, it would add immeasurably to the project. Please send me this information.

I can be reached at [addresses and phone numbers follow].

If you plan to be anywhere in the Willamette Valley, please let me know, and we could arrange a meeting.

Could you send me a permanent mailing address in the enclosed envelope? Also, if you have a minute, maybe you could jot down what you are feeling *right now* about Bhagwan and Rajneeshpuram.

My permanent address is:
Here are some of my feelings about Bhagwan and Rajneeshpuram:

Follow-Up Questions, January 1997

Introduction

This is a follow-up after a dozen years. I am talking with about twenty women whom I met at Rajneeshpuram or who are friends of people I knew at the ranch.

This is for the epilogue of a book I am working on about women who lived at Rajneeshpuram.

I am interviewing a number of people, both sannyasins and women who dropped sannyas, in order to preserve everyone's privacy. No names are used at all, and there is complete anonymity. I am trying to consider how people have been in the world for the last dozen years, since the ranch collapsed. This interview is not taped, and you may refuse to answer any questions you like. Also, please feel free to ask me questions about my research or about myself.

Questions

1. Did you do anything special for Osho Celebration on January 19 this year or for Osho's birthday this winter?
2. Do you ever reflect on Rajneeshpuram?
3. If so, how? What?
4. In retrospect, did Rajneeshpuram affect your life? If so, how?
5. What spiritual path do you follow now?
6. What kind of work on the outside do you do now?
7. Do you run a center/meditations/groups?
8. Do you do any networking with sannyasins—formal/informal? For example, are you someone people in Pune might call for some information about the United States?
9. (If applicable) Would I recognize you now? Would people from Rajneeshpuram recognize you?
10. How do you look?
11. What color hair?
12. What dress size are you now?
13. How has your health been?
14. Are you in a long-term relationship? With a sannyasin or a similar seeker or with someone who is not very spiritual? How long?
15. Are any kids living with you?
16. Do you live with any other sannyasins? Any former sannyasins?
17. Do you see other sannyasins/ex-sannyasins often?
18. (If applicable) What are your kids doing? Did they ever take sannyas?
19. Describe where you live. Are there any pictures of Osho in your home?
20. Do you meditate? How often?
21. Have you been to Pune recently? How frequently do you visit and for how long?
22. Have you visited or do you plan to visit Viha in Mill Valley or the Osho Academy in Sedona? If so, when and for how long?
23. Do you have any plans to visit Pune or one of the centers?
24. Would you ever want to live in an intentional community again?
25. Do you have anything else to say about Osho/Friends of Osho (your center)?
26. Anything else?

Appendix B
Decisions for Constructing Composites and Using Quotations

Composites

1. All of the women in this study were American citizens whose primary language was English.

2. All of the women had graduate or professional degrees and/or personal incomes over $40,000 in 1995 dollars.

3. All of the women had been sannyasins for at least two years, and they had lived at the ranch for at least four months.

4. Each woman's transcript was used for one and *only* one composite.

5. Protection of anonymity was a central consideration in constructing all of the composites.

6. Accurate depiction of sannyasins' personal accounts was the other major consideration.

7. All names were changed both for sannyasins and for the outsiders whom they identified as part of their personal lives.

8. Respondents were given sannyasin names other than their own. The names were other sannyasins' names, which could be construed to have a meaning similar to that which Bhagwan and one or more individuals in each composite attributed to her or their name(s). A number of individuals sometimes had been given the same sannyas name, a practice that created difficulties for both devotees and the Rajneesh organization's central office. Sometimes people adopted adjectives to distinguish themselves. Thus, four different women with the same name could be called Big Shanti, Little Shanti, New York Shanti, and Laughing Shanti. In other cases, several people used the same name. Thus, I could use alternative names from other sannyasins, because names seldom denoted only one person.

The three composite women's names were selected from published darshan diaries. Bhagwan's remarks regarding those names are quoted directly from those diaries. They were:

Shanto from Bhagwan Shree Rajneesh. 1981. *The tongue tip taste of Tao: A darshan diary,* 170–72. Poona: Ma Yoga Laxmi, Rajneesh Foundation Ltd.

Tanmaya from Bhagwan Shree Rajneesh. 1979. *For madmen only: A darshan diary,* 18–20. Poona: Ma Yoga Laxmi, Rajneesh Foundation Ltd.

Yashodara from Bhagwan Shree Rajneesh. 1979. *For madmen only: A darshan diary,* 434–45. Poona: Ma Yoga Laxmi, Rajneesh Foundation Ltd.

9. I disguised unique or widely known incidents in individuals' life histories. This was critical because the Rajneesh therapy groups and published darshan diaries had made some individual's definitive experiences widely recognizable. When those experiences could be disguised and they also applied to at least two sannyasins

within a composite, they were used with modifications, for confidentiality.

10. Composites were grouped in terms of women's dates of birth because of their common historical experience, which transcended social class and other major demographic variables.

11. Locations were changed for all major events. Regions were kept the same, however, as were city sizes. The only exceptions to this rule were the Los Angeles area and the San Francisco Bay area. So many sannyasins had lived in these cities, it was possible to describe them without identifying individuals. Moreover, the West Coast's booming spiritual and personal growth marketplaces were central to many sannyasins' spiritual careers.

12. Key life events, such as marriage and divorce, were included in composites only when they had been shared by the majority of sannyasins in a group.

13. Appendix C indicates demographic and social characteristics of the sann-yasins in this study. To preclude identification, the information is not organized in categories for each composite.

Quotations

1. Quotations for each composite woman were assembled only from individ-uals who belonged to the age group under consideration and not from all of the respondents.

2. References to names and locations in quotations were changed without notation of that change.

3. Minor grammatical errors and pauses or extraneous colloquialisms, such as "you know," were omitted without notation.

4. Interviewer's questions, prompts, or comments were omitted without notation.

5. All quotations in the composites were verified by checking transcriptions against tapes of the original interviews.

Appendix C

General Demographic Information about Composites

Age at Time of Interview
Shanto: 49, 47, 46.
Dara: 42 (2), 40, 39, 35.
Tanmaya: 34, 33 (2).

Parents' Social Class (Income, Occupation, Ethnicity)
Shanto: upper-middle class (3).
Dara: upper class (1), upper-middle class (1), working class (3).
Tanmaya: upper-middle class (1), middle class (2).

Number of Siblings
Shanto: 0 (1), 2 (2).
Dara: 2 (1), 3 (3), more than 4 (1).
Tanmaya: 1 (1), 2 (2).

Religion Raised
Shanto: Orthodox Jewish (2), culturally Jewish (1).
Dara: Roman Catholic (4), liberal Protestant (1).
Tanmaya: liberal Protestant (2), conservative Jewish (1).

Highest Educational Degrees
High School (2).

Junior College (1).
College (1).
M.A. or M.S. (3).
Ph.D. (2).
J.D. (2).

Annual Household Income in 1984 Dollars in Last Year before Sannyas
Over $200,000 (3).
Over $100,000 (1).
$75,000–$99,000 (1).
$50,000–$74,000 (3).
$25,000–$49,000 (3).

Number of Children
Shanto: 2 (1), 3 (1), 4 (1).
Dara: 0 (2), 1 (3).
Tanmaya: 0 (2), 1 (1).

Marital Status Immediately before Taking Sannyas
Shanto: divorced (2), separated (1).
Dara: single (1), married (1), divorced (3).
Tanmaya: single (2), married (1).

Notes

Chapter 1

1. I refer to Bhagwan Shree Rajneesh or Rajneesh or Bhagwan throughout this book, interchanging all three names. The media favored "Rajneesh," while sannyasins preferred "Bhagwan," but I have made no distinction, other than using "Bhagwan" when narrating the sannyasins' stories. I also use "Osho," his current name, where that is appropriate. I have also used both Poona and Pune throughout, since the town's name changed a decade after my first interviews.

2. Satya Bharti Franklin (1992) convincingly described Bhagwan Shree Rajneesh's collusion in criminal activities. Yet George Meredith (1988), who was Bhagwan's personal physician with the sannyasin names of Devaraj and later Amrito, suggests with equal certainty that Bhagwan knew nothing specific about Sheela and her circle's many nefarious plots. According to Meredith, the master was aware of her lust for power but did nothing to stop Sheela, because sannyasins had much to learn from their own responses to her.

3. Janet Jacobs (1989) discusses the two-step process of detachment in which individuals who leave new religions by themselves are first disillusioned with other members and later come to criticize the leader. The process of attachment may have a different emphasis. Lofland (1981) underscores the importance of sustained interaction with other members in order to cement commitment to the group. The leader remains in the background during this process but may become increasingly important as time goes on. Sannyasins often came to Rajneesh before knowing other devotees. After taking sannyas, however, they usually became involved in intense relationships. The master-disciple bond, however, continued to supersede those interpersonal ties, and it was often the foundation on which enduring attachments to other sannyasins were built. When the ranch collapsed, sannyasins judged one another's actions in terms of whether or not individuals had always placed Bhagwan and his welfare first. If someone disaffiliated but still manifested intense love for Bhagwan, he or she was still considered to be part of the movement.

4. For a full discussion of shifting views of children, see the following site available on the Internet: *Viha Connection V8#1,* "Special Section on Meditation and Procreation," <http://www.oshoviha.org>.

Chapter 2

1. Some of Rajneesh's writing published before 1979 lucidly describe both his philosophy and his personal history. The books that were most useful to me and which were mentioned by sannyasins as being important to them were *The Book of Secrets* (Rajneesh 1974), *Meditation: The Art of Ecstasy* (Rajneesh 1976), and *I Am the Gate* (Rajneesh 1977). The best of the books by apostates is *The Promise of Paradise* (Franklin 1992). While she was still a sannyasin, Franklin, then known as Satya Bharti, edited a number of Bhagwan's most influential books and wrote two accounts of the ashram published as trade books in the West: *Drunk on the Divine* (Bharti 1980) and *Death Comes Dancing* (Bharti 1981).

Two of the most readable, albeit contested, books by apostates are *Bhagwan: The God That Failed* (Milne 1987) and *The Ultimate Game* (Strelley and San Souci 1987). In *The Rajneesh Files* Win McCormack (1985) has compiled and edited the confrontational articles from *Oregon Magazine*.

In *Bhagwan: The Most Godless Yet the Most Godly Man* Meredith (1988) critiques many of the apostates' charges in his account of Bhagwan, from the standpoint of being his personal physician. Meredith's book and Satya Bharti's two books from 1981 offer extraordinary insights into the master-sannyasin dyad.

2. Carter (1990) is meticulous, perceptive, and rigorous in his organizational history of the Poona Ashram and Rajneeshpuram. Gordon (1987) addresses social-psychological issues, and he was the only outsider who wrote about the World Tour in 1986.

3. See appendix A for interview questions and the questionnaire sent shortly after Rajneeshpuram disintegrated.

4. The Thematic Apperception Test cards used were numbers 1, 2, 3BM, 4, 13M, and 16. For detailed discussion, see Sundberg, Goldman, Rotter, and Smythe 1992.

5. *Writing Culture: The Poetics and Politics of Ethnography,* a collection edited by James Clifford and George E. Marcus (1986), presents rich postmodernist approaches to ethnography and life histories without dismissing more traditional academic styles. Laurel Richardson (1990) suggests new, creative ways of structuring accounts and moving beyond traditional ethnographic styles.

Chapter 5

1. Macrobiotics involves diet and meditation to promote physical health and spiritual growth. Special recipes and menus emphasize minimal cooking and all natural ingredients. A macrobiotic diet is vegan, with no animal products of any kind. Meals include sea vegetables, whole grains, beans, vegetables, and fruits.

2. Fritz Perls was the resident seer and psychotherapist at the Esalen Institute, a well-known personal growth retreat in Big Sur, California. His work was extremely popular in the late 1960s and 1970s. He offered readers possibilities for personal growth and self-actualization. *Gestalt Therapy Verbatim* (Perls 1969) explained his approach to existential therapy. Verbatim transcripts of therapy sessions, along with

commentaries on those sessions, followed the brief explanation. Rajneesh therapists adopted a number of Perls's techniques.

3. Ram Dass (Richard Alpert), along with Timothy Leary, brought LSD to mainstream attention in the mid-1960s. Alpert dropped out of academia after a successful record of research, publication, and teaching at Harvard and Stanford and briefly became part of the psychedelic Left. In the late 1960s he journeyed to India and sat at the feet of a holy man as one of a number of Americans trying to attain enlightenment. He returned to the United States, reborn as Ram Dass. Considerably subdued, Richard Alpert now strives to promote peace and serve the world through the nonprofit Seva Foundation headquartered in New Mexico. See Ram Dass 1971.

Epilogue

1. After she was arrested in Germany on one federal charge of attempted murder, Sheela faced a number of additional criminal charges. She was eventually returned to the United States in February 1986. The terms of extradition were renegotiated because of new charges, and there were complicated sets of plea bargains involving Sheela's cooperation in amending them. The long list of formal accusations finally included charges related to hundreds of salmonella poisonings in The Dalles, attempted murders of state and federal officials, arson, and wiretapping (Carter 1990, 234–36).

2. Sannyasins made a distinction between Milne (1987), Strelley and San Souci (1987), on the one hand, and Franklin (1992), on the other. They saw Milne as a sexually obsessed turncoat and Strelley as a minor player who vastly overestimated her own importance. Both of these apostates criticized Bhagwan and portrayed him as a charlatan. On the other hand, Franklin, a more sympathetic defector, still spoke of him with some reverence. Most sannyasins responded to Franklin's deference to Rajneesh and explained her criticisms in terms of the fact that Sheela had exploited and mistreated her.

3. The following 1998 Internet address brings seekers into hundreds of Osho-related links: <http:/osho.org/>.

References

Aguirre, Adelberto, and Jonathan Turner. 1998. *American ethnicity*. New York: Prentice-Hall.

Bainbridge, William Sims. 1997. *The sociology of religious movements*. New York: Routledge.

Barker, Eileen. 1984. *The making of a moonie*. London: Basil Blackwell.

Becker, Howard S. 1967. Whose side are we on? *Social Problems* 14:239–47.

———. 1970. *Sociological work: Method and substance*. Chicago: Aldine.

———. 1986. *Writing for social scientists: How to start and finish your thesis, book, or article*. Chicago: University of Chicago Press.

Beckford, James. 1975. *The trumpet of prophecy: A sociological study of Jehovah's Witnesses*. New York: John Wiley.

Bellah, Robert N., Richard Madsen, William M. Sullivan, Ann Swidler, and Steven Tipton. 1985. *Habits of the heart: Individualism and commitment in American life*. Berkeley: University of California Press.

Benjamin, Jessica. 1988. *The bonds of love: Psychoanalysis, feminism, and the problem of domination*. New York: Pantheon.

Bharti (Franklin), Satya. 1980. *Drunk on the divine: An account of life in the ashram of Bhagwan Shree Rajneesh*. New York: Grove Press.

———. 1981. *Death comes dancing: Celebrating life with Bhagwan Shree Rajneesh*. London: Routledge & Kegan Paul.

Bion, William. 1959. *Experiences in groups*. New York: Basic Books.

Bird, F., and B. Reimer. 1983. Participation rates in new religions and parareligious movements. In *Of gods and men: New religious movements in the West*, ed. Eileen Barker, 215–38. Macon, GA: Mercer University Press.

Bissinger, Buzz. 1998. Shattered glass. *Vanity Fair* (September): 176–90.

Black, Claudia. 1991. *It will never happen to me*. New York: Ballantine.

Blau, Peter M. 1964. *Exchange and power in social life*. New York: John Wiley.

Bloch, Marc. 1953. *The historian's craft*. New York: Vintage Books.

Brown, Karen McCarthy. 1991. *Mama Lola: A Vodou priestess in Brooklyn*. Berkeley: University of California Press.

Browning, Christopher. 1992. *Ordinary men: Reserve Police Battalion 101 and the Final Solution in Poland*. New York: HarperCollins.

Camic, Charles. 1987. Charisma: Its varieties, preconditions, and consequences. In

Advances in psychoanalytic sociology, ed. Jerome Rabow, Gerald Platt, and Marion Goldman, 238–77. Malabar, FL: Krieger.

Carter, Lewis F. 1987. The new renunciates of Bhagwan Shree Rajneesh. *Journal for the Scientific Study of Religion* 26:148–72.

————. 1990. *Charisma and control in Rajneeshpuram.* New York: Cambridge University Press.

Chernin, Kim. 1985. *The hungry self: Women, eating, and identity.* New York: Harper & Row.

Chodorow, Nancy. 1978. *The reproduction of mothering.* Berkeley: University of California Press.

————. 1989. *Feminism and psychoanalytic theory.* New Haven: Yale University Press.

Christensen, Mark. 1985. Rancho Rajneesh. *Penthouse: The International Magazine for Men* 16:40–44, 72–74, and 106.

Clarke, Ronald O. 1985, Fall. The teachings of Bhagwan Shree Rajneesh. *Sweet Reason: A Journal of Ideas, History, and Culture* 4:27–44.

————. 1988. The narcissistic guru: A profile of Bhagwan Shree Rajneesh. *Free Inquiry* 8:33–45.

Clifford, James, and George E. Marcus, eds. 1986. *Writing culture: The poetics and politics of ethnography.* Berkeley: University of California Press.

Coles, Robert. 1977. *The privileged ones.* Boston: Little, Brown.

D'Emilio, John, and Estelle B. Freedman. 1988. *Intimate matters.* New York: Harper and Row.

Davidman, Lynn. 1991. *Tradition in a rootless world: Women turn to Orthodox Judaism.* Berkeley: University of California Press.

Davidson, Sara. 1977. *Loose change: Three women of the sixties.* Garden City, NY: Doubleday.

de Beauvoir, Simone. 1953. *The second sex.* New York: Knopf.

Denzin, Norman K. 1989. *Interpretive interactionism.* Newbury Park, CA: Sage.

Denzin, Norman K., and Yvonne S. Lincoln, eds. 1994. *Handbook of qualitative research.* Thousand Oaks, CA: Sage.

Dunier, Mitchell. 1992. *Slim's table: Race, respectability, and masculinity.* Chicago: University of Chicago Press.

Durkheim, Emile. 1958. *Rules of the sociological method.* Trans. J. H. Mueller and S. A. Solovay. New York: The Free Press.

Ebaugh, Helen Rose Fuchs. 1977. *Out of the cloister: A study of organizational dilemmas.* Austin: University of Texas Press.

Erikson, Kai T. 1966. *Wayward Puritans: A study in the sociology of deviance.* New York: John Wiley.

Evans, Sara. 1979. *Personal politics: The roots of women's liberation in the Civil Rights Movement and the New Left.* New York: Vintage Books.

Faludi, Susan. 1991. *Backlash.* New York: Simon & Schuster.

Fanon, Frantz. 1963. *The wretched of the earth* (Les damnes de la terre). New York: Grove Press.

Ferrell, Jeff, and Mark S. Hamm, eds. 1998. *Ethnography at the edge.* Boston: Northeastern University Press.

Festinger, Leon, Harold W. Reicken, and Stanley Schachter. 1956. *When prophecy fails.* New York: Harper & Row.

Finke, Roger, and Rodney Stark. 1992. *The churching of America: 1776–1990.* New Brunswick: Rutgers University Press.

Firestone, Shulamith. 1970. *The dialectic of sex: The case for feminist revolution.* New York: William Morrow.

Fitz Gerald, Frances. 1986. *Cities on a hill: A journey through contemporary American cultures.* New York: Simon & Schuster.

Franklin, Satya Bharti. 1992. *The promise of paradise: A woman's intimate story of the perils of life with Rajneesh.* New York: Station Hill Press.

Frazer, Kennedy. 1985. *The fashionable mind: Reflections on fashion, 1970–1982.* Boston: David R. Godine.

Friedan, Betty. 1963. *The feminine mystique.* New York: Norton.

Galanter, Mark. 1989. *Cults: Faith, healing, and coercion.* New York: Oxford University Press.

Gallese, Liz Roman. 1985. *Women like us.* New York: William Morrow.

Gangaji (Antoinette Varner). 1996. *You are that!* Vol. 2. Boulder, CO: Satsang Press.

Gardiner, Judith Kagan. 1987. Self-psychology as feminist theory. *Signs: A Journal of Women in Culture and Society* 12:761–78.

Geertz, Clifford. 1973. *The interpretation of cultures.* New York: Basic Books.

———. 1988. *Works and lives: The anthropologist as author.* Stanford: Stanford University Press.

Gilbert, Elizabeth. 1996. Dale Evans: Homebody on the range. *New York Times Magazine,* November 24, 62–23.

Gilligan, Carol. 1982. *In a different voice.* Cambridge: Harvard University Press.

Gilligan, Carol, Nona Lyons, and Trudy Hammer. 1990. *Making connections.* Cambridge: Harvard University Press.

Glaser, Barney, and Anselm Strauss. 1967. *The discovery of grounded theory.* Chicago: Aldine.

Goffman, Erving. 1963. *Stigma: Notes on the management of spoiled identity.* Englewood Cliffs, NJ: Prentice-Hall.

Goldberg, Arnold. 1978. *The psychology of the self.* New York: International Universities Press.

Goldman, Marion S. 1988. The women of Rajneeshpuram. *CSWS Review* 2:18–21.

———. 1990. A review essay on *S* and *A Bliss Case. Society* 27:94–96.

———. 1995a. Continuity in collapse: Departures from Shiloh. *Journal for the Scientific Study of Religion* 34:342–53.

———. 1995b. From promiscuity to celibacy: Women and sexual regulation at Rajneeshpuram. In *Sex, lies, and sanctity,* ed. Mary Jo Neitz and Marion S. Goldman, 203–21. Greenwich, CT: JAI Press.

———. 1997. Alice Miller's insights into the sociology of seekership. In *Religion, society and psychoanalysis,* ed. Donald Capps and Janet L. Jacobs, 200–217. Boulder, CO: Westview Press.

———. 2000. The ethnographer as holy clown. In *Reflexive ethnography,* ed. Lew Carter. Greenwich, CT: JAI Press.

Goldman, Marion S., and Jack Whalen. 1990. From the New Left to the New Enlightenment: Implications of public attention on private lives. *Qualitative Sociology* 13:85–107.

Gordon, James S. 1987. *The golden guru.* Lexington, MA: Stephen Grenne Press.

Greer, Germaine. 1971. *The female eunuch.* New York: McGraw-Hill.

Haaken, Janice. 1993. From Al-Anon to ACOA: Codependence and the reconstruction of caregiving. *Signs: Journal of Women in Culture and Society* 18:321–45.

Hoge, Dean R., Benton Johnson, and Donald A. Luidens. 1994. *Vanishing boundaries: The religion of mainline Protestant baby boomers.* Louisville: Westminster/John Knox Press.

hooks, bell. 1989. *Talking back: Thinking feminist, thinking black.* Boston: South End Press.

———. 1990. *Yearning: Race, gender and cultural politics.* Boston: South End Press.

Horwitz, Mardi J., ed. 1991. *Hysterical personality style and the histrionic personality disorder.* Northvale, NJ: Jason Aaronson.

Iannaccone, Laurence. 1995. Risk, rationality, and religious portfolios. *Economic Inquiry* 33:285–95.

Jaccoby, Russell. 1975. *Social amnesia: A critique of contemporary psychology from Adler to Laing.* Boston: Beacon.

Jacobs, Janet Liebman. 1989. *Divine disenchantment.* Bloomington: Indiana University Press.

Johnson, Benton. 1992. On founders and followers: Some factors in the development of new religious movements. *Sociological Analysis* 53 (supp.): S1–S13.

Johnson, Miriam M. 1975. Fathers, mothers, and sex-typing. *Sociological Inquiry* 45:319–34.

———. 1991. *Strong mothers, weak wives.* Berkeley: University of California Press.

Kernberg, Otto. 1975. *Borderline conditions and pathological narcissism.* New York: Jason Aronson.

Kilbourne, Brock, and James T. Richardson. 1984. Psychotherapy and new religions in a pluralistic society. *American Psychologist* 39:237–51.

Kohut, Heinz. 1984. *How does analysis cure?* Chicago: University of Chicago Press.

Krueger, Derek. 1996. *Symeon the holy fool.* Berkeley: University of California Press.

Laing, R. D. 1968. *The politics of experience.* New York: Pantheon Books.

Lasch, Christopher. 1979. *The culture of narcissism.* New York: Norton.

Latkin, Carl A. 1987. Rajneeshpuram, Oregon: An exploration of gender and work roles, self-concept, and psychological well-being in an experimental community. Ph.D. diss., University of Oregon.

———. 1990. Research note: The self-concept of members of an experimental community: Rajneeshpuram. *Journal for the Scientific Study of Religion* 29:91–98.

Latkin, Carl A., Richard Hagan, Richard Littman, and Norman Sundberg. 1987. Who lives in utopia: A brief report on the Rajneeshpuram Research Project. *Sociological Analysis* 48:73–81.

Levine, Saul V. 1984. Radical departures. *Psychology Today* 18:20–27.

Lipstadt, Deborah. 1993. *Denying the holocaust: The growing assault on truth and memory.* New York: The Free Press.

Lowen, Alexander. 1977. *The way to vibrant health.* New York: Harper Colophon.

Lofland, John. 1981 [1966]. *Doomsday cult: A study of conversion, proselytization, and maintenance of faith.* New York: Irvington.

Mahler, Margaret S. 1968. *On human symbiosis and the vicissitudes of individuation.* New York: International Universities Press.

Masterson, James F. 1981. *The narcissistic and borderline disorders.* New York: Brunner Mazel.

McClelland, David. 1985. *Human motivation.* New York: Scott-Foreman.

McCormack, Win. 1985. *The Rajneesh files: 1981–1986.* Portland: New Oregon Publishers.

McGuire, Meredith. 1982. *Catholic pentecostalism.* Philadelphia: Temple University Press.

Mehta, Gita. 1979. *Karma Kola: Marketing the mystic East.* New York: Simon & Schuster.

Melton, J. Gordon, and Robert L. Moore. 1982. *The cult experience: Responding to new religions.* New York: Pilgrim.

Meredith, George. 1988. *Bhagwan: The most godless yet the most godly man.* Poona: Rebel Publishing House.

Milgram, Stanley. 1974. *Obedience to authority: An experimental view.* New York: Harper & Row.

Miller, Alice. 1981. *The drama of the gifted child.* New York: Basic Books.

———. 1983. *For your own good: Hidden cruelty in childrearing and the roots of violence.* New York: Farrar, Straus & Giroux.

Mills, C. Wright. 1959. *The sociological imagination.* London: Oxford University Press.

Milne, Hugh. 1987. *Bhagwan: The god that failed.* New York: St. Martin's Press.

Mitchell, Richard. 1993. *Secrecy and fieldwork.* Newbury Park, CA: Sage.

Morrison, Andrew, ed. 1986. *Essential papers on narcissism.* New York: New York University Press.

Murray, Harry. 1943. *Thematic apperception test.* Cambridge: Harvard University Press.

Neitz, Mary Jo. 1987. *Charisma and community: A study of religious commitment within the charismatic renewal.* New Brunswick: Transaction Books.

———. 1998. Walking between the worlds: Writing about Wicca. Paper presented at the meetings of the Society for the Scientific Study of Religion, Montreal.

Norwood, Robin. 1988. *Letters from women who love too much.* New York: Pocket Books.

Ofshe, Richard. 1980. The social development of the Synanon Cult. *Sociological Analysis* 41:109–27.

Osho (Bhagwan Shree Rajneesh). 1993. *The everyday meditator: A practical guide.* Boston: Charles E. Tuttle.

———. 1996. *Meditation: The first and last freedom.* New York: St. Martin's Press.

Palmer, Susan. 1987. Therapy, charisma, and social control in Rajneeshpuram. Paper presented to the Association for the Sociology of Religion, Chicago.

Palmer, Susan, and Arvind Sharma. 1993. *The Rajneesh papers: Studies in a new religious movement.* Delhi: Motitlal Banarsidass.

Park, Robert E. 1925. *The city.* Chicago: University of Chicago Press.

Perls, Frederick S. 1969. *Gestalt therapy verbatim.* Lafayette, CA: Real People Press.

Pipher, Mary. 1994. *Reviving Ophelia: Saving the selves of adolescent girls.* New York: G. P. Putnam's Sons.

Pollock, G. H. 1975. On mourning, immortality, and utopia. *Journal of the American Psychoanalytic Association* 23:334–62.

Punch, Maurice. 1985. *The politics and ethics of fieldwork.* Beverly Hills, CA: Sage.

Ragin, Charles C., and Howard S. Becker, eds. 1992. *What is a case? Exploring the boundaries of social inquiry.* New York: Cambridge University Press.

Rajneesh, Bhagwan Shree. 1974. *The book of secrets.* Comp. Ma Yoga Astha. Poona: Ma Yoga Laxmi, Rajneesh Foundation.

———. 1975. *No water, no moon.* Poona: Ma Yoga Laxmi, Rajneesh Foundation.

———. 1976. *Meditation: The art of ecstasy.* Ed. Ma Satya Bharti. New York: Harper & Row.

———. 1977. *I am the gate.* Ed. Ma Satya Bharti. New York: Harper & Row.

———. 1979a. *The Buddha disease: A darshan diary.* Poona: Ma Yoga Laxmi, Rajneesh Foundation.

———. 1979b. *For madmen only: A darshan diary.* Poona: Ya Yoga Laxmi, Rajneesh Foundation.

———. 1979c. *The open door: A darshan diary.* Poona: Ma Yoga Laxmi, Rajneesh Foundation.

———. 1981. *The tongue tip taste of Tao: A darshan diary.* Poona: Ma Yoga Laxmi, Rajneesh Foundation Ltd.

———. 1983. *Rajneeshism: An introduction to Bhagwan Shree Rajneesh and his religion.* Ed. Academy of Rajneeshism. Rajneeshpuram: Ma Anand Sheela, Rajneesh Foundation International.

———. 1985a. *Glimpses of a golden childhood.* Ed. Swami Devaraj. Rajneeshpuram: Rajneesh Foundation International.

———. 1985b. *The Rajneesh Bible.* Vol. 1. Ed. Academy of Rajneeshism. Rajneeshpuram: Rajneesh Foundation International.

———. 1990. *I leave you my dream.* Supplement to the *Osho Times International* 3, no. 2.

Ram Dass (Richard Alpert). 1971. *Remember: Be here, now.* New York: Crown.

Reinharz, Shulamit. 1992. *Feminist methods in social research*. New York: Oxford University Press.

Richardson, James T. 1990. Jewish participation in so-called cults: Spiritual seduction or active agency. Paper presented at the Society for the Scientific Study of Religion, Washington, DC.

Richardson, James T., Mary Stewart, and Robert Simmonds. 1978. Researching a fundamentalist commune. In *Understanding new religions,* ed. Jacob Needleman and George Baker, 235–51. New York: Seabury Press.

Richardson, Laurel. 1990. *Writing strategies: Reaching diverse audiences*. Newbury Park, CA: Sage.

Robbins, Thomas. 1988. *Cults, converts, and charisma*. Beverly Hills, CA: Sage.

Rockland, Michael A. 1989. *A Bliss case*. Minneapolis: Coffee House Press.

Romero, Mary. 1995. Life as the maid's daughter. In *Feminisms in the academy,* ed. Domina Stanton and Abigail Stewart, 157–79. Ann Arbor: University of Michigan Press.

Rosaldo, Renato. 1989. *Culture and truth: The remaking of social analysis*. Boston: Beacon.

Runyan, William McKinley. 1982. *Life histories and psychobiography*. New York: Oxford University Press.

Schoenherr, Richard, and Andrew M. Greeley. 1974. Role commitment processes and the American Catholic priesthood. *American Sociological Review* 39:407–26.

Sennett, Richard, and Jonathan Cobb. 1972. *The hidden injuries of class*. New York: Knopf.

Shibley, Mark A. 1996. *Resurgent evangelism in the United States: Mapping cultural change since 1970*. Columbia: University of South Carolina Press.

Skolnick, Arlene S. 1991. *Embattled paradise: The American family in an age of uncertainty*. New York: Basic Books.

Skolnick, Jerome H. 1966. *Justice without trial*. New York: John Wiley.

Stark, Rodney. 1996a. *The rise of Christianity: A sociologist reconsiders history*. Princeton: Princeton University Press.

—————. 1996b. Why religious movements succeed or fail: A revised general model. *Journal of Contemporary Religion* 11:133–46.

Stark, Rodney, and William Bainbridge. 1985. *The future of religion*. Berkeley: University of California Press.

Strelley, Kate, with Robert D. San Souci. 1987. *The ultimate game: The rise and fall of Bhagwan Shree Rajneesh*. New York: Harper & Row.

Sundberg, Norman D. 1987. Survey data on Rajneeshpuram collected in 1983–84.

Sundberg, Norman D., Marion Goldman, Nathan Rotter, and Douglas Smythe. 1992. Personality and spirituality: Comparative TAT's of high achieving Rajneeshees. *Journal of Personality Assessment* 59:326–39.

Sundberg, Norman D., Carl Latkin, Richard Littman, and Richard Hagan. 1990. Personality in a religious commune: CPI's in Rajneeshpuram. *Journal of Personality Assessment* 55:7–17.

Suttles, Gerald D. 1972. *The social construction of communities.* Chicago: University of Chicago Press.

Task Force on the DSM-IV of the American Psychiatric Association. 1994. *Diagnostic and statistical manual of mental disorders,* 3d rev. ed. Washington, DC: American Psychiatric Association.

Temerlin, Maurice, and Jane W. Temerlin. 1980. Psychotherapy cults: An iatrogenic perversion. *Psychotherapy: Theory, Research, and Practice* 19:131–39.

Tipton, Steven M. 1982. *Getting saved from the sixties.* Berkeley: University of California Press.

Wallis, Roy. 1979. *Salvation and protest.* London: Francis Pinter.

———. 1984. *Elementary forms of new religious life.* London: Routledge & Kegan Paul.

Weber, Max. 1968 [1922]. *Economy and society: An outline of interpretive sociology.* Vol. 3. New York: Bedminster Press.

Weiss, Joseph. 1993. *How psychotherapy works: Process and techniques.* New York: Guilford Press.

Whittier, Nancy. 1995. *Feminist generations: The persistence of the radical women's movement.* Philadelphia: Temple University Press.

Winnicott, D. W. 1964. *The child, the family, and the outside world.* New York: Penguin.

Wolfe, Tom. 1976. *Mauve gloves and madmen.* New York: Farrar, Straus & Giroux.

Wright, Stuart A. 1987. *Leaving cults: The dynamics of defection.* Washington, DC: Society for the Scientific Study of Religion.

Index